SEEING IS DECEIVING:
The Psychology of Visual Illusions

SEEING IS DECEIVING:
The Psychology of Visual Illusions

STANLEY COREN
University of British Columbia

JOAN STERN GIRGUS
Princeton University

 LAWRENCE ERLBAUM ASSOCIATES, PUBLISHERS
1978   Hillsdale, New Jersey

DISTRIBUTED BY THE HALSTED PRESS DIVISION OF
JOHN WILEY & SONS
New York   Toronto   London   Sydney

Lawrence Erlbaum Associates, Inc., Publishers
62 Maria Drive
Hillsdale, New Jersey 07642

Distributed solely by Halsted Press Division
John Wiley & Sons, Inc., New York

Library of Congress Cataloging in Publication Data
Coren, Stanley.
  Seeing is deceiving.

  Bibliography: p.
  Includes indexes.
  1. Optical illusions. 2. Optical illusions—
Psychological aspects. I. Girgus, Joan S., 1942–
joint author. II. Title.
QP495.C67   152.1'48   78-13509
ISBN 0-470-26522-1

Printed in the United States of America

This book is dedicated to
Leon Festinger and Julian Hochberg

Contents

Preface

In the past century and a quarter over 1,000 articles have been published dealing with visual illusions. Despite this obvious evidence of interest, only three serious books have appeared dealing with these puzzling perceptual phenomena. The authors of these books include a lighting engineer, a physicist, and a psychologist, and their principle concern was with the presentation, or cataloging, of the basic visual distortions rather than with an integrated attempt at explanation. This book provides such an attempt. It brings together much of the known data and offers explorations and evaluations of the theoretical viewpoints that are exerting an influence on contemporary thought about visual illusions. We attempt to demonstrate that these illusory distortions do not represent a breakdown in the normal processes of perception but rather are the end product of many well-known perceptual mechanisms working in consort to produce a percept different from the physical reality.

The book opens with a treatment of how illusions have played an important part in the history of psychology. Few individuals are aware of the fact that Wundt used the existence of visual illusions as one major justification for his proposal that psychology should be a science separate from physiology and physics. Following the historical discussion, two chapters present a relatively complete catalog of visual geometric illusions. At least the prototype of each of the major distortions that can be elicited by lines drawn on paper is illustrated and described in these pages, as well as many of the important variants of the basic configurations.

Beginning with Chapter 4, three chapters provide a discussion of how the optical characteristics of the eye, the neural interactions that occur on the retina, and the analysis of input in the primary visual centers of the cortex play a role in the formation of many visual illusions. Beginning with Chapter 7, we consider a number of cognitive-judgmental or information-processing strategies that can lead to discrepancies between the conscious percept and the measured relationships in the environment. The eight chapters from Chapter 4 to Chapter 11 make it quite clear that illusions arise from many different sources and at many different levels in the perceptual process. In Chapter 12 these many divergent sources are brought together, and, at least at the demonstration level, it is shown how an illusory distortion may be dissected to show the contributions of various causal components. Chapter 13 takes this multicausal approach one step further and demonstrates how it might be used to establish a meaningful classification system for illusions. The last chapter attempts to reintegrate the study of illusions into the main body of psychological and perceptual theorizing and to demonstrate the usefulness of illusions as a tool for the investigation of visual processes.

Since this book occupied our attention for more than three years, many individuals have been involved with it at various stages. It would be virtually impossible to credit all those who have assisted in the preparation of the manuscript or who have interacted with us concerning the various ideas contained in it. It is certainly the case that three institutions played an invaluable role in providing us with assistance: The University of British Columbia, The City College of the City University of New York, and Princeton University. Their respective department heads, Dr. Peter Suedfeld, Drs. Donald Mintz and Louis Costa, and Dr. Sam Glucksberg, provided us with space and support during varying phases of the preparation of this manuscript. Much of the research was supported by grants from the National Research Council of Canada (A9783) and the National Science Foundation of the United States (74-18599). The mechanical aspects of manuscript preparation were handled by a number of people. Roberta M. L. Brustin helped with many of the figures. Lois Citron assisted in the preparation of the index, and James Walker found us a particularly elusive photograph. Thanks also go to the many people who assisted in the preparation of the bibliography, figures, duplicating, and other tasks too numerous and varied to mention but nonetheless vital. This group included Ann Daniels, Keith Humphrey, Jeannie Garbor, Richard Fraenkel, Rosalind Wu, Joe Porac, Lucille Spivak, and Richard Cropp. The typing and organizational tasks were well handled by Joyce Coninx-Wright, Susan Dixon, Sheryl Riley, Maureen Skuce, Melanie Wallace, Marilyn Santomauro, and Eileen Donohue. Two colleagues in particular, Clare Porac and Laurence M. Ward, read, commented on, and disagreed with early drafts of the manuscript, thus providing much-needed stimulation and support. To all these individuals, as well as to all the members of our research teams working in our laboratories, we offer our appreciation. We further wish to thank all our colleagues in the field who have provided us with the data and theoretical viewpoints that form the foundation of this book.

STANLEY COREN
JOAN STERN GIRGUS

SEEING IS DECEIVING:
The Psychology of Visual Illusions

1
A Brief History of Visual Illusions

In 1854 a rather unusual paper was published by J. J. Oppel. This paper was unusual because it devoted 10 pages of serious psychological analysis to an array of lines. These lines did not form a complex picture or graph but rather a simple figure shown in Figure 1.1. At first glance this figure appears to be nothing more than two horizontal extents. The upper extent is divided into a number of segments and appears to be slightly longer than the lower. Actually, it is this apparent difference in length that motivated Oppel's analysis since, as a ruler will quickly demonstrate, the two extents are physically equal. Oppel noted that there had been occasional mention of other instances where the relationships represented in consciousness are systematically different from what might be expected on the basis of direct physical measurement. For those instances that could be represented by lines drawn on paper, he coined the phrase *geometrisch-optishe Tauschung* which we generally translate as *geometrical optical illusion.*

Oppel's paper was not to be an isolated treatment of such illusory phenomena. Soon the literature contained contributions by many of the most important researchers in physics, physiology, philosophy, and psychology, each attempting to explain the existence of such systematically fallacious percepts. The list included such notables as Baldwin, Brentano, Ebbinghaus, Helmholtz, Jastrow, Judd, Lipps, Muensterberg, Titchener, and Wundt. In addition to analysis, these luminaries presented many new configurations in which simple lines drawn on paper led to percepts at variance with reality. The interest aroused was quite intense. The 50 years after Oppel's treatise first appeared saw the publication of over 200 papers dealing with illusions, and the next 50 years saw this number rise to over 1,000. One might very well wonder why there has been so much fuss over the misperception of the size or shape of a few lines in a drawing.

FIG. 1.1. An illusory distortion in which the divided space appears longer than the undivided space (after Oppel, 1855).

Perhaps this question is best answered by noting that the only contact we have with the world around us comes through our senses. We put total reliance on the correspondence between our conscious experience of the environment and its physical reality in order to perform such simple tasks as estimating how far we have to jump to get over a puddle without getting wet as well as for such complex life-and-death matters as estimating the distances between ourselves and other vehicles as we drive a car on a highway at mile-a-minute speeds. We have continual verification of the accuracy of our senses. When we reach for objects in view, they are always at the place where they appear to be. We use vision to keep ourselves from bumping into walls, falling over cliffs, or being run down by oncoming cars. Our experience has taught us that our sensory impressions are dependable and trustworthy. This confidence in the veracity of perception has become part of our cultural heritage and is expressed in such common phrases as "Seeing is believing" and "I didn't believe it until I saw it with my own two eyes." Thomas Reid clearly stated this position of faith in the senses in 1785 when he wrote:

By all the laws of all nations, in the most solemn judicial trials, wherein men's fortunes and lives are at stake, the sentence passes according to the testimony of eye or ear, witnesses of good credit. An upright judge will give a fair hearing to every objection that can be made to the integrity of a witness, and allow it to be possible that he may be corrupted; but no judge will ever suppose that witnesses may be imposed upon by trusting to their eyes and ears. And if a skeptical counsel should plead against the testimony of the witnesses, that they had no other evidence for what they declared than the testimony of their eyes and ears, and that we ought not to put so much faith in our senses as to deprive men of life or fortune upon their testimony, surely no upright judge would admit a plea of this kind. I believe no counsel, however skeptical, ever dared to offer such an argument; and, if it were offered, it would be rejected with disdain (Essay 2, Chapter 5).

It is because we have such faith in the ability of our senses to reproduce the external world accurately in consciousness that drawings such as Figure 1.1 are disturbing and excite our interest. The very root of the word used to describe such phenomena manifests this disturbance. The Latin root of the word *illusion* is *illudere,* which means "to mock." Thus these phenomena mock our trust in our senses.

Although it was simply the existence of a discrepancy between percept and reality that began the serious investigation ot these phenomena, (as early researchers puzzled over the fact that a few lines drawn on paper could deceive the beautifully complex sensory and perceptual system that allows us to coordinate in the world), it was the theoretical implications that sustained the research. Such phenomena clearly demonstrate that the eye is not a simple camera passively recording stimuli. They provide evidence that perception is an active process that takes place in the brain and is not directly predictable from simple knowledge of the physical relationships. In this context it is not at all surprising that visual illusions comprised an important class of behaviors studied in the last quarter of the nineteenth century by the new science of mental phenomena named *psychology.*

THE BEGINNINGS

One can only speculate about which of the common everyday discrepancies among sense, impression, and reality was the first to be noticed. Perhaps it was an afterimage caused by glancing at the sun, which would appear phenomenally as a dark orb hovering in the field of view, always just out of reach. Perhaps it was a stick, half in and half out of a pool of water, which looked bent but felt straight. Surely phenomena of this kind must have presented a dilemma for primitive people whose knowldge about the world was almost completely limited to information gained through direct perception of the environment, without the benefit of any measuring instruments. We do know that by the time we reach the height of the Greek period, perceptual errors and illusions were being ascribed to some inner processing error. Thus Parmenides (ca. 500 B.C.) (Diogenes Laertius, 1925) explains the existence of perceptual illusions by saying, "The eyes and ears are bad witnesses when they are at the service of minds that do not understand their language."

The Greek writers and philosophers wrote about the problems of perception at great length. In general, they seemed to espouse one of two viewpoints:

1. Sensory inputs are variable and inaccurate, and one of the major functions of the mind is to correct these inaccuracies to provide an accurate representation of the external environment.

2. The senses are inherently accurate and thus responsible for our veridical picture of the environment, and it is the mind or judgmental capacities that are limited.

From the first point of view, perceptual errors arise when the senses are relied on more than the mind, whereas from the second point of view, perceptual errors arise when the mind interferes with the work of the senses. These two opposing viewpoints were both quite popular in ancient Greece and were to dominate thought about perception and cognition for more than 2,000 years. For example, Plato (ca. 300 B.C.) argued that we should talk of perceiving objects *through* the senses but *with* the mind, since the senses give only an imperfect copy of the world. Properties of objects, such as their identity, are taken to be the result of the action of the mind or intellect working on the sensory impression. Thus an error of perception could arise only through some mental miscalculation, perhaps due to inattention. The most succinct statement of this position comes from Epicharmus (ca. 450 B.C.) (Spearman, 1937) who says, "The mind sees and the mind hears. The rest is blind and deaf." An investigator with this orientation would study higher level information-processing strategies rather than the sense organs themselves in order to understand perceptual errors and illusions. The alternative doctrine, based on a total trust in the senses, can be exemplified by a statement from Protagoras (ca. 450 B.C.), who said, "Man is nothing but a bundle of sensations (Freeman, 1953)." In this view any errors or inaccuracies in perception must arise from distortions in the basic materials supplied to the receptors (i.e., the bending or tearing of visual rays).

Aristotle (384–322 B.C.) (Beare, 1931) seems to have adopted a compromise position, incorporating elements of both these viewpoints. He begins by arguing that there are some perceptual qualities that are immediately and accurately perceived by the senses: "Each sense has one kind of object which it discerns, and never errs in reporting that what is before it is color or sound (although it may err as to what it is that is colored or where it is, or what it is that is sounding or where it is)." There are, however, other qualities such as movement, number, figural qualities, and magnitude, that are not the exclusive property of any one sense but are common to all. These qualities, according to Aristotle, require intellectual mediation to assure accuracy of representation. As an example of how perception can be led astray, Aristotle describes an environmental version of the Oppel–Kundt illusion (which is the distortion we showed in Figure 1.1), noting that extents filled with many objects tend to appear greater than empty extents.

Greek architects of the classical era were also cognizant of the existence of visual illusions. Figure 1.2A shows a schematic diagram of the east face of the Parthenon. Although it looks quite square, this should not be the case. Consider the angle between the roof and the architrave, which forms the configuration schematically shown as Figure 1.2B. This array is actually a variant of the Jastrow–Lipps illusion, which we will describe more fully later. For the moment it will suffice if the reader notes that the horizontal line in the diagram appears to sag slightly away from the point of the angle. On the basis of this illusory distortion, we might expect that the building would look like Figure 1.2C, in which we depict an exaggerated composite of what the percept should be. In fact, however, the building's proportions were altered to compensate for this distortion. A schematic version of the pattern of these alterations is shown in Figure 1.2D.

Such corrections were apparently made quite consciously. Vitruvius (ca. 30 B.C.) (Granger, 1931) specifically says, "The stylobate must be so levelled that it increases toward the middle with unequal risers; for if it is set out to a

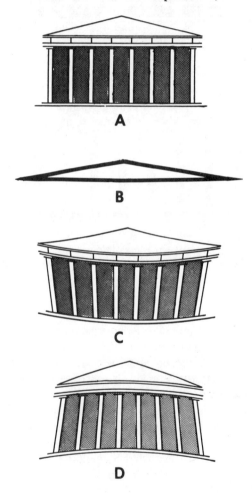

FIG. 1.2.   Architectural illusions; (A) A schematic diagram of the east face of the Parthenon; (B) a simplified diagram of the Jastrow–Lipps illusion that is present between the roof and architrave; (C) a schematic representation of how the building should look, given the illusory distortion; (D) an exaggerated version of alterations made in the shape of the building in order to offset the illusion.

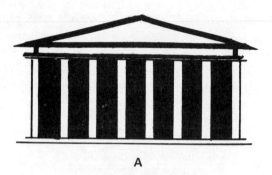

A

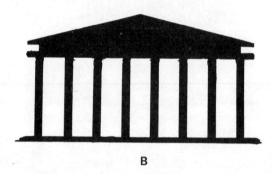

B

FIG. 1.3.   The irradiation illusion causes the set of columns imaged against a dark background to look thicker than the columns imaged against the light of the sky.

level it will seem to the eye to be hollowed."The fact that such a correction was necessary as well as the magnitude of the correction required, was probably determined on the basis of trial and error.

The builders of the Parthenon also corrected another set of distortions. Because of brightness contrast, columns imaged against the dark of the interior are seen as light objects on a dark background, whereas columns imaged against the bright sky are seen as dark objects on the light background. There is an illusory effect known as the *irradiation illusion* (see pages 41–42), in which bright objects seem larger than dark ones. Figure 1.3 shows how this irradiation illusion would make columns imaged against a dark background look thicker than columns imaged against a light background. To offset this illusion, the Parthenon is constructed so that the angle columns, which are normally seen against the bright sky, are considerably thicker than the columns normally seen against the dark cella wall.

It is thus clear that information about visual distortions played an important role in design in early Greece. To quote Vitruvius again, "For the sight follows gracious contours; and unless we flatter its pleasure by proportionate alterations of the modules (so that by adjustment there is added the amount to which it suffers illusion), an uncouth and ungracious aspect will be presented to the spectators."

The general trends of thought outlined by the Greek philosophers survived the Middle Ages more or less intact. Thus Descartes' (1596–1650) position is not that different from Aristotle's, when he notes that there is both a registration stage and an interpretation stage in the perceptual process. Perceptual error or illusion may intrude at either of these two steps along the road to consciousness. The philosophers of the seventeenth and eighteenth centuries accepted these two levels of perceptual processing and concentrated their efforts on ascertaining which attributes of perception are given at birth and which are learned through experience. With reference to this issue, Reid (1719–1796) and Kant (1724–1804) argued that almost all knowledge of the external world comes directly through the senses and is interpreted by innate mechanisms, whereas Locke (1632–1704), Berkeley (1685–1753), and Hume (1711–1776) argued that virtually all perceptual qualities are learned through experience with the environment. Regardless of their theoretical biases concerning the importance of experience versus heredity, both groups assumed that some sensory impressions, such as color and brightness, are given and do not require further elaboration. The dispute tended to focus on the relational attributes that allow us to ascertain the size and location of stimuli. For those attributes mediated by innate mechanisms, perceptual errors can arise only if the light rays are interfered with before they reach the eyes or if the neural message is disrupted. On the other hand, for those attributes learned through experience, presumably using the *a priori* attributes as building blocks, perceptual errors or illusions can also arise because the input has been misinterpreted.

THE EXPERIMENTAL FOUNDATIONS

In 1826 Johannes Mueller (1801–1858) published two books, the first on the physiology and the second on the phenomenology of vision. The second volume contained discussions of a number of phenomena that Mueller called *visual illusions.* These visual illusions were not distortions found in two-dimensional line drawings. They were such things as afterimages, phantom limbs, and the fact that the impression of white may be produced by mixing any wave length with its complement, with the resultant percept carrying no evidence of the individual components.

Mueller's major contribution to psychology, however, rests in the several volumes comprising his *Handbuch der Physiologie des Menschen* (1833–1840), some 15% of which was devoted to problems of sensation and perception. It was in this work that Mueller enunciated the doctrine of specific nerve energies, which argues that each nerve is coded for a specific sensation in consciousness.

Thus the stimulation of a visual nerve will always lead to the sensation of sight, no matter what the source of the stimulation. As evidence for this, Mueller offers another "illusion," namely, the fact that the sensation of light often results from mechanical stimulation of the eye such as occurs when it is rubbed or hit.

Mueller reasoned that, since the mind is located in the head, it could have no contact with the external world but only with the neural activity produced by stimulation of sensory receptors. Implicit in the theorizing from antiquity to Mueller had been the assumption of some sympathetic bond between the object and the eye, whereby the internal physiological process could be said to reproduce the external objective reality and its relationships in some fashion. Thus the importance of Mueller's law of specific nerve energies lies in its explicit denial of any necessary, qualitative connection between the physical stimulus, the physiological changes in the nervous system, and the resultant changes in consciousness. Before Mueller, perception had been conceived of as a process by which the receptors took the equivalent of a photograph of the stimulus and carried it to the sensorium for analysis. In Mueller's conception, the physiological processes translate the image into a pattern of neural activity equivalent to the observer's translating the visual image into words. Since the act of translating involves some interpretation and selection, the opportunity now exists for perceptual distortions to arise during this stage of processing.

During the same period, E.H. Weber (1834) was wrestling with a set of systematic discrepancies between physical reality and the conscious percept. He observed that adding 10 mm to a line 10 mm in length is seen to be a large increase in the extent, whereas adding the same 10 mm to a line 1,000 mm in length is, at most, seen as a minimal increase and may not even be noticed. The increase in apparent extent does not seem to be exclusively dependent on the absolute stimulus length that is added; it also seems to depend on the context or base stimulus to which the addition is made. Weber chose an approach to these observations that is quite different from that used by Mueller. Rather than attempting to explain *why* such an illusion occurred, he adopted the methodology of the physicist and sought simply to evolve a quantitative description of the distortion. The existence of a systematic quantitative relationship — namely, that the size of the difference that is just perceptible is a fixed fraction of the size or intensity of the stimulus being increased — seems to justify this approach. Fechner (1860) elaborated these findings and this approach into the system we now know as classical psychophysics.

It is interesting to note that the psychophysical approach essentially denies the existence of visual illusions. All illusions are reduced to quantitatively predictable discrepancies between the conscious percept and the physical stimulus. Of course, if there were no systematic errors or illusions, there would be no need for a field of psychophysics to establish the relationship between consciousness and reality.

In many respects the two most dominant forces in nineteenth century thought about perception were Hermann von Helmholtz (1821–1894) and Ewald Hering (1834–1918). It is often said that there are two major viewpoints in contemporary studies of perception. The first emphasizes the structural properties and process of transduction in the receptors themselves and tends to deemphasize higher level cognitive processing. The second focuses on higher level cognitive processing strategies and their effects on the final percept. Helmholtz characterizes the latter view whereas Hering characterizes the former. It is easy to see that these viewpoints are natural extensions of the dichotomy we first observed in Greek thought.

In his emphasis on visual information processing strategies, Helmholtz offered a theory of perception that is similar to many that we discuss in later chapters. He proposed that, in general, perception in the adult observer is based on unconscious inferences that the mind makes about the pattern of excitation in the nervous system. Since most stimulus arrays are ambiguous, the observer must interpret the sensory stimulation arriving in the brain in light of his knowledge of the environment. Thus perception is an inductive process wherein the observer uses his experience to interpret the patterns of excitation in his receptors. Because most adults are not aware of this interpretive process, Helmholtz calls it *unconscious inference*. As a means of studying these inferential processes, illusions prove to be very useful. Helmholtz (1881) argues, "The study of what are called illusions of the sense is, however, a very prominent part of the psychology of the senses; for it is just those cases which are not in accordance with reality which are particularly instructive for discovering the laws of those processes by which normal perception originates." Thus illusory errors that appear in consciousness may expose the nature of the inferential process that went into their formulation and thus give us a better understanding of the inferential processes and strategies that normally guarantee veridicality in perception. This viewpoint has been reiterated many times. For example, Baldwin (1895) contended that the study of pathological perception, or more simply illusions, is just as important to the understanding of normal veridical perception as the study of pathological states of the body is to the understanding of normal bodily functioning. Helmholtz (1881) summarizes his position on the formation of visual illusions in the following way: "The explanation of the possibility of illusions lies in the fact that we transfer the notion of external objects, which would be correct under normal conditions, to cases in which unusual circumstances have altered the retinal picture." Thus for Helmholtz illusions simply represent normal mechanisms that lead to a distorted percept because of unusual circumstances in the stimulus array or the viewing situation.

On the other hand, Hering (1861) argued that the pattern of stimulation on the retina and excitation in the nervous system could account very well for nearly all percepts. He assigns to each retinal locus a specific sign containing information about the height, breadth, and depth of the target and argues that this information is then automatically extracted. To explain the variety of visual illusions, he looks for peripheral structural mechanisms that might lead to that particular distortion, independent of higher level processing. For example, he postulates lateral interactions on the retina to explain brightness contrast (which he considered an illusory distortion). Later research has shown that such lateral inhibitory and facilitory neural interactions do, in fact, occur. Hering argues that linear illusions occur from equally automatic retinal interactions.

In many respects we have done a disservice to both Helmholtz and Hering. Both of these investigators were much more eclectic than we have indicated. Helmholtz devotes nearly half of his *Treatise of Physiological Optics* (1856, 1860, 1866, 1962) to optical and neural mechanisms. In a similar fashion, whenever anatomical considerations did not seem adequate to the task, Hering resorted to cognitive judgmental strategies. It should thus be clear that the difference between these two positions is one of emphasis rather than one of substance. Nonetheless, the cogency of the arguments these two theorists advanced is reflected in the fact that both of these viewpoints are still found among contemporary researchers.

THE RISE OF VISUAL ILLUSIONS

The middle of the nineteenth century was marked by the separation of psychology as a distinct intellectual enterprise different from philosophy, physiology, or physics. It also marked the beginning of a spate of interest in visual illusions.

In 1855 Oppel published three papers in which he included a number of interesting perceptual distortions that could be easily represented as two-dimensional linear displays. These included the Oppel–Kundt illusion, which we showed as Figure 1.1, and several others. Five years later, in the same year that Fechner published his *Elements of Psychophysics,* Zoellner (1860) presented a new set of visual distortions that were later to bear his name. Between 1860 and 1900, over two hundred papers demonstrating and analyzing various visual distortions appeared. All these distortions could be represented as simple lines on paper, and all of them were virtually unknown before 1855 when Oppel first introduced his famous figures and named this class of effects *visual geometric illusions.*

There had been earlier sporadic reports of visual distortions, usually in reference to environmental configurations. For example, Smith (1738) describes an example of an illusory distortion, later to be studied by Baldwin, in the following fashion:

> We are frequently deceived in our estimates of distances by an extraordinary magnitude of objects seen at the end of it: as in travelling towards a large city or castle or a cathedral church or a mountain larger than ordinary, we think that they are much nearer than we find them to be upon trial (Remarks, paragraph 314).

In a similar vein, he describes a size contrast effect: "Animals and small objects seen in valleys, contiguous to large mountains, appear extraordinarily small."

These descriptions do not seem to carry the same weight or impact as a simple graphic display such as that shown as Figure 1.4 where the two circles (which are simply surrogates for two animals) are the same size, yet the circle surrounded by large forms (which are merely graphic analogues of mountains) seems to be somewhat smaller than its counterpart, which is not near large objects. Such juxtapositions of environmental elements do not occur very frequently and, of course, cannot be arranged and rearranged at will. The major advantage of lines drawn on paper lies in their flexibility. To begin with, one can easily bring large and small objects in close proximity to one another in the picture plane. One can also, select stimuli, such as circles, squares, or lines, which have no necessary and familiar size. Add to these benefits the fact that the observer can easily verify the dimensions of the figural components with a ruler, and we see why experimentation with drawn configurations is much more easily accomplished than similar experiments in the environment.

We will probably never know precisely why the sudden surge of publications of visual illusions occurred in the middle of the nineteenth century. It is possible that part of the explanation lies with the better writing instruments available at about this time, thus permitting the sort of casual sketching or "doodling" that might lead to the accidental discovery of some illusion patterns.

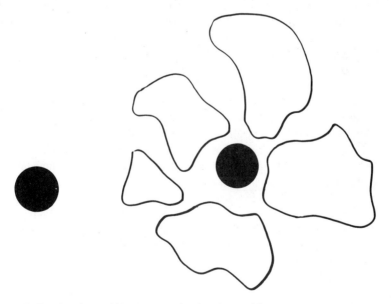

FIG. 1.4. A graphic representation in which subjects in close proximity to large objects appear diminished in size. The central dark circles are physically equivalent, although the one surrounded by large figures appears smaller.

Certainly the interest in visual illusions was fostered and nourished by a general interest in sensation and perception that had already engendered many new optical gadgets and instruments, including the stroboscope, the kaleidoscope, and the stereoscope. These devices became quite popular with the public, and illusions may have been seen as simply another kind of perceptual "magic." It is thus perhaps not surprising that an array of people, drawn from a number of different disciplines, all turned to the study of these interesting and surprising perceptual effects. New illusion configurations began to appear in a vast unsystematic flood. There were new distortions described by the astronomer Zoellner, the sociologist Mueller-Lyer, the physiologist Loeb, and the philosopher—psychologist Brentano. It is interesting to note that Brentano was introduced to linear illusions, not by a fellow psychologist, but by a physicist friend who was intrigued by one such distortion. Many psychologists whose major interests seem to lie far from perception also took their turn at producing illusion configurations. Included in this group are Judd and Binet, both interested in education and child development; the philosophically oriented Baldwin and James; the clinician Jastrow; the founder of applied psychology, Muensterberg; as well as a host of workers in the area of aesthetics, including Stumpf and Lipps. This is not to say that specialists in perception were excluded. We find papers by Wundt, Hering, Helmholtz, Stratton, Sanford, and Delboeuf, all of which presented new illusion configurations or variants of already known distortions. This tradition of both the specialist and nonspecialist working in the area of visual geometric illusions continues to the present. Of the three serious books written on visual illusions in the twentieth century, only one was written by a psychologist (Robinson, 1972); one was written by a physicist (Tolansky, 1964); and the third was written by a lighting engineer (Luckiesh, 1922).

Besides being easy to draw, illusions are apparently easy to theorize about. Thus along with the proliferation of illusion-producing configurations, there was a proliferation of theories. Most theories were "proven" by means of demonstrations, which consisted of nothing more than additional variants of the original distortion and comments on the phenomenology thus evoked. When experiments were done, they usually consisted of the introspective report of one subject, usually the author, making generalization difficult.

The Mueller—Lyer illusion, shown as Figure 1.5, has been one of the most popular configurations since its introduction. The upper horizontal line is usually seen as longer than the lower, although both are equal in length. This illusion, first introduced in 1889, provides an excellent case history of the proliferation of theories (Carter & Pollack, 1968). By 1902, 12 major theories had been proposed to explain this illusion, with a number of minor variations on the major themes. Each theory reflected the general orientation and biases of its theorist. Thus the more cognitively oriented theorists based their explanation on total impression (Mueller—Lyer, 1889), or on the tendency to form closed figures (Laska, 1890), or on the interpretation of possible perspective cues in

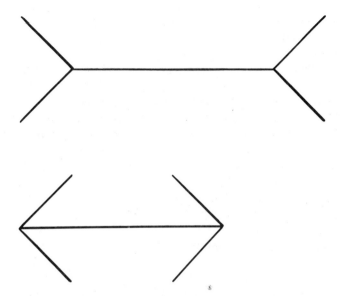

FIG. 1.5.   The Mueller–Lyer illusion in which the upper horizontal line appears longer than the lower, although they are in fact equal in length.

the figure (Thiery, 1896), or even on aesthetic feelings of freedom or constraint (Lipps, 1897). The more physiologically oriented theorists suggested mechanisms such as actual or implied eye movements (Heymans, 1896; Wundt, 1898) or the optical limitations of the eye (Einthoven, 1898). To compound the problem, as Carter and Pollack (1968) point out, most researchers did not communicate with one another personally but carried the controversy about theories of illusions into the journals. Thus Sanford (1901) reviews a number of such dyadic interactions, such as Lasha against Lipps, Mueller-Lyer against Heymans, or Lipps against Brentano and Jastrow.

THE ERA OF WUNDT

In the midst of all of this, the science of psychology was being born. Structuralism was probably the first formal school of psychological thought, and its founder, Wilhelm Wundt, was probably the first person who formally called himself a psychologist. Wundt spent the first 20 or so years of his academic life in the same department at Heidelberg where Helmholtz was then teaching. By the time Wundt was appointed to Fechner's chair in Leipzig in 1875, his thinking and writing had evolved into something clearly identifiable as psychology. In 1879 he founded the first formal administrative unit for psychological research. The work done in this laboratory during the next 30 years by Wundt and his students, primarily using the technique of analytic introspection, profoundly influenced the psychological thought of this period. Students came to study with Wundt from all over western Europe and America and carried the new psychology away with them.

Although Wundt himself believed that psychology should use different experimental techniques for different problems, the primary technique on which the theory of structuralism was based was that of analytic introspection. Structuralism adopted the atomistic viewpoint that earlier in the nineteenth century had proved so successful in physics, biology, and chemistry. It seemed reasonable to assume that consciousness could be viewed as the sum of basic elements, much as biologists had come to view living organisms as the combination of basic units called cells. Structuralism argued that the total sensory impression must be composed of the sum of simple sensory impressions, which might be analogous to the qualities described by Mueller in his doctrine of specific nerve energies. Analytic introspection presumably trained observers to isolate these simple sensory impressions in consciousness and thus reveal the irreducible elements of each conscious experience.

With this emphasis on the careful and analytic analysis of the conscious states evoked by various physical stimuli, it is little wonder that many of Wundt's students — including the Americans, Stratton, Judd, and G. Stanley Hall, the Englishman, Titchener, the German, Muensterberg, the Frenchman, Bourdon, and the Belgians, Thiery and Michotte — engaged in the detailed analysis of various visual illusions. Each of these investigators, at one time or another, was surprised by the discrepancy between some aspect of the carefully observed conscious experience and the actual stimulus array and felt it important and interesting enough to warrant further investigation and study.

Since the technique of analytic introspection was designed to reduce consciousness to basic sensory elements, it seemed reasonable to assume that visual illusions, when dealt with in this manner, would disappear. Surely introspection would yield an accurate estimate of the length of the horizontal in the Mueller—Lyer illusion, and the illusion itself would turn out to be nothing more than a judgmental error added to the basic sensory elements by not-so-careful observers.

There did seem to be some evidence that argued that illusory distortions were nothing more than judgmental artifacts. Heymans (1896) had shown that simply viewing the Mueller—Lyer illusion for a while, with free eye movements, reduced the size of the illusory distortion considerably. Furthermore, when the observer restricted his attention to the critical parts of the figure and ignored the inducing elements, the magnitude of the illusion was considerably reduced (Benussi, 1904). This line of evidence led Schumann (1904) to comment:

> The fundamental fact is that most geometric optical illusions are considerably reduced, or disappear altogether, as soon as we inspect the figure in question more often and try always to compare them as exactly as

possible. This definitely supports the assumption that, at least with many of the illusions, we are dealing with pure errors of judgment.

Unfortunately, these experiments seemed to lead to a reduction in the size of the distortion rather than to the total disappearance of the illusion that the structuralists would have preferred. In addition, there were other data that seemed to contradict the structuralist point of view. Seashore (1961) reports the following example:

> Up to that time the theory had prevailed that a person who was subject to such gross illusions was abnormal or at least a weakling. A supercilious element in my attitude, as well as the attitude of my associates, was illustrated by the fact that I selected Divinity students as my subjects for these experiments, it being generally conceded that these gentlemen, as a class, might be regarded as suggestible; but I produced a rather telling shock and reaction to this by turning the guns on professors and brilliant graduate students, showing that the normal illusion obtained for them quite in the same manner and degree [p. 249].

Since analytic introspection failed to eliminate visual illusions, even in trained observers, Wundt suggested that the final conscious percept might be a "creative synthesis" between sensory and nonsensory elements. Specifically, Wundt suggested that proprioceptive feedback from eye movements might interact with our conscious experience of the visual stimulus. He suggested that the eye may expend more energy in moving over some parts of the configuration than in moving over other parts. If feedback were available from such movements, they might be incorporated into, and hence distort, the final conscious percept. Helmholtz (1866), Heymans (1896), Judd (1902), Muensterberg (1897) and Van Biervliet (1896), rapidly adopted this position. There was, in fact, a heroic experiment conducted by Delabarre (1897), which seemed to support eye movement involvement in visual illusions. Delabarre affixed a plaster cap to his cornea. The cap had a hole in it to permit the entrance of light into the eye and was attached by a series of levers to a pen scribing the surface of a smoked drum. The direction and extent of pen movements thus provided a record of the direction and relative extent of the eye movements. Delabarre found that his eye movements were, in fact, longer when he was scanning the overestimated segment of the Mueller—Lyer illusion than when he was scanning the underestimated segment. These data were taken as confirmation of eye movement involvement in illusion formation, despite the fact that it is as likely that the distorted percept evokes the erroneous eye movements as it is that the eye movements "cause" the illusion observed in consciousness.

By this time, the technique of analytic introspection was under strong attack. Psychologists seemed to be unable to agree on the major attributes of a sensation, and there was no objective way to adjudicate between conflicting reports. Watson (1913) described the prevailing state of affairs in the following way: "I doubt if any one psychologist can draw up a set of statements describing what he means by sensation which will be agreed to by three other psychologists of different training."

This situation led to two separate revolutions, one in the United States, led by Watson, and the other in Germany, led by Wertheimer, Koffka, and Koehler. These revolutions had different bases. Watson's behaviorist position questioned the fruitfulness of trying to study consciousness but failed to challenge the underlying atomistic assumptions of structuralism. The Gestalt revolution retained the phenomenological approach while questioning the underlying atomistic assumptions. In their determination to discard the method of analytic introspection and to displace the old structuralist doctrines, they also rejected many of the questions and issues raised during the height of Wundt's influence, including the problem of visual illusions.

TWO REVOLUTIONS

The two revolutionary theoretical schools that sprang to life in the beginning of this century nearly sounded the death knell for research on visual illusions. Behaviorism wished to discard this area of research for methodological reasons, whereas Gestalt psychology wished to discard it for theoretical reasons.

It would be inappropriate to dwell too long on the behaviorist approach to perceptual phenomena such as visual illusions since the behaviorists themselves refuse to dwell on perception. According to Watson, subjective reports are nonverifiable, and, since perception must use subjective reports to describe the conscious experience, perception was no longer to be considered a part of the scientific study of behavior known as psychology. As Watson wrote in 1919:

> The reader will find no discussion of consciousness and no reference to such terms as perception, attention, will and the like. These terms are in good repute, but I have found that I can get along without them. . . . I frankly do not know what they mean, nor do I believe that anyone else can use them consistently.

Watson is true to his word. In his 1930 book, *Behaviorism,* the words sensation, perception, and illusions do not even appear in the index.

For the behaviorist, one must analyze all phenomena in terms of stimulus–response links. The function of the stimulus is not to evoke a conscious experience but rather to elicit a response. As Watson (1919) put it, "In a system of psychology completely worked out, given the response the stimuli can be predicted; given the stimuli the response can be predicted." Clearly, there is no need for, or indeed room for, either perception or illusion in such a system. In some respects, Watson seems to assume the veridicality of the registration of sensory information by taking the registration of the stimulus completely for granted. In contemporary behaviorism, the emphasis has not shifted very much. Skinner, writing on behaviorism in 1974, does not include a chapter on perception, but he does include one on perceiving in which he talks of the perceptual response in terms of stimuli that elicit various behaviors.

The Gestalt school, on the other hand, retained the structuralist emphasis on the phenomenology of the observer, while rejecting the atomistic assumptions. The configuration, rather than any element within it, served as a unit of analysis.

Although Wertheimer's paper on apparent motion in 1912 is cited as the beginning of Gestalt psychology, its roots actually lie deep in the nineteenth century. The German philosopher, Ehrenfels, noted in 1890 that reduction of the percept to basic units could not adequately describe the conscious experience. The description of a visual array as being composed of four dots does not tell us how to reconstruct either the percept or the stimulus. Ehrenfels argued that the relationship among the elements of the array must be specified as well. Thus we must talk about four dots arranged in a square or a trapezoid, since it is this organization among them that determines the form of the conscious percept. If we change the color or shape of the dots, this does not noticeably alter our perception of the array as being a square. Ehrenfels called the relationship among the stimuli their form—quality (*Gestalt—qualitaet*). Schumann (1900), who conducted the first experimental studies based on this mode of analysis, argued that the observers' pattern of attention organized the stimulus elements into unitary patterns. Thus according to his interpretation the Mueller—Lyer illusion is caused by the fact that the observer directs his attention to the overall length of the figure rather than to the length of the horizontal alone.

For Schumann, attention is a continuous, dynamic process. This can be shown in Figure 1.6, which presents a grid pattern composed of an array of equally spaced elements. If one studies the pattern for a while, groups of elements begin to organize themselves in the percept. One sees groupings of squares or lines of diagonals in successive momentary aggregates, all popping in and out of consciousness. Notice that the stimulus itself is unchanging; it is the perceptual representation that is undergoing change. Schumann might well have called these fluctuating patterns illusions. He does not because of his belief that illusory percepts are merely manifestations of normal processes in the observer, which happen to produce occasional percepts in disagreement with the physical reality.

Wertheimer's (1912) analysis of the phenomenon of apparent movement represented both a continuation of the line of thought stemming from Ehrenfels and a sharp break with it. The data for this paper were collected in Schumann's laboratory, with Koffka and Koehler serving as the main observers. However, the analysis of the data by these three leaders of the Gestalt movement rejected all prior notions, including Schumann's concept of acts of attention. The analysis

FIG. 1.6.   A grid of equally spaced elements in which the perceptual organization continually fluctuates from columns to rows to diagonals according to fluctuations in attention (after Schumann, 1904).

contended that perceptual organizations are not intellectual in nature but, rather, are the result of innate sensory processes acting on the stimulus input. Thus they would argue that one does not learn, or intellectually decide, to group Figure 1.7A into two pairs of dots but, rather, that the organization occurs because of the unlearned principle that objects in close spatial proximity tend to be organized as parts of common units. In fact, learned or intellectual processes do not seem very powerful in the organization of the percept. Thus in Figure 1.7B, observers do not usually spontaneously report the familiar learned figures, namely an M and W, which are embedded in it. The internal organization of the configuration outweighs our past experience.

It is interesting that the Gestalt movement based its theoretical position on a set of stimulus arrays that demonstrated that the final percept was not predictable from knowledge of the stimulus elements alone. At the same time, there seems to be little interest in the study of visual geometric illusions per se, as shown by the fact that Koffka (1935) spends less than five pages out of a total of 720 discussing any of the classical illusion configurations. At the same time, he devotes over 200 pages to perceptual demonstrations that could be called illusory, in the sense that the relationships manifested in the conscious representation of the stimulus are not the same as those existing in the physical array. The Gestaltists avoided the use of the word "illusion" when discussing these grouping phenomena, in order to show the generality of the underlying perceptual processes and to avoid any predispositions toward judgmental explanation of these perceptual data. This position is perhaps best illustrated by Koehler's (1967) discussion of Wertheimer's original study of apparent movement. In his last series of lectures, Koehler (1967) argues that the phenomenon, although well known, had not been seriously studied before 1912 because it had been classified as an illusion, which ". . . meant that stroboscopic movement was not accepted as a perceptual fact at all; it was held to be the product of a mistake in the observer's thinking."

Since, for the Gestalt psychologist, all perception involved a noncorrespondence between the conscious representation and the physical array and, for the behaviorists, simple stimulus registration and overt response rather than the conscious experience were to be the only proper study of psychology, no room for the study of illusions remained. For the Gestalt psychologist, an illusion was merely another manifestation of normal perception, whereas for the behaviorist, an illusion was a content of consciousness and hence not available for study. The hundreds of illusion-producing configurations and the dozens of theories used to explain them were all discarded or de-emphasized as research in this area went into a dramatic decline in the second decade of this century.

THE REBIRTH

The years between 1915 and 1950 were relatively inactive ones for research in visual illusions. Although the number of articles appearing in the psychological literature averaged about 4,500 during these years, the number of papers on visual illusions averaged somewhat less than four a year. Since that time, the

A   B

FIG. 1.7. (A) Four dots that tend to be phenomenally organized into two groups because of the operation of the principle of proximity; (B) a nonsense figure in which observers do not spontaneously report the familiar learned elements it contains, which are the letters M and W.

number of papers published on visual geometric illusions has risen steadily. It is difficult to determine exactly why this contemporary resurgence has occurred, since we are too close to the events in time to gain any perspective. It is interesting to note, however, that the resurgence of interest in illusions parallels the decline of Gestalt psychology and Watsonian behaviorism and the rise of several new theories of perception.

By 1940 both the behaviorist and the Gestalt psychologist were being forced to reconsider their positions. Behaviorists were encountering numerous instances where the responses were at variance with the expectations based on the stimulus input. To explain this, they were forced to propose an intermediate, nonobservable, response, called the *perceptual response*. The nature of this nonobservable, perceptual response could only be ascertained by means of overtly recordable verbal responses. At this point, it becomes difficult to distinguish between simple phenomenological reports and verbal indicators of an internal perceptual response. Once one allows such phenomenological reports, the stage is set for the rediscovery of illusory phenomena.

The Gestalt position had been gradually becoming more physiological. In 1944 Koehler and Wallach presented an elaborate model of electrochemical brain fields which they sought to use to explain a variety of perceptual phenomena. They maintained that the conscious percept was isomorphic with the pattern of stimulation in the brain. Thus any change in the pattern of excitation in the brain should result in a corresponding change in the conscious experience. To verify their position, they turned to the field of visual illusions, noting some of the dynamic changes in the magnitudes of these distortions that occur over time. Thus nearly 40 years after the rejection of visual illusions as a valid area of study, we find Koehler actually using such distortions to test his newly elaborated theoretical position (Koehler & Fishback, 1950a, 1950b).

Other investigators, allied with neither the Gestaltists nor the behaviorists, began to become more aware of illusory phenomena and their importance for the study of visual processing. Helson (1964a, 1964b) used a set of systematic distortions obtained in psychophysical judgments as the basis for his *adaptation level theory*. Werner and Wapner (1952, 1954) and Werner, Wapner, and Chandler (1951) utilize a distortion in the orientation of a line as evidence for their *sensory tonic theory*. Brunswik (1934) suggests that we learn to put greater or lesser reliance on certain cues in the environment in our attempt to form a veridical picture of the world and that illusory distortions can be used to demonstrate the nature of our cue selection. Ames (1951) extended Brunswik's notion, pointing out that the same image in the eye may be produced by an unlimited number of targets that differ in their size orientation, and location relative to the observer. Figure 1.8 shows five objects of different sizes, shapes, and distances from the observer, all of which cause the same size square image on the retina. Ames suggests that our conscious experience represents a "bet" or hypothesis about the meaning of a particular proximal stimulus, with the particular "bet" depending on the observer's previous experience. Thus illusions may be viewed simply as a "wrong guess" about the distal object. All these theorists are operating in a realm of ambiguity in which discrepancies between the physical relationships and the conscious representation of the array are to be expected as a function of the normal operation of the perceptual system. Since illusory distortions are expected, they are valid phenomena for research and further study.

It should be noted that some researchers in perception still viewed illusions as minor aberrances to be ignored or brushed aside. Gibson (1959) writes that his theory ". . . is concerned in the first place with veridical perception and only in the second place with illusions and errors. It presupposes that if a satisfactory explanation of the former can be given, an explanation of the latter will be easy." However, an equally strong case can be made that, if we first understand how illusions and errors arise, an explanation of veridical perception will be easy.

In this brief historical survey we have attempted to set the context out of which the contemporary study of illusions emanates. Many of the themes that emerged throughout the early theorizing on illusions recur in contemporary speculation. As we turn to the theories in later chapters, it is interesting to compare them with their historical antecedents.

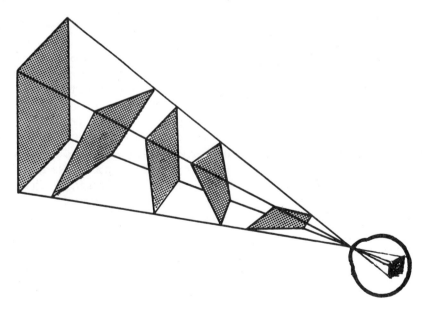

FIG. 1.8. Five objects of different sizes, shapes, and distances from the observer, all of which cause the same size square image on the retina.

2 Size Illusions

Before turning to an analysis, or even a presentation, of the set of phenomena called visual illusions, it is important to specify what is meant by an illusory distortion. Unfortunately, this is not as easy a task as one might think, since it brings one face to face with intensely complicated philosophical questions such as "What is the nature of reality?" or "What shall we define as true or veridical?" Since we are primarily interested in psychological questions rather than philosophical issues, we have decided simply to specify a tentative working definition. This may be less intellectually satisfying than trying to tackle the broad issue of reality, but it should temporarily suffice to provide an indication of the scope and nature of the phenomena we wish to discuss.

To begin with, let us recognize that the primary function of the visual system is to provide the organism with information about the environment. This information includes specification of a variety of stimulus relationships such as the size, distance, and shape of objects. Our percepts usually are reasonably accurate reconstructions of the real world stimulus relationships. Sometimes, however, they are in error. It is possible to delineate four major classes of perceptual error. The first is caused by limitations in the sensitivity of the receptive organ itself; the second involves direct distortion of the stimulus input; the third is composed of certain systematic perceptual errors; the last is visual illusions. The obvious question that arises is how one decides which perceptual errors should be included in each category.

There is little difficulty in determining which perceptual errors result from receptor limitations. Such an error occurs, for example, when an observer responds that no light was present in the field merely because the light was too dim to be detected by his receptor apparatus. Similarly, it is usually easy to determine which perceptual errors result from a direct distortion of the stimulus input as, for example, when the use of magnifying or minifying lenses leads to erroneous estimates of size. Such "errors," in fact, represent an accurate description of a distorted input. It is extremely difficult, on the other hand, to distinguish between certain systematic perceptual errors and visual illusions.

Let us consider the simple situation where two pieces of gray paper are cut from the same stock and one is placed on a black background while the other is placed on a white background. Under these conditions, the piece of gray paper on the white background looks darker than the piece of gray paper on the black background. This is the familiar phenomenon known as brightness contrast. This phenomenon obviously respresents a discrepancy between the phenomenal appearance of the stimuli and the physical reality, since the light reaching the eye from the two patches is identical. This difference does not appear to be due to limitations in the receptor apparatus nor is there any external transformation of the optical array. Should brightness contrast be classified as a visual illusion? Many older texts do, in fact, classify brightness contrast in this way. Lotze (1852) refers to brightness contrast as an illusion, and Luckiesh (1922) includes this phenomenon in his book on visual illusions. By 1964, however, Tolansky no longer lists brightness contrast effects as illusions. Thus, over the years, brightness contrast was apparently removed from the class of visual illusions and placed in the category of systematic perceptual errors. This change in classification probably occurred because between 1922 and 1964 we learned a great deal about neural inhibitory networks in the visual system. It became generally accepted that the interplay between excitatory and inhibitory components on the retina could explain brightness contrast. Hence, workers in perception are no longer surprised to find that the apparent brightness of a piece of paper varies as a function of the background on which it is placed. In fact, by 1972, Robinson is using brightness contrast to explain other illusory phenomena.

Illusions seem to be distinguished from perceptual errors by the existence of an *apparently inexplicable* discrepancy between the appearance of the stimulus and its physical reality. In other words, an illusion may be said to exist when the percept surprises the observer, when he can think of no explanation for why the visual world should behave in that particular fashion. This obviously means that a phenomenon that would be classified as an illusion by one group of observers might not be classified as an illusion by a second group. For example, the nonpsychologist might well consider brightness contrast an illusion. He might also view some aspects of color mixing, such as the combining of red and green beams of light to produce the phenomenal appearance of yellow, as illusions. To the psychologist these phenomena are explicable and expected and hence not illusions. There is an additional consequence of such a definition of illusion. As our understanding of visual phenomena increases, the range and scope of the effects known as visual illusions should contract. Ultimately, when we know exactly how the visual system works, visual illusions should no longer exist.

Such a statement might cause one to pause for a moment to ask why visual illusions should attract such interest and warrant such extensive research if they are doomed ultimately to disappear from the psychological literature. There are several reasons. First, illusory phenomena are extremely prevalent in the world outside the laboratory. The size of lines, for instance, may be over- or under-estimated by 25% or more, depending on the context of the stimuli in which they are embedded. The indicator needle on some poorly constructed dials may be misjudged by several degrees as a function of an illusory distortion. For many years, the cross hairs used to align targets in measuring microscopes were so arranged that a systematic illusion of misalignment could be expected. Illusions that occur in the everyday world can also be useful. As we noted in the previous chapter, for many centuries architects have been using illusory effects to make buildings appear more pleasing to the eye. Package designers distort the shape of bottles so that they seem to contain more product than they actually do. Denton (1971) has even suggested that illusions could be used in traffic control. He has devised a method of road marking that causes drivers to overestimate the speed at which their cars are traveling. He suggests that this could be used at freeway exits to provide a subtle urge to slow down. In our pragmatic interactions with our environment, some knowledge of visual illusions seems useful.

Second, although it is true that the separate study of visual illusions may disappear when we completely understand the operation of the visual system, the converse proposition is also true. The more completely we understand why these distortions occur, the more perfect will be our understanding of visual functioning. If, by manipulating the cues in an illusion figure, estimates of length can be more or less distorted, we may have discovered something about the factors that normally enter into our perception of extent. Perhaps learning why we err in any given illusion figure will tell us something about why we are normally so accurate in our estimates of stimulus relations.

Finally, illusions are fun! Students in introductory psychology classes are usually more intrigued by illusions than by any other part of the chapter on perception. Illusions are the demonstrations that convince artists, architects, engineers, and the average person in the street that psychologists may have something interesting to say about the functioning of the eye. Although some investigators seem to consider illusions as a side eddy in the current work on the psychology of perception (though it is somewhat difficult to see how over 1,000 articles on a topic can be considered a side eddy), illusions have helped to define psychology as an independent discipline separate from philosophy and medicine, as we have seen in our historical survey. Numerous important mechanisms have been discovered, confirmed, and disconfirmed during the study of illusions. Many perceptual theories have been fathered by data from illusions, and many others have been refuted by this same body of knowledge.

In this book we are concerned with a particular subset of the general class of visual illusions. The illustrations in this book all consist of surprising discrepancies in the perception of two-dimensional line drawings. There are many other perceptual situations in which illusions arise, but the visual distortions that occur in two-dimensional configurations are, by far, the most numerous and most frequently studied in the psychology laboratory.

CLASSIFICATION OF TWO-DIMENSIONAL VISUAL ILLUSIONS

The beginning of any scientific discipline involves the naming and classification of the objects or concepts to be studied. A name serves as a shorthand specification of the properties of the named object. Scientific labels are usually based on an underlying classification scheme. They usually designate the properties that make the labeled object similar or dissimilar to other objects of its type.

Unfortunately, no general organizing principle of nomenclature has emerged for visual illusions, mainly because no underlying form of classification is yet apparent. Most illusion forms derive their names from their originators. If a person named Mueller–Lyer invents an illusion, we refer to this figure as the *Mueller–Lyer illusion*. When a person named Brentano varies the figure slightly, we have the *Brentano form of the Mueller–Lyer illusion*. Sometimes the fact that one figure is a variation on another is never made clear in the name. Unless one is familiar with both patterns, it is difficult to tell that the *Wundt illusion* is a variant of the *Hering illusion*. However, a rational system of nomenclature must await a rational system of classification.

Nonetheless it is necessary to group illusions in some manner if we are speak of them. Previous writers have tended to group illusions on the basis of configurational similarities. Robinson (1972) takes a well-known configuration, such as the Mueller–Lyer illusion (Figure 1.5), and groups all the configurations that seem similar under the general heading of the *Mueller–Lyer effect*. Similarly, Tolansky (1964) notes that one group of illusion patterns has converging or diverging lines and refers to *convergence–divergence* illusions.

In this book we have chosen to divide all illusion figures into two classes based on the kind of distortion they produce. It should be noted, however, that this classificaton is simply a matter of convenience and is meant to imply nothing about the causes or mechanisms involved in the formation of the distortions. We return to the problem of classification in a later chapter, when we can deal with it in terms of the data and theories we will have discussed to that point. For the moment, we simply choose to group rather than to classify.

Since we have limited the material in this book to illusion configurations that can be depicted with lines on paper, all possible distortions that we might consider reduce to shifts in the apparent position of points in space. These shifts can manifest themselves as distortions in the size, area, direction, or shape of lines and objects. Boring (1942) has suggested that most illusion patterns can be decribed as manifesting *distortions of size* or *distortions of direction.* Illusions of direction may be subdivided into distortions involving the direction of a simple line element and distortions in the shape of an object (which may be seen as the sum of directional distortions in the line segments that make up the contour of the shape). These groupings roughly follow those suggested by Wundt (1898) in the first serious attempt to classify illusory distortions.

It is important to note that this classification scheme is solely for the purposes of exposition. We must be careful to avoid assuming more homogeneity in the class than is, in fact, the case. It should not be assumed that the mechanisms that cause the overestimation of a line in one figure have anything in common with the mechanisms that cause the overestimation of a similar line in another figure.

In this and the next chapter, we present some of the most common forms of visual illusions in a picture book, or catalog, fashion. The difficult task of explanation will be set aside for the moment, as we simply browse through a set of interesting and deceiving patterns.

Let us begin with illusory distortions in which the apparent size of objects is erroneously perceived when compared to what we would expect on the basis of actual physical measurements. We subdivide this form of distortion into two general types. In the first, a single linear extent, such as the length of a line or the space between two figural elements, is distorted. The actual form of the distortion is usually an over- or underestimation of the line length or the judged distance. Although we are speaking only of this one simple effect, it should be clear that it may result in other perceptual consequences because the distortion of even one line length can lead to an alteration in the shape of the figure. For example, if we begin with a square, the contraction of one horizontal extent will make it look like a trapezoid, whereas the contraction of both horizontal extents will make it appear to be rectangular. Thus a distortion in extent may well lead to a distortion in shape as well.

The second type of size distortion involves the misperception of area. In these configurations, the overall area of a figure is erroneously judged as too large or too small. It should be clear that this group of effects is very similar to the linear distortions that form the first group of size illusions, only here all the dimensions of the figure are distorted to the same degree. This leads to a uniform change in the apparent size of the figure.

ILLUSIONS OF LINEAR EXTENT

The Oppel—Kundt Illusion

The first illusion to be systematically studied in the psychological literature was an illusion of linear extent. It was the configuration shown as Figure 1.1, in which the divided extent is seen as being longer than the undivided extent. This figure was introduced by Oppel (1855) and later parametrically studied by Kundt (1863), and it bears both their names. Figure 2.1 shows some variations of the Oppel–Kundt illusion. In Figure 2.1A, a square area is divided by an increasing number of lines. This tends to elongate the divided extent (which here is the horizontal dimension). The number of lines and their spacing in the configuration are important in this effect. Kundt (1863), Aubert (1876), Piaget and Osterrieth (1953), Obanai (1933), and Oyama (1960) all report that the maximum illusion is found when the number of dividing lines is intermediate. Too many or too few divisions results in diminished effects. This can be seen in Figure 2.1B, which shows a series of divided extents with an increasing number of dividing lines. Notice that the apparent length of the extent increases at first, as the number of elements increases, and then begin to decrease, as the density of the divisions continues to increase. It is possible to vary the size of the figures and spaces without altering the number of divisions by propping the figure up and stepping back a few feet, thus reducing the size of the image on the retina. When you do this, you will find that with more distant viewing the figure that appeared to be the longest at normal reading distance no longer appears so. The longest stimulus now appears to be one with fewer divisions, indicating that it is the spacing between the dividing lines rather than the number of dividing lines that is most important in determining the effect.

This effect seems fairly simple so far; however, do not be deceived. Figure 2.1C presents a special case of the Oppel–Kundt illusion. In this configuration the open undivided space on the left is compared with a space of the same size on the right, which contains only one central dividing element. In this pattern the usual effect is reversed, with the divided space being underestimated relative to the undivided space. Obonai (1954) has shown that the magnitude of this underestimation can be altered by varying the size of the dividing element and the spacing of the dots. Thus it becomes clear that even this simple distortion contains a built-in problem for the theorist. Why should an extent divided by one element lead to an effect exactly opposite from that produced by an extent divided by several elements?

The Horizontal-Vertical Illusion

Historically, the illusion configuration that next captured the attention of psychologists involved an even less complex array than the Oppel–Kundt figure. Two forms of this distortion, usually called the horizontal-vertical illusion, are shown in Figure 2.2A. In these figures the vertical line appears to be longer than the horizontal line although both are physically equal in length. In this illusion the vertical line is apparently 7% to 14% longer than the horizontal line (Kuennapas, 1955a). Intermediate inclinations between horizontal and vertical orientations produce intermediate illusory effects (Girgus & Coren, 1975). This figure was first described by Fick (1851), who merely used it as an example of asymmetry in the visual field. Oppel (1855) began the first psychological investiga-

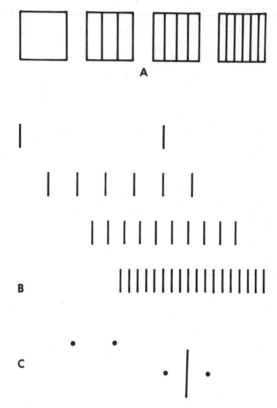

FIG. 2.1.   Variations of the Oppel–Kundt illusion. (A) The horizontal extent of a square is increased by adding additional vertical lines; (B) the overestimation of extent varies as a function of the number of divisions; (C) a single dividing element reverses the effect, causing underestimation of the divided extent.

tions of this figure. Wundt (1898) recognized the theoretical importance of this distortion and used it as an example of the fact that psychological processes must combine with physical stimulation in forming the conscious percept.

Figure 2.2B shows two variants of the distortion, using line drawings of real objects. In both these patterns the horizontal extent is physically equal to the vertical extent. The identity of the object whose dimensions are to be assessed seems to make little difference.

Figure 2.2C is the form of the illusion that is most frequently presented in textbooks as the horizontal-vertical illusion. The reason for its selection is clear; it produces a stronger distortion than either of the variants in Figure 2.2A. Unfortunately, Figure 2.2C is really a combination of two effects: the horizontal-vertical illusion and the special case of the Oppel–Kundt illusion shown in Figure 2.1C. The fact that the vertical line serves as a single dividing element contributes to the underestimation of the horizontal line. This bisection effect

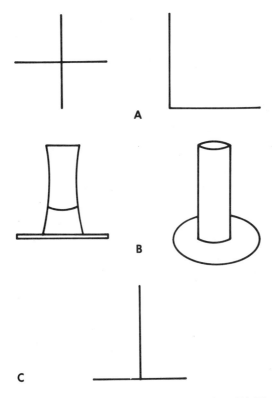

FIG. 2.2. Variation of the horizontal-vertical illusion. (A) The vertical line is seen as being longer than the horizontal line; (B) the vertical extent of objects is overestimated relative to the horizontal extent; (C) the most popular form of this illusion, which is actually a compound of the horizontal-vertical illusion and the special form of the Oppel–Kundt illusion shown in Figure 2.1C.

seems to be considerably stronger than the horizontal-vertical effect, which can be seen by tilting the page 90 degrees so that the bisected line is now vertical and the formerly vertical line is now horizontal. When you do this, you are pitting the two effects (horizontal-vertical and divided-undivided) against each other. Under these circumstances, the divided (vertical) line still looks shorter than the undivided (horizontal) line. It is difficult enough to accept the fact that a configuration consisting merely of two lines in different orientations can lead to consistent errors of perceptual judgment. It is even more difficult to accept the idea that this error may actually be the sum of several sources of distortion.

The horizontal-vertical illusion seems to be dependent on the orientation of the lines on the retina (Avery & Day, 1969; Kuennapas, 1958). You can demonstrate this for yourself by propping this book up vertically and laying your head flat on the table in front of it to look at Figure 2.1A again. Now the images of the lines that were formerly vertical run horizontally across the retinal surface. Since you know your head is tilted, you will still perceive environmentally vertical lines (including those in Figure 2.1A) as running up and down in the real world, despite the fact that they now run horizontally across your retina. You will see that under these conditions it is the retinally vertical lines (which are environmentally horizontal) that appear to be longer.

The Mueller—Lyer Illusion

Even the briefest journey into the study of visual illusions is bound to bring one into contact with the pattern shown in Figure 2.3A. In this configuration, the horizontal shaft of the figure with the wings turned out appears to be longer than the horizontal shaft of the figure with the wings turned in. This configuration was first presented by Mueller—Lyer in 1889 and bears his name. More work has been done on this illusion than on virtually all other illusion configurations combined. One of the reasons for the popularity of this figure is the tremendous strength of the obtained distortion. The apparently longer segment is usually seen as 25% to 30% longer than the apparently shorter segment.

There are myriad variations of this figure. Figure 2.3B shows the most popular variant, which was first introduced by Brentano (1892). Figure 2.3C shows

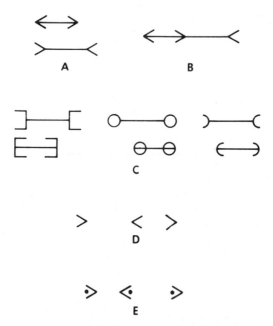

FIG. 2.3. Variations of the Mueller—Lyer illusion. (A) The horizontal shaft with wings turned out appears to be longer than that with wings turned in; (B) the Brentano form of the illusion; (C) variations in wing shape alter illusion magnitude; (D) the illusion still occurs with the shaft removed; (E) the expected effect reverses for dots placed in proximity to the wings.

how variations in the shape of the wing affect the size of the distortion. In general, as the wings become less angular, the distortion decreases. Figure 2.3D shows that the distortion apparently involves an alteration in the extent of the space between the vertices of the angles, since the illusion is still present when the horizontal shafts are removed.

However, consider the configuration shown in Figure 2.3D. One would predict that the distance between the outward pointing wings would be overestimated and that the distance between the left-hand dot and the middle dot would appear to be longer than the distance between the right-hand dot and the middle dot. (The distances are, in fact, equal.) Yet in this interesting figure created by Ebbinghaus in 1902, the opposite effect occurs.

Variations in the size of the angle between the wings also affects the illusion strength dramatically. Although there is some disagreement about the size that produces the maximal distortion, in general the evidence indicates that smaller angles produce greater over- and underestimation than do larger angles (Auerbach, 1894; Brentano, 1892; Dewar, 1967a, 1967b; Heymans, 1896; Lewis, 1909; Nakagawa, 1958; Wundt, 1898).

Altering the length of the wings also affects the strength of the distortion. The size of the illusion increases as wing length increases, up to some optimal length. Increases in wing length beyond this point lead to a decrease in illusion strength. The strongest effect is obtained when the length of the wings is between 20 and 35 percent of the length of the shaft (Dewar, 1967b; Hayami & Miya, 1937; Lewis, 1909; Nakagawa, 1958).

The Mueller—Lyer figure will reappear many times as we discuss the theories of illusions. It is a favorite of illusion theorists, and often their downfall.

The Baldwin Illusion

We seldom judge a stimulus in isolation. Most perceptual judgments seem to involve a comparison between the target stimulus and the stimuli surrounding it. This fact has often been used by special effects experts. They take a normal-size actor and make him look like a giant by surrounding him with tiny pieces of furniture or tiny replicas of houses. Or they make him appear to shrink by surrounding him with oversized trees, chairs, and so on. The subjective experience that the actor is actually larger or smaller is quite compelling. In general, any stimulus surrounded by larger stimuli seems smaller than it really is, whereas any stimulus surrounded by smaller stimuli seems larger than it really is. The general process is usually called *size contrast*. Notice that we are not explaining the perceptual effect by applying this label but simply describing it. There are a number of illusion configurations that can best be described as showing some sort of size contrast effect. The oldest of these is the configuration first studied by Baldwin in 1895.

Figure 2.4A shows the basic Baldwin illusion patterned after Restle and Merryman (1968a, 1968b). In this configuration, the line flanked by large squares seems smaller than the line flanked by small squares. The actual measurements in Baldwin's study were taken on the pattern reproduced as Figure 2.4B, in which a line is flanked by two squares differing in size. The hatch mark indicates the midpoint of the line, dividing it into two equal segments. Yet the midpoint seems to be too close the large square. It actually looks as if the line segment near the large figure had been reduced in extent.

As in the Mueller—Lyer illusion, it is easy to show that it is not the line per se but the space between the components that is distorted. Figure 2.4C shows a series of increasingly large rectangles, each separated by the same size gap. Notice how, as the figures increase in size, the space separating them appears to shrink (Schumann, 1900).

There is nothing particularly special about squares as the inducing figures. Wundt (1898) noted a variant of the Baldwin illusion, which is shown in Figure 2.4D. Here we have two pairs of horizontal parallel lines. The height of the gap

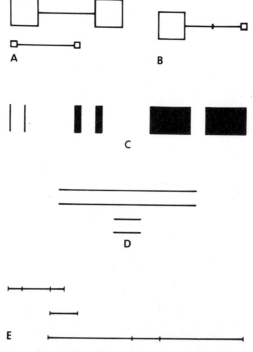

FIG. 2.4.   Variations of the Baldwin illusion. (A) The line segment flanked by large squares is underestimated relative to the segment flanked by small squares; (B) the hatch mark divides the shaft in half, but the segment next to the larger square seems smaller; (C) space surrounded by larger masses is seen as being apparently smaller; (D) space enclosed by long parallel lines seems narrower; (E) the line component surrounded by small segments seems larger than the line component surrounded by large segments.

in the two pairs is identical, but the space between the longer lines seems smaller than the space between the shorter lines.

Figure 2.4E shows a deceptively simple configuration that is probably a variant of this same illusion principle. The central segment of each of the two divided lines is equal in length to the segment presented alone. Yet when the line is flanked by small line segments (top line), it is overestimated and when it is flanked by larger line segments (bottom line), it is underestimated. Thus the central region seems to be contrasted against the size of the flanks, which provide the context for judgment. A number of Japanese researchers have studied this simple configuration. Oyama (1960) and Obanai (1954) report that the maximum overestimation of the center segment is obtained when the flanks are each about half as long as the central extent. The maximal underestimation seems to occur when each of the flanks is approximately twice as long as the central region. There is some evidence that the overall size of the configuration may affect the strength of the illusion, with slightly stronger distortions obtained for smaller figures.

The Ponzo Illusion

One of the illusion configurations that has received a good deal of attention recently is shown in Figure 2.5A. Koehler and Wallach (1944) attributed this figure to Ponzo (1928). The actual primary source for this illusion has not been clearly established. Luckiesh presented a variant of it in 1922, (republished in 1965) and Titchener presented a version in 1901. Unfortunately, neither of these authors cited the source where he first obtained it. Since Ponzo's name is so intimately associated with this configuration in most current writings, we refer to it as the Ponzo illusion in line with the contemporary nomenclature. The basic pattern of the distortion is that lines closer to the apex of an angle are overestimated relative to lines farther down in the body of the angle. Figure 2.5B shows that there is actually a gradient of distortion. As we move closer and closer to the vertex, the lines seem to become progressively longer (Fisher, 1968). Figure 2.5C shows that it is not necessary to have a complete angle to obtain the illusion; rather, the important variable seems to be the proximity of the test lines to another line in the field. With only half the angle present, as in 2.5C, the magnitude of the obtained distortion is almost precisely halved (Fisher, 1968). Figure 2.5D points out more clearly that the critical variable for elicitation of the illusion is the proximity of the test element to adjacent contours rather than the presence of slanted lines in the field (Fisher, 1968).

Looking at Figure 2.5D, one is reminded of the Baldwin illusion in that the length of the horizontal line seems to decrease as the size of the space between it and the contour increases, an effect that has been demonstrated on a variant of the Baldwin (Restle & Merryman, 1968b). Notice that, if we attempt to understand the Ponzo illusion as a form of the Baldwin illusion in this fashion, we are

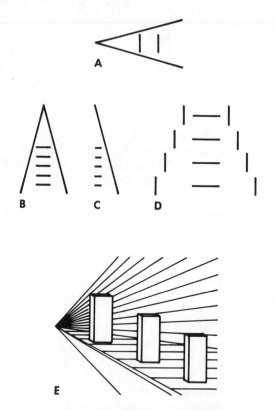

FIG. 2.5.   Variants of the Ponzo illusion. (A) The linear nearer the apex appears larger; (B) as lines approach the apex, they grow steadily larger; (C) the illusion still occurs with only one converging line; (D) in the absence of line convergence, varying the proximity of adjacent lines still produces the effect; (E) a perspective drawing version of the basic Ponzo configuration.

actually simply assuming a symmetry between lines and spaces. In Figure 2.4C, we showed that depicted extents could affect our judgment of the size of spaces; now we simply assume that the size of spaces may also affect our judgment of depicted extents. This kind of speculation, which reduces an illusion pattern to a variant of another pattern, is exceedingly common in the literature. Unfortunately, such attempts have not been particularly successful, partly because it is invariably difficult to specify which is the basic pattern and which is the variant. Is the Ponzo a variant of the Baldwin or is the Baldwin a variant of the Ponzo?

The reader will undoubtedly have noticed that the presence of the converging lines in Figures 2.5A and 2.5B suggest a perspective drawing. In fact, one of the most frequently reproduced variants of the Ponzo configuration is really simply a drawing of a possible three-dimensional scene, as shown in Figure 2.5E. Notice that the posts are all physically the same length, yet the ones that appear to be

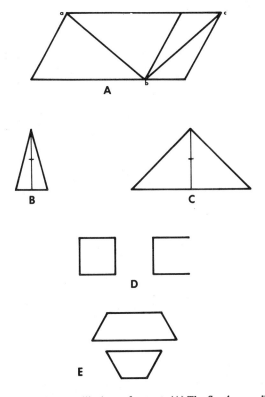

FIG. 2.6. Miscellaneous illusions of extent. (A) The Sander parallelogram, in which the diagonal *ab* is seen as longer than *bc* although they are physically equal; (B) the hatch mark divides the vertical line in half but appears to be too high; (C) for an obtuse angle, the illusion reverses and the midpoint appears too low; (D) the open width of the square on the right is overestimated relative to the closed width of the square on the left; (E) the upper line of the top figure is equal in length to the upper line of the bottom figure, although it appears longer.

closer to the apex of the angle (and hence seem to be farther away) look larger. At a later point in the text, we discuss a popular theoretical position that is based on this type of analysis.

Some Miscellaneous Illusions of Linear Extent

There are a number of illusions of extent that are difficult to group. Some of these, however, result in fairly strong and interesting effects. Probably the most impressive is shown as Figure 2.6A. This figure is usually credited to Sander (1926) although, as with the Ponzo illusion, there are earlier representations of it (Luckiesh, 1922/1965). The length of the two diagonals labeled *ab* and *bc* is actually the same, although *ab* seems to be considerably longer. The apparent difference between the two lines is often as large as 20 to 25% of their length.

Figures 2.6B and 2.6C show two isosceles triangles. In Figure 2.6B the hatch mark on the altitude of the triangle appears to be closer to the apex than to the base, although it actually divides the line into two equal segments. This effect was first noted by Wundt (1898) and has been recently explored by Piaget and Pene (1955). They noted that this effect is strongest when the angle that the line bisects is around 55°. When the angle is made very obtuse, as in Figure 2.6C, the effect reverses itself. This reversal is strongest when the angle is around 140°.

Figure 2.6D is an example of another general class of distortions. If we consider the apparent width of the open and closed equare, it is quite apparent that the width of the open squares appears to be larger than the width of the closed square. Mueller–Lyer (1889) was the first to notice that the size of an open or unbounded dimension is usually overestimated. Such overestimation of the unbounded dimension is also found in curved figures (Coren & Festinger, 1967).

Figure 2.6E is an interesting and somewhat puzzling distortion of length, which was introduced by Titchener (1901). In this figure, the upper line of the top figure and the upper line of the bottom figure are both the same length. The top line belonging to the larger figure, however, appears to be considerably longer than the top line belonging to the smaller figure. It is possible to analyze this figure in a number of different ways. For example, one could think of it as a variation of the Mueller–Lyer configuration in which the angles between the sides of the trapezoid and the top line are equivalent to the turned-in and turned-out wings. It is also possible to analyze this configuration as a special case of the Ponzo illusion by arguing that the sides of the trapezoid simply represent truncated angles. If you mentally complete the angle, you will see that the top line on the upper figure is closer to the apex of its angle than is the top line on the lower figure. It is also possible to analyze this figure as a special case of the Baldwin illusion in which the short upper line of the bottom figure is contrasted with the long lower line of the figure above it. Needless to say, the distortion could involve all three illusions or, for that matter, none of them.

ILLUSIONS OF AREA

Many of the same principles and pattern manipulations that cause distortions of linear extent also cause distortions in area. For example, Figure 2.7A shows a variant of the Ponzo illusion in which the circle closer to the apex of the angle is seen as uniformly larger than the circle farther back in the body of the angle. Notice that this figure is an areal variation of Figure 2.5A. Similarly, the ubiquitous Baldwin illusion can be drawn as an illusion of area. In Figure 2.7B, the square flanked by large squares appears to be smaller than the square flanked by small squares. Figure 2.7C shows a special case of this figure, which was probably first presented by Ebbinghaus (1902) and generally bears his name, although it is sometimes referred to as *Titchener's circle illusion*, probably because Titchener (1901–1905) reprinted this figure as part of an exercise in his book on experimental psychology. Notice that Figure 2.7C is nothing more than a Baldwin illusion with more than two inducing figures surrounding the central test figure. It is not surprising, therefore, that this Ebbinghaus or Titchener's circle illusion shows the same type of distortion as the Baldwin illusion in that a target surrounded by large objects appears phenomenally smaller than one surrounded by small objects. The effect is considerably stronger when there is a large number of figures around the test object (Massaro & Anderson, 1970; Morinaga, 1956). Girgus, Coren, and Agdern (1972) have shown that the distance between the test circle and the surrounding elements is important. They report that, as the inducing elements are moved farther away, the apparent size of the central circle decreases, irrespective of the size of the inducing circles. This finding could have easily been predicted from the next illusion we will discuss, the Delboeuf.

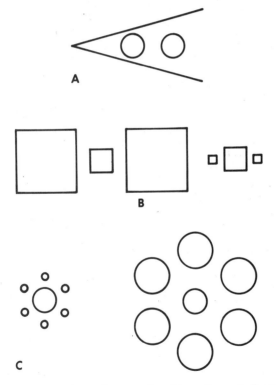

FIG. 2.7.   Some illusions of area produced by patterns similar to extent distortions. (A) An areal version of the Ponzo illusion in which the circle near the apex appears to be larger (B) a variant of the Baldwin illusion in which the square flanked by large squares appears to be smaller than the square flanked by small squares: (C) the Ebbinghaus illusion in which the apparent size of the central circle surrounded by small circles is larger than the apparent size of the central circle surrounded by large circles.

The Delboeuf Illusion

Figure 2.2A shows an illusion of area originally introduced by Delboeuf in 1892. In this illusion the apparent size of a circle is altered by the size of a concentric circle. In Figure 2.8A, the central circles on the right and left are the same size as the circle shown alone. However, when surrounded by a large circle, the central figure appears to be reduced in size, whereas it is apparently expanded when surrounded by a smaller circle. Piaget, Lambercier, Boesch, and von Albertini (1942) and Morinaga (1955) have shown that the maximum overestimation occurs when the diameter of the surrounding circle is about 50% larger than the diameter of the inner circle. The maximum underestimation seems to occur when the diameter of the outer circle is five or six times as large as the diameter of the inner circle (Oyama, 1960).

Figure 2.8B shows that the apparent size of both the outer and the inner circle are distorted. The circles in the Delboeuf illusion appearing alone on the right and left are the same size as the circles arranged concentrically in the center.

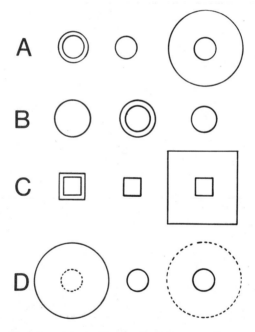

FIG. 2.8.   Variations of the Delboeuf illusion. (A) The central circle surrounded by the large concentric circle appears to be smaller than the circle alone, whereas the central circle surrounded by a smaller concentric circle seems to be enlarged; (B) when placed concentrically, the outer circle is apparently contracted, whereas the inner is expanded; (C) the same illusion occurs for forms other than circles; (D) the distortion is increased when the central test element is reduced in contrast and decreased when the outer inducing circle is reduced in contrast.

When the two elements are combined, the smaller circle seems expanded whereas the larger circle seems contracted. Figure 2.8C demonstrates that there is nothing particularly special about circles, since the Delboeuf affect can occur with other concentrically arranged shapes.

There is at least one other stimulus parameter that seems to affect the strength of this distortion. If the contrast of the central circle is reduced, the magnitude of the distortion increases; however, if the contrast of the outer circle is reduced, the magnitude of the distortion decreases (Oyama, 1962; Weintraub & Cooper, 1972; Weintraub, Wilson, Greene, & Palmquist, 1969). This effect is demonstrated in Figure 2.8D using a dotted line to mimic lower contrast.

It is possible to conceive of the Delboeuf illusion as a special case of the Baldwin illusion. Consider a linear measurement taken across the diameter of the circles in Figure 2.8A. Compare the results of such a measurement arranged along a line with the Baldwin figure variants shown as Figure 2.4E. It is clear that the contours of the circles in Figure 2.8A divide the enclosed space in a manner similar to the way the hatch marks in Figure 2.4E divide the line.

If we look at the quantitative relationships in these two distortions, speculations of commonality between these distortions seem further supported. For the line version of the Baldwin figure (2.4E), the maximum overestimation of the central segment seems to occur when the central region is about 50% of the whole line (Oyama, 1960), whereas the maximum overestimation of the central circle in the Delboeuf figure (2.8A) occurs when its diameter is about 65% as long as the diameter of the surrounding circle. For underestimation, the correspondence is even closer. Both figures achieve maximum underestimation when the larger extent is about five times as large as the smaller.

The reader should note that, although we have spoken of the Delboeuf illusion as a variant of the Baldwin illusion, we could have as easily presented them in the opposite order. For the purposes of our discussion, when one illusion is spoken of as a variant of another, it should be interpreted as simply meaning that the two illusions manifest similar types of distortion and seem to vary similarly when figural parameters are altered.

The Wundt-Jastrow Illusion

There is a striking set of illusions in which two figures of equal size are placed in proximity to each other as shown in Figure 2.9A. When oriented in the pictured manner, the upper figure appears considerably smaller than the lower. This can be demonstrated very effectively by cutting two figures, similar to those in 2.9A, out of heavy white cardboard and holding them up against a dark background so that they are clearly visible. If one shows this to an audience, they readily agree that the lower figure is larger than the upper. When one slowly exchanges the positions of the two cut-out forms, the audience is usually quite astonished as the upper figure reaches the lower position and the formerly smaller figure looks like the larger of the pair.

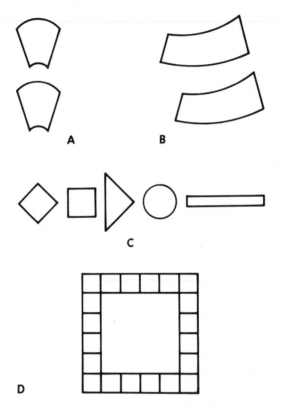

FIG. 2.9.   Some variations of illusions of area. (A) The Wundt—Jastrow illusion in which the upper figure appears to be smaller than the lower; (B) regardless of shape or orientation, the figure whose short side is in proximity to the long side of its counterpart tends to be underestimated; (C) these figures differ in the perceived amount of area that they enclose, although all are equal; (D) the garden path illusion in which the area enclosed in the central square seems greater than that of the surrounding walk, although both are equal.

This illusory distortion of size seems to be relatively independent of the shape of the objects, provided they have one side that is longer than the other side. The figure whose short side is placed next to the long side of its counterpart is seen as the smaller object. As can be seen in Figure 2.9B, this effect is not dependent on which figure is above or below. Invert the book to see.

This type of illusion clearly demonstrates how little we know about how people estimate area. The shape of any object clearly interacts with our estimate of the area that it encloses. For instance, Figure 2.9C shows five different, yet very common figures. Most observers will find it difficult to believe that they all enclose the same area. It seems that the presence or absence of angles, the length of the longest and shortest lines in the array, and the juxtaposition of the test configuration with other configurations all interact with our judgment of the amount of the enclosed area.

Tolansky (1964) presents an interesting demonstration of an illusion based on the misjudgment of area. He calls it the *garden path illusion*. This illusion is shown in Figure 2.9D, which is a schematic representation of a square garden with a paved pathway (represented by the hatched lines) going around it. The actual area covered by the "paved path" is equal to the area of the clear "lawn," yet the lawn looks much larger. It would be useful for architects and landscape designers to know about this distortion.

The Irradiation Illusion

There is a very old area illusion that we noted previously when we were talking about architecture (page 6). This illusion was extensively analyzed by Helmholtz (1856, 1860, 1866/1962) and is based on brightness differences in the field rather than on contour interactions. The basic form of the illusion is shown in Figure 2.10A, in which the two central squares are equal in size, although the white square appears to be considerably larger than the black square. Pierce (1898) described this effect as being characterized by the white areas "boring into" the black areas. Helmholtz (1856, 1860, 1866/1962) is responsible for the currently used label for this effect: the *irradiation illusion*.

Tolansky (1964) presents a most interesting variant on this effect (Figure 2.10B), in which the spaces between the discs are exactly equal to the diameters of the discs. In the figure on the left, however, the black interstices look considerably smaller than the diameter of any one disc whereas in the figure on the right, where the brightnesses are reversed, the white interstices look considerably larger than the diameter of any one disc.

The presence of the irradiation effect is frequently acknowledged in popular lore. For instance, people wear black clothes so that they will look slimmer. Presumably, given the nature of the stimuli that produce this illusion, they will look even slimmer when they are standing in front of white walls.

The BOOM!–SQUISH! Illusion

One never quite gets away from the effects of the media in today's culture. There are a number of interesting pictorial effects that are characteristic of current advertising illustrations, comic book illustrations, and television cartoons. Suppose you wish to show that something is about to explode. This is usually done by drawing a circle on a piece of paper with an array of outward-pointed arrows around it. The point is often emphasized by writing "BOOM!" in big block letters nearby. If something is rapidly contracting or about to be crushed, it is commonly indicated by a circle surrounded by inward-pointing arrows (and maybe the word "SQUISH!"). Such configurations are shown in Figure 2.11.

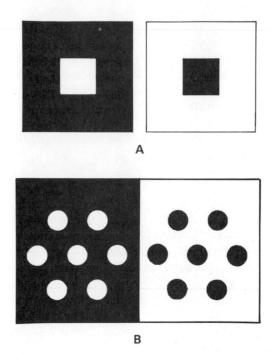

A

B

FIG. 2.10.   Variants of the irradiation illusion. (A) The white square on
the black background appears to be larger than the black square on white;
(B) the diameter of the circles is equal to the size of the spaces between the
circles, yet the spaces seem larger when the circles are black and smaller
when they are white.

Clearly, the exploding circle seems larger than the imploding circle. Unfortunately, it is difficult to know whether to classify the apparent size difference in the
two circles as an illusion or as a stylized representational picture. We leave this
choice to the reader.

Illusions of Size in the Natural and Man-Made Environment

Visual illusions of size and area are not confined to lines drawn on paper. As we
noted in the previous chapter, there are many man-made or naturally occurring
situations in which our visual sense is deceived. These instances of environmental
illusions are quite frequent and often striking. One example is a rather remark-
able metal structure in St. Louis, Missouri, called the Gateway Arch. This structure looks as though it were about twice as tall as it is wide. It is, however, exactly 630 feet tall and 630 feet wide. Figure 2.12 is a photograph of the arch. As
a ruler will readily demonstrate, the height and width of the arch are equal on
the page. Yet even here the effect persists. St. Louis has created the world's

largest horizontal-vertical illusion, a variant of the same distortions we saw in Figure 2.2, only many times larger in size and magnitude of distortion.

Actually, the Gateway Arch is not an exceptional case. Illusions abound in the natural environment. For instance, the horizontal-vertical illusion can be seen in a number of different contexts. It is the reason a tree looks much shorter when it has been felled than when it is standing. Chapanis and Manken (1967) had observers estimate the height of vertical objects such as lamp posts, parking meters, and buildings by means of a horizontal line. Using this technique, they found that the height of a four-story building was overestimated by approximately 25%.

A

B

FIG. 2.11.   The circle drawn with lines of action representing expansion appears to be larger than that drawn with lines representing contraction.

FIG. 2.12. The Gateway Arch in St. Louis, in which the height equals the width but appears to be much greater.

Other illusory distortions of extent are also common. For instance, contrast illusions similar to the Baldwin or Ebbinghaus illusions (Figures 2.4 and 2.7) are all around us. If one sees a three-story house standing between two ranch-style, single-story dwellings, it might appear to be quite tall. If this same three-story building is sandwiched between two forty-story office buildings, it suddenly looks very small indeed.

Architects and interior design experts often use illusory effects without even knowing it. For example, they may elect to install a floor covered in linoleum tile rather than a sheet of linoleum of a single color because the former makes the room appear to be larger. It seems likely that the lines demarcating the boundaries of the square tiles serve the same function as the dividing elements in the Oppel–Kundt illusion (Figure 2.1), thus expanding the room's dimensions.

FIG. 2.13.   The moon illusion in which the horizon moon seems overestimated relative to the moon at its zenith. (A) the moon on the horizon;
(B) when depicted as the same size at its zenith, the moon appears too
large; (C) a more phenomenally correct depiction of the moon at its zenith.

Perhaps the best known of the environmental illusions relates to the size of
the sun and moon. The rising or setting sun or moon always looks considerably
larger than the same heavenly body when it is high in the sky. Artists have long
recognized this fact and accentuated this effect by drawing scenes in which a
huge harvest moon sits on the horizon overlooking fields and farms below, as in
Figure 2.13A. If we were to place the same size moon high in the sky over this
landscape, it would look much too large, as can be seen in Figure 2.13B. To
match our usual perceptual experience in the environment, we have to reduce
the size of the moon dramatically, as shown in Figure 2.13C.

These few examples make it clear that illusions of size are readily found in nature. Their presence is often recognized, albeit not explicitly, in everyday actions
and advice, as when a tailor or clothing salesman suggests some particular striped

pattern to make you appear taller, shorter, fatter, or thinner in direct application of the Oppel—Kundt effect (Figure 2.1). Food packagers know that a bottle with a pinched waist looks taller and thus appears to hold more cooking oil. The hour-glass contours mimic the apparently longer segment of the Mueller—Lyer illusion (Figure 2.3). Although they may not realize it, by altering the appearance of the size of objects without changing the physical dimensions, these individuals are working in the realm of illusions.

3 Direction, Location, and Shape Illusions

In the preceding chapter we catalogued a series of illusions in which the apparent length or size of a stimulus was distorted. In this chapter we present a series of illusions in which the apparent shape or orientation of stimuli systematically differs from what would be expected on the basis of actual physical measurements. As we noted earlier, however, judgments of size, shape, and orientation are not independent of one another. The way in which these dimensions interact can be easily demonstrated in a simple closed figure, such as the outline square shown in Figure 3.1A. If we now alter the direction of the vertically oriented sides, the figure is no longer seen as square but appears as the rhombus in Figure 3.1B. If, on the other hand, we simply alter the length of one side, the square becomes the trapezoid shown as Figure 3.1C. Thus the simple alteration of one length not only changes the global shape of the figure but also forces changes in the orientation and inclination of adjacent pattern elements. In this vein, one might look back at Figure 2.1A, which was a variant of the Oppel–Kundt illusion. Although we discussed this pattern as an illusion of extent, we have obviously altered the shape of the square to that of a rectangle by elongating it in one dimension.

This analysis suggests that configurations which produce illusions of extent could be altered to create shape distortions. For instance, when we look at Figure 3.1D, we see a variant of the Ponzo illusion (described in Figure 2.5), which was introduced by Ehrenfels (1890). He added additional converging lines to the usual array, thus increasing the size of the distortion, and used a square instead of two lines. Notice that we obtain the expected alteration in the apparent length of the verticals. This, however, results in a changed perception of the square. It now appears to be trapezoidal, with concomitant tilting of the horizontal lines. Therefore, in this configuration, we have a shape distortion or an illusion affecting the direction of lines, in addition to the usual Ponzo extent illusion.

The Baldwin illusion can be modified so that it also affects the orientation of contours. In Figure 3.1E, we show such a pattern in which the dark areas are constructed so that they increase in width toward their base, which is analogous to a continuous increase in square size for Figure 2.4C. This results in a distortion such that the white space between the dark areas seems to be continually contracting as one moves down the figure. Under these circumstances, the inner contours, although physically vertical, appear to be tilting away from each other.

Another interesting set of shape distortions can be created using the Delboeuf illusion. As we saw in Figure 2.8A, the Delboeuf involves an expansion of space toward near contours and a contraction or shrinking away from distant contours. In Figure 3.1F, we combine these two effects by using an asymmetrical (here oval) inducing figure. This leads to an expansion of the vertical dimension and a contraction of the horizontal dimension of the central circle, thus making this circle appear slightly egg shaped, with its major or longer axis oriented vertically. Figure 3.1G shows that such a shape distortion can also be produced by placing the asymmetrical inducing element within the test circle. In Figure 3.1H, we see that the same principle may be used to distort other geometrical shapes. In this figure, the square looks slightly rectangular after the introduction of an oval inducer into its interior.

If we can alter the shape of figures and the direction of contours by some of the same manipulations of extent that we have already presented, one might ask why we need to categorize these illusions as a separate class. However, there are some distortions of shape and orientation that are not readily reducible to simple distortions of extent. Thus even though all illusions are ultimately reducible to apparent shifts in the location of points in space, there is a certain phenomenal independence between shape, inclination, and size.

ILLUSIONS OF DIRECTION AND LOCATION

Illusions of direction and location are quite striking when encountered. Illusions of direction involve distortions in which the direction or orientation of a contour or figure is altered. Thus, for instance, a vertical line may be made to appear to be tilted. In illusions of location, the actual location of lines and figures is shifted in space although the orientation or inclination of lines remains unaffected. Thus, for example, a square may appear to be a few millimeters farther to the right than it actually is.

It is interesting to note that the first examples of an illusion of direction and an illusion of location were published by the same individual, an astronomer from Leipzig named Zoellner, who was neither a psychologist nor a specialist in vision.

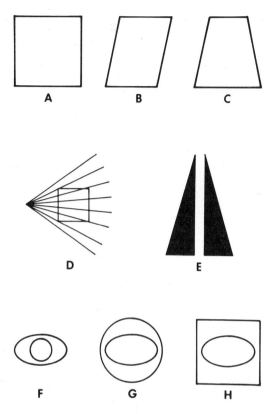

FIG. 3.1.   (A) An outline square; (B) whose apparent shape changes when one simply alters the orientation of lines; (C) or their length; (D) a variant of the Ponzo illusion in which the shape of a square is distorted; (E) a variant of the Baldwin illusion in which the vertical lines appears to be tilted; (F) a variant of the Delboeuf illusion in which the inner circle appears to be oval; (G) here the outer circle appears oval; (H) here the outer square appears to be slightly rectangular.

The Zoellner Illusion

In 1860 Zoellner noticed an interesting illusion of direction. If a line is intersected by a number of other lines that form acute angles with it, the main line seems to be tilted in the direction opposite to the direction of these intersecting elements. The simplest form of this effect is shown in Figure 3.2A in which three long lines are all vertical and parallel to one another. The presence of the short intersecting lines makes the long lines appear to be tilted in different directions.

Zoellner contended that the thickness of the lines makes little difference in the magnitude of the effect, as can be seen in Figure 3.2B, which is composed of wider lines but still manifests the distortion. There are, however, some stimulus parameters that do seem to affect the magnitude of the distortion. For instance,

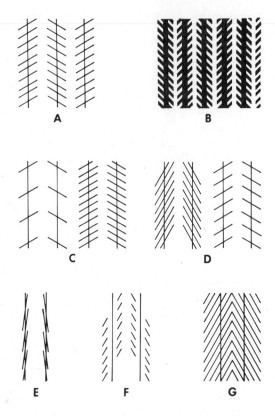

FIG. 3.2.   Variations of the Zoellner illusion. (A) The three vertical lines are parallel but appear to be tilted; (B) a variation of the same effect with thicker lines; (C) as more crossing lines are added, the apparent tilt becomes greater; (D) the tilt is larger when the angles of the oblique crossing lines are more acute; (E) when the angles of the obliques become very small, the direction of apparent tilt reverses; (F) obliques do not have to intersect verticals to obtain the apparent tilt; (G) the herringbone variant of the Zoellner illusion.

increasing the number of oblique lines intersecting the test line seems to increase the magnitude of the illusion, as can be seen by comparing the two arrays in Figure 3.2C. The critical feature appears to be the density of the intersecting lines, which is defined in terms of the number of lines per unit area in the retinal image (Wallace & Crampin, 1969).

The illusion is strongly dependent on the angle of intersection between the test line and the oblique lines. In general, as the angle becomes more acute, the amount of inclination of the lines increases (Maheux, Townsend, & Gresock, 1960; Morinaga, 1933; Wallace & Crampin, 1969) as can be seen in Figure 3.2D. This sort of observation might lead one to believe that we could describe the Zoellner illusion as one of directional contrast, where the apparent direction of the test line is contrasted against the direction of inclined inducing lines in much the same way that the size of the test circles is contrasted against the size of the inducing circles in the Ebbinghaus illusion (Figure 2.7C). Although this seems to be an adequate description for the distortions found in most Zoellner patterns, it proves to be inadequate when the angles of intersection are small. If the acute angle between the test line and the oblique line is less than 10°, the illusion reverses. Now the main lines seem to tilt toward the inducing oblique lines instead of away from them (Adam, 1964; Imai, 1962; Wallace & Crampin, 1969). This effect, which is maximal for very small angles of around 2°, is shown as Figure 3.2E. This unexpected reversal serves to point out the complexity of what at first appears to be a simple and systematic effect.

Figure 3.2F shows that the oblique lines need not pass through the test line to produce the distortion. Figure 3.2G shows the effect when the oblique lines are extended until they intersect. This configuration is more than a minor variant. It is often called the *herring bone illusion,* and we will return to it later in this chapter.

The Poggendorff Illusion

In 1860 Zoellner submitted the paper describing the illusion shown in Figure 3.2 for publication. Poggendorff, the editor who reviewed the paper, noticed that there was more than a simple tilt effect to be found in these figures. If you look carefully at Figure 3.2B, you will notice that the oblique intersecting lines appear to be slightly disrupted. As each oblique line crosses the central line, it seems to be displaced upward or downward, depending on its inclination. The resultant percept is that the two line segments do not appear to line up exactly. Poggendorff alerted the author to this distortion and Zoellner amended his manuscript to include an analysis of this effect, which he named the *Poggendorff illusion.*

The basic Poggendorff effect can be seen more dramatically in Figure 3.3A, in which a single transversal is shown crossing a black bar. Although both segments of the transversal are colinear, the right-hand portion clearly appears to be too high. There is nothing special about a heavy opaque bar. The figures in 3.3B and 3.3C show transversals intersecting pairs of parallel lines. Again the displacement effect is obvious.

The illusion is sensitive to the size of the angle between the transversal and the parallels. When the transversal intersects the parallels at 90°, there is no apparent distortion. As the angle between the transversal and the vertical becomes more acute, the illusory effect appears to increase (Cameron & Steele, 1905; Krantz & Weintraub, 1973; Wagner, 1969; Weintraub & Krantz, 1971), as shown in Figures 3.3B and 3.3C.

The size of the separation between the parallels also affects the illusion magnitude. As the width of the separation increases, so does the illusion magnitude, as shown in Figure 3.3D. The effect of the relationship between transversal

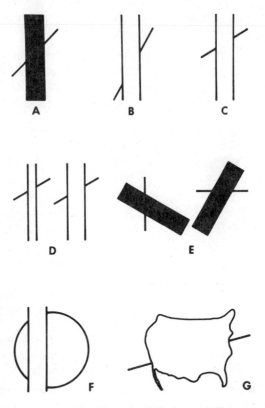

FIG. 3.3.   Variations of the Poggendorff illusion. (A) The segments of the oblique transversal actually form a continuous straight line, but the segment on the right seems too high; (B) and (C) the apparent displacement of the transversal is increased when the angles are more acute; (D) increasing the separation between the parallels increases the effect; (E) orienting the transversal horizontally or vertically reduces the illusion; (F) a curve looks discontinuous when interrupted by parallel lines; (G) the separating elements does not have to have straight lines to produce the distortion.

angle and size of separation on the magnitude of the Poggendorff illusion is regular enough to allow mathematical description. Weintraub and Krantz (1971) report an empirical equation of $I = 0.162 \ (W/\tan A)$ where I is illusion magnitude, W is the width of the separation between the parallels, and A is the acute angle between the transversal and the parallels. Although this equation seems to describe the illusion reasonably well, it is actually limited to the special case in which the parallel lines are vertical. The figures shown in Figure 3.3E are identical to Figure 3.3A, except that they are rotated so that the transversal line is either horizontal or vertical. Under these conditions, the magnitude of the illusion is considerably reduced (Green & Hoyle, 1965; Leibowitz & Toffey, 1966; Weintraub & Krantz, 1971). It thus becomes clear that one cannot begin to quantify illusory effects until all the relevant variables are accounted for, or at least enumerated.

Figures 3.3F and 3.3G show that neither the transversal nor the contours that interrupt the transversal need be straight. A curve passing behind a bar will look discontinuous because of the operation of the Poggendorff effect (Figure 3-3F) as will a straight line intersecting a random shape (Figure 3.3G).

The Twisted Cord Illusion

In 1908 Fraser presented a series of striking and complicated illusion figures. As a group they are among the strongest orientation effects to be found in the literature. Figure 3.4A shows one of these illusions, in which all the letters are made up of vertical sides and horizontal tops and bottoms. Perceptually, they seem to be clearly tilted. These figures are called *twisted cord illusions* because one can actually construct these patterns using a cord made of a uniform twist of dark and light strands laid on a checkered pattern. Figure 3.4A is actually a photograph of such a construction. The complexity of this pattern and Fraser's specific instructions for its production makes one wonder if this illusion was a serendipitous discovery that came about when someone tried to align some twisted cords on a table covered with a checkered tablecloth.

Such complexity seems to invite simplification. Let us first simplify the background by removing all the gray squares, leaving only black and white squares and thus reducing the brightness levels from three to two (Figure 3.4B). Under these circumstances, the effect is obviously still apparent. Now let us remove all the background squares that are not in direct contact with the contours of the letters (Figure 3.4C). It is clear that the distortion still remains. Now let us remove the remainder of the background, leaving only the twisted cords (Figure 3.4D). As strange as it may seem, the illusory tilt remains, although it is somewhat reduced in magnitude.

When the twisted cord illusion is presented in this form, the direction of the distortion reminds one of the Zoellner illusion (Figure 3.2A). The configuration shown in Figure 3.4D could easily be interpreted as a simple modification of the Zoellner. However, one must be careful not to jump to the conclusion that there must be a relationship between these two illusions on the basis of the apparent similarities between Figures 3.2A and 3.4D. Figure 3.4D was derived from Figure 3.4A, using a rather large number of pattern changes. We have not measured the magnitude of the illusion as we moved through the four illusion variants represented in Figures 3.4A through 3.4D. Thus we do not know whether our systematic removal of the background had any effect on the magnitude of the illusion, although we do know that it did not destroy it entirely. Suppose we now remove the twist from the cord, as shown in Figure 3.4E. This clearly reduces the illusion to zero. This, then, makes it reasonable to hypothesize that it is primarily the alternating light and dark lines making up the letters that support

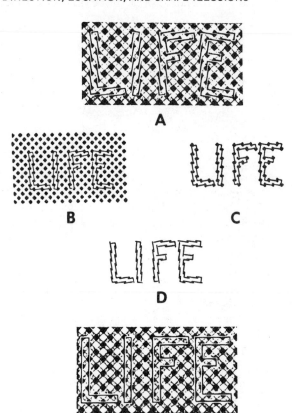

FIG. 3.4.   Variations of the twisted cord illusion. (A) The letters appear
to be tilted although they are actually vertical and parallel to one another;
(B) the illusion persists when the gray is removed from the background;
(C) it also remains when the nonadjacent squares are removed from the
background; (D) even if the background is white, the illusion remains; (E)
the illusion is still observable when no background squares are present;
(F) when the twist is removed, the effect disappears.

this illusion, with perhaps some small contribution from the checkerboard background. If this is correct, it would seem to strengthen the supposition that there
is a kinship between the Zoellner and the twisted cord illusions.

The Kindergarten Patterns

Figure 3.5A shows a mat woven out of two colors of heavy braid, with the two
colors shifted relative to each other to create a broken or wavelike pattern. Such
a mat always looks as if the weaving were alternately too tight and too loose so
that each vertical braid seems to vary in width. The difficulty, however, lies not
in the workmanship but in the eye appraising it.

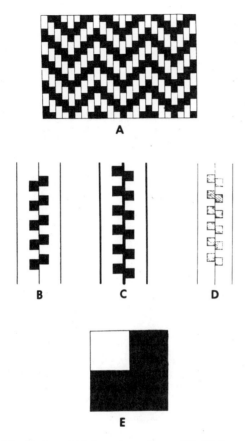

FIG. 3.5.   The illusion of kindergarten patterns. (A) All the vertical lines
are parallel although they do not appear to be so; (B) the basic component
of the illusion showing how the vertical lines come to appear to be tilted;
(C) thickening the lines reduces the distortion; (D) reducing the contrast
of the adjacent elements reduces the effect; (E) Pierce's irradiation illusion
in which the white sector appears to be larger than one quarter of the area,
and the lower right corner of the white sector appears to be more acute
than 90°.

If you tip this book so that you can sight down the vertical lines in Figure
3.5A, you will at once see that all the lines are straight and parallel. This interesting effect was discussed by Lipps (1897) and Muensterberg (1897), who
called it the *shifted chequerboard figure.* Pierce (1898), in an interesting and
careful analysis of this distortion, dubbed it the *Illusion of the kindergarten
patterns,* presumably because such mats are frequently woven by young children.
It seems to be a directional effect due to the displacement of the squares relative
to one another.

If we attempt to dissect this figure, we find that the basic unit of distortion
is that shown in Figure 3.5B. Notice that the line on which the squares abut
appears to be slightly tilted rather than vertical. If we mentally connect the

centers of each pair of squares, a series of short, parallel, oblique lines intersecting the main vertical is formed, which gives the impression of a kind of Zoellner illusion. The same thing may be accomplished more easily by squinting or shifting the accommodation of the eye so as to blur the image. Viewed this way, Figure 3.5B looks much like a blurred Zoellner illusion. However, it is dangerous to try to equate illusory distortions based on perturbations or amputations of stimulus elements. It is not at all clear what processes we are manipulating when we alter features of the array. A small change in one stimulus parameter may evoke a totally different mechanism. For example, equation of this illusion with the Zoellner is easily negated by the manipulation of further stimulus elements. In Figure 3.5C we have merely thickened the vertical lines. We know from Figure 3.2B that the Zoellner illusion works perfectly well with thick lines, yet in the kindergarten pattern this results in a massive reduction in the effect. Another stimulus manipulation that makes the same point is shown in Figure 3.5D, in which we have reduced the contrast of the offset squares. This manipulation also does not seem to affect the magnitude of the distortion in the Zoellner illusion (Zoellner, 1860), but it reduces the magnitude of the distortion of this pattern. Thus it seems unlikely that the kindergarten pattern is simply a variant of the Zoellner illusion, despite the existence of a plausible configurational similarity in the two stimuli.

Pierce (1898) proposed that the kindergarten illusion is composed of the sum of a number of small distortions like the one shown in Figure 3.5E, in which the white sector is exactly one quarter the size of the overall square, and the contours bounding it meet in a perfect right angle. Notice that the white area appears to be distorted in two ways. First, it looks as if it is slightly larger than one quarter of the area of the larger square, and second, the interior or lower left angle of the white square seems to be smaller than a right angle. The sum of such angular distortions in a configuration like Figure 3.5A would produce an overal distortion in the correct direction. Pierce suggested that this distortion might be a variant of the irradiation illusion shown in Figure 2.1C. If this were the case, then one would expect the reduction in the illusion with a reduction in contrast that we found in Figure 3.5D.

Frame of Reference Illusions

There are many situations in which the orientation of a surrounding field seems to alter the orientation of an enclosed object. In Figure 3.6A, for example, both lines have exactly the same inclination, yet they seem to tilt in different directions as a function of the tilt of the surrounding square. This illusory effect has been extensively studied since Gibson's first mention of it in 1937 (Beh & Wendroth, 1972; Beh, Wendroth, & Purcell, 1971; Gibson, 1937; Morant & Aronoff, 1966; Wendroth, 1973; Witkin & Asch, 1948a, 1948b). Since it is usually measured by means of an adjustable rod in a tilted frame, the illusion is usually referred to as the *rod and frame effect*. Witkin believes that certain personality types are more susceptible to this illusion than others. He has found, for example, that women and hysterics tend to show greater illusion magnitude where men and obsessive-compulsives tend to show less of this distortion (Witkin, Dyk, Faterson, Goodenough & Karp, 1962).

The magnitude of this effect seems to be increased if the frame fills the visual field. Some of the most spectacular results have been found when a model room is used as the frame. In this situation, the room is mechanically tilted while subjects seated inside the room are asked to make perceptual estimates of the verticality of their own bodies (Witkin, 1949). The effect on the perceived orientation of the self is similar to that observed on the lines in Figure 3.6A.

Rotation effects induced by a surrounding frame can occur with objects as well as with lines. In Figure 3.6B, the square looks like a slightly tilted parallelogram when it is surrounded by a tilted rectangle, but it is obviously an upright square when the rectangle is oriented with its long side horizontal. We have probably all been caught by this distortion while trying to hang a picture. Sometimes we have great difficulty getting it to look straight, only to discover a decided slant in the ceiling or the floor of the room which, in turn, apparently tilts the picture.

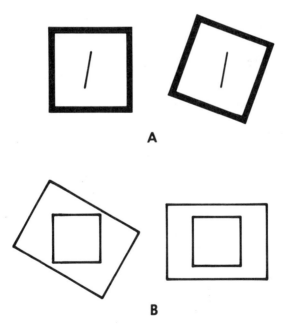

FIG. 3.6. Variations of frame reference illusions. (A) The inclination of a line is apparently changed, depending on the orientation of the surrounding frame; (B) the orientation of the frame also affects the apparent tilt of the central square.

The Jastrow-Lipps Illusion

An angle may be defined as the shape or space enclosed by two intersecting straight lines or plane surfaces. An angle is such a simple geometric configuration that it is usually easy to derive the mathematical laws that specify its relationship to other geometric components. Although the mathematical situation may be simple, the perceptual situation is considerably more complex.

A large number of investigators, beginning with Jastrow (1891, 1892), have concerned themselves with illusions in the estimation of the size of an angle. In general, the results indicate that small angles tend to be overestimated, with the maximum overestimation for angles of 10 to 20°, whereas large angles tend to be underestimated, with the maximum underestimation in angles of 125 to 160° (Blakemore, Carpenter, & Georgeson, 1970; Morinaga, 1933; Wallace & Crampin, 1969). At 90°, most researchers report neither over- nor underestimation. As in the Poggendorff illusion, orientation plays a role. If one of the sides of the angle is oriented either horizontally or vertically, we find an overestimation for small angles as before. However, at about 45°, the effect weakens and then shifts to an underestimation until it reaches 90°. Then this distortion also disappears (Hofmann & Bielchowsky, 1909; Day, 1965; Fisher, 1969a; Gibson, 1937). This cycle of over- and underestimation seems to repeat itself again between 90 and 180°.

These angular distortions are not very strong, and the reader may find that quick glances at the configurations in Figure 3.7, rather than a steady fixation, will improve the illusion slightly. The major perceptual effect found in angles is shown in Figure 3.7A. In both configurations shown, the isolated line is actually parallel to the side of the angle. The side of the angle apparently deviates from parallel as a function of the size of the angle. For an acute angle, the end of the side seems to be closer to the isolated line than the vertex, suggesting that the angle has been perceptually opened out, whereas the converse is true for an obtuse angle, suggesting a closing of the angle. Figure 3.7B shows how a vertical line may appear tilted through the addition of angles at its ends. This distortion may be predicted from an opening out of acute angles, although a few additional assumptions may be necessary to make the prediction work.

The most powerful illusion based on angular expansion and contraction was introduced by Lipps (1897). It is shown in Figure 3.7C in which the central line segments are all parallel to one another. The addition of the wings that form the obtuse angles at the ends of these central segments makes the segments appear to be tilted toward and away from one another. It is possible to suggest that these angles at the ends of the central line segments may serve the same function as the oblique lines in the Zoellner illusion.

If acute angles tend to be overestimated, then a group of acute angles placed together ought to be overestimated even more than one angle alone, through summation of the individual distortions. In Figure 3.7D there are two right

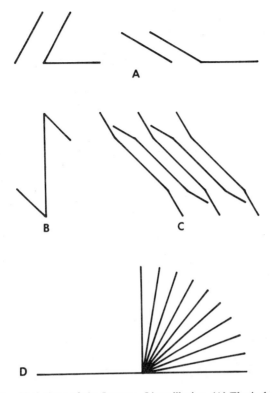

FIG. 3.7.   Variations of the Jastrow–Lipps illusion. (A) The isolated lines are parallel to the sides of each angle, yet appear to be tilted toward the wing tip, due to the overestimation of the acute angle, or toward the vertex, due to the underestimation of the obtuse angle; (B) addition of acute angles apparently tilts a vertical line; (C) the Lipps illusion in which parallel lines do not appear to be parallel, due to the addition of obtuse angles; (D) a right angle made up of a series of acute angles is overestimated relative to a simple right angle.

angles. One of these, however, is composed of a number of acute angles. Notice that the compound angle on the right appears to be larger than the simple angle on the left (Blix, 1902; Helmholtz, 1856/1962).

Angular Illusions of Location

All pattern distortions can be interpreted as distortions in location. To alter the apparent extent of a line, we must alter the location of its end points. To alter the shape of any object, we must alter the location of the points that make up its contour. There are, however, some instances of illusory distortion in which the phenomenological impression seems to entail a shift in the location of a point or points, without any concomitant distortion in the size or shape of the configuration. These distortions are seldom noticed because they are small in magnitude, yet they occur in abundance in many very simple configurations.

Let us begin by considering an angle, such as the one shown in Figure 3.3A. There is certainly nothing special about this angle. It simply consists of two lines, one of which is horizontal and one of which is slanted up and to the right. Of course, we know that the size of this angle may tend to be somewhat distorted by the Jastrow–Lipps effect. However, there is an additional distortion present in this figure that can easily be seen by looking at the two additional lines that appear in the field. Mentally extend the horizontal line on the left and see where you think it will pass in relation to the horizontal side of the angle. Similarly, mentally extend the isolated line that points upward until it intersects the angle; most observers report that this line passes to the left of the side of the angle (Jastrow, 1891; Luckiesh, 1922/1965). Needless to say, the sides of the angle are colinear with the isolated lines. This can easily be seen by sighting down the page. The effect seems to be a simple displacement of the apparent locus of the angle in space, as if someone had taken the angle and pulled it a millimeter or so in the direction of the vertex. Since the isolated line and the side of the angle continue to appear parallel to each other, even though they do not appear to be colinear, this effect cannot be caused by the apparent opening up of the sides of the angle which we described in the previous section.

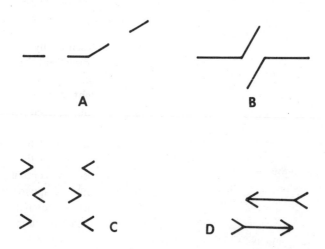

FIG. 3.8   Some angular illusions of location. (A) The line segments do not seem to be colinear with the sides of the angle, as if the angle were displaced in the direction of the vertex; (B) the displacement seems to shift the horizontal sides of the angles out of colinearity; (C) Morinaga's paradox in which the upper and lower horizontal extents are overestimated relative to the center, yet the upper and lower vertices seem displaced toward each other relative to the center pair; (D) the figures appear displaced horizontally in the direction in which the arrows point.

We can amplify this effect by using two angles, as shown in Figure 3.8B. Physically, the horizontal sides of the two angles are colinear; however, the horizontal side on the right now seems to be considerably higher than the horizontal side on the left.

Illusions of locus and illusions of extent can apparently be perceptually independent of each other. Figure 3.8C consists of a stack of Mueller–Lyer components in the form we depicted earlier as Figure 2.3D. If we estimate the size of the open extent between the inward pointing angles, it is clearly longer than the extent between the outward pointing angles, which is nothing more than the usual Mueller–Lyer distortion of extent. Given this extent illusion, one would expect that the vertices of the inward-pointing angles should be seen as farther apart than the vertices of the outward-pointing angles. However, based on the distortions that we have been discussing in this section, we would predict an apparent displacement of the vertices in the opposite direction. All the vertices in Figure 3.8C are vertically aligned. If we now ignore the extents and attend only to the placement of the angles, we find that the vertices of the inward-pointing angles appear to be nearer to each other than the vertices of the outward-pointing angles. In other words, the apparent displacement of the vertices in this situation can be predicted from the distortion shown in Figure 3.8A but not from the Mueller–Lyer distortion of extent. This is frequently called *Morinaga's paradox,* after its discoverer (1954). This phenomenon would clearly seem to imply that judgments of locus and judgments of extent may be independent of each other.

Figure 3.8D simply confuses the issue even more. This figure shows a variation of a displacement effect patterned after one first presented by Judd (1898). There are two arrow-like figures pointing in opposite directions. The two horizontal lines are equal in length with their endpoints vertically aligned. Phenonenally, the upper figure appears to be placed to the right of the lower figure, as if the entire figure, including the angles and connecting horizontal lines, were displaced in space.

It should be pointed out that the illusions described in this and the previous section involve relatively small distortions. In addition, some of the patterns of distortion shown in Figure 3.7 seem to produce opposite perceptual effects to those shown in Figure 3.8, despite the fact that they involve apparently similar elements. It may well be that these two types of distortions compete with each other in some situations, with each subtracting from the observed magnitude of the other, thus reducing the overall effect.

ILLUSIONS OF SHAPE

For the most part, the transition from illusions of location and direction to illusions of shape does not comprise a very large step. If we change the location or direction of one part of a figure, while keeping the location and direction of the other parts constant, we have altered its shape. This seems to be the under-lying principle of a number of shape distortions.

The Wundt–Hering Illusion

Whenever a geometric form is superimposed on a field of lines in such a way that the angles of intersection between the boundaries of the shape and the lines that make up the field vary for different parts of the figure, we usually find some report of shape distortions. One of the oldest and the most familiar is the Wundt–Hering illusion shown in Figure 3.9A (Hering, 1861). The two horizontal lines are drawn straight and parallel, yet they appear to be curved, such that the lines bow out at the center.

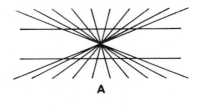

A

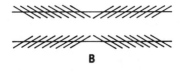

B

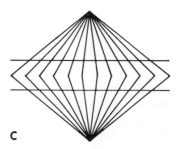

C

FIG. 3.9.   Variations of the Wundt–Hering illusion. (A) In the Hering variant, two parallel straight lines appear to be bowed outward in the center; (B) the Zoellner illusion may be used to mimic this effect; (C) the Wundt form, in which the lines appear to be bowed inward.

We can approximate this shape distortion using a variant of the ubiquitous Zoellner configuration. In Figure 3.9B, we have oriented the inducing obliques in opposite directions for the two halves of the horizontal lines. The two parallel lines appear to be bent outward at the center, thus creating a crude reproduction of Figure 3.9A. Both the intensity of the effect and the smoothness of the curvature of the horizontal lines are greater in Figure 3.9A, probably because the angle of intersection of the background lines with the horizontals is continuously changed in the basic configuration. We know from Figure 3.2D that the angle inclination of the vertical lines in the Zoellner illusion increases as the angle of intersection with the obliques becomes more acute. Thus, in Figure 3.9A, we might expect the ends of the horizontals to be bent downward a large amount because of the very acute angles of intersection, whereas the center of the horizontals should show practically no distortion because the angle of intersection is nearly 90°. The gradual shift in the angle of intersection, from the ends to the center of the horizontal, produces a smooth curve in the distortion. Wundt (1898) modified this pattern to show that the lines can be made to appear to bend toward each other rather than away from each other (Figure 3.9C). The bending of a straight line is one of the simplest forms of shape illusion. This illusion forms the basis for a variant called the *herringbone illusion.*

The Herringbone Illusion

Suppose that we fill a field with Zoellner-like inducing elements. It might easily result in a herringbone pattern like that used in suit fabrics. It is easily predictable that such a geometric array will distort any outline shape superimposed upon it, as shown in Figure 3.10A.

A figure does not have to be surrounded by this field of lines in order to be distorted. Figure 3.10B shows that figures which contain this array of lines will also be distorted, as will solid figures placed against such a background (Figure 3.10C).

The Orbison Illusions

The shape distortions we have been looking at seem to have a common characteristic. In each a form is altered when it interacts with a systematic field of lines. This format was first exploited by Orbison (1939a, 1939b), who created a number of illusion configurations by placing outline forms on repetitive backgrounds consisting of diverging lines or concentric circles that he called *geometric fields.* He found that shapes seemed to alter dramatically as he moved them from position to position over such a background. In Figure 3.11A, we have centered a square on a field of concentric circles. The reader will notice that the sides of the square seem to be curved inward in this situation. Displacing the square

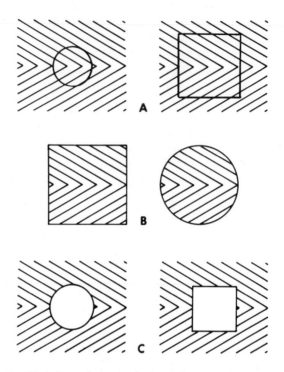

FIG. 3.10.   Variations of the herringbone illusion. (A) The square and circle are distorted out of their normal symmetrical shapes; (B) this works equally well when the figure encloses the lines or; (C) when the lines do not cross the boundary of the figure.

toward the periphery alters the distortion, as can be seen in Figure 3.11B. Now two of the sides seem to be bowed in the same direction whereas the other two sides seem to be straight but no longer parallel. Different patterns of distortion occur if the figure is placed on other geometric fields such as one consisting of diverging lines. When centrally placed on such a field, the sides of a square seem to be bowed outward, as shown in Figure 3.11C. When we displace this square to one side, it appears to be trapezoidal in shape, as shown in Figure 3.11D.

It is fairly easy to create such configurations, and the effects can be quite startling. First, draw a field of concentric circles or diverging lines on a piece of paper. Next, take a clear sheet of acetate, a thin piece of plastic or glass, or a fairly transparent piece of tracing paper, and draw a regular geometric figure on it with a felt-tipped pen. Now lay the geometric shape on the field of lines and move it around. As you slide the shape around over the background, it seems to change from moment to moment. You have the impression that the sides of the form are made of rubber and are in a constant state of contraction and expansion. The only changes actually occurring, of course, are changes in the stimulus relationships between the contours of the form and the background. As you move the overlay, you change the orientation, angle, and direction of the line elements that intersect the lines defining the form. This is equivalent to a continually changing and complex variant of the Zoellner, Wundt—Hering, or herringbone illusions. Because the changes continuously occur, the effect is even more dramatic than those in a static presentation, and it provides one of the most startling experiences in the field of visual illusions.

Some of these effects are reminiscent of what might be expected if one summed a series of distortions, similar to the Jastrow—Lipps illusion (Figure 3.7). As you will recall, this illusion could be described as an increase in the apparent size of acute angles and a decrease in the apparent size of obtuse angles. To see how this effect might result in shape distortions, consider Figure 3.12A, which shows a horizontal line touched in the center by the vertex of an obtuse angle. The Jastrow—Lipps illusion predicts that the acute angles will appear to open slightly and the obtuse angle will appear to close slightly. This is best seen from the apparent downward tilt at the ends of the horizontal line. There should also be an apparent upward rotation of the ends of the oblique lines, which is not easily detected in this array.

In Figure 3.12B, the obtuse angle is displaced downward in relation to the horizontal line. Now there are four acute angles — all of which should expand perceptually. This should lead to a slight bowing of the horizontal line, and indeed such a bowing may be easily observed in the figure. Figure 3.12C is based

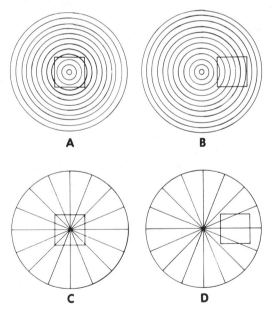

FIG. 3.11. Variations of the Orbison illusion, in which the apparent shape of the square varies as it is superimposed over different parts of a geometric field of lines.

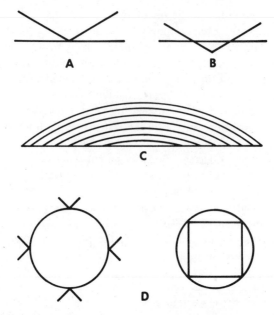

FIG. 3.12.   Some other variations of the Jastrow–Lipps illusion. (A) Here
the ends of the horizontal line seem to tilt downward as though the acute
angles were opening up; (B) this effect can make the horizontal line appear
to be slightly curved; (C) the horizontal line seems to sag downward in the
center; (D) the circles appear to be deformed in the regions near where
they make contact with the angles.

on the same principle. It shows a series of arcs, all of which end at a single
horizontal line. In this configuration, each arc forms an acute angle with the
horizontal line at each of its end points. The apparent expansion of these acute
angles might explain the slight sag in the horizontal line.

Berliner and Berliner (1948) have suggested that all angular distortions can
be described by a single mathematical expression. Using data from the standard
version of the Zoellner illusion (Figure 3.2A), they have proposed that these
distortions can be described by the mathematical relationship

$$d = c \sin 4a$$

where d represents the magnitude of the distortion, c is a constant that changes
sign to suit the observed direction of the distortion, and a is the angle between
the judged line and the intersecting line. Unfortunately, in actual practice, the
constant c seems to vary a bit with the variations in the angle a. Nonetheless,
Kristof (1960) was able to show a reasonable directional agreement between this
expression and the observed distortion for background fields of diverging lines.

This implies that every time contours meet the angle of intersection should
appear to extend or contract, thus producing an illusory distortion. Such effects

must, in fact, exist in great number but may be generally ignored. They frequently intrude on our consciousness only when they alter the shape of a regular geometric figure. Figure 3.12D shows two examples of the distortion of a circle through contact with the vertices of angles. Both of these configurations could be described in terms of the opening up of acute angles, thus producing apparent bumps or kinks in the smooth arc of the circle.

The Twisted Cord Illusion

In an earlier section, we presented the twisted cord illusion as an illusion of direction (Figure 3.4). This effect can also be used to produce some dramatic shape distortions. In 1908 Fraser presented the figure shown as Figure 3.13A. Virtually all observers viewing this pattern report that they see a set of spirals converging inward toward the center of the configuration. Actually, the pattern consists of a set of concentric circles created by using alternating light and dark lines. The circularity of the patterns may best be shown by placing your finger on any one line and tracing around it. You should end up back at your starting point.

A

B   **C**

FIG. 3.13.   Some twisted cord shape illusions. (A) The black and white lines seem to form a spiral, although they are actually concentric circles; (B) a simplified version of the illusion (C) a form of the illusion only slanted lines, which greatly weakens the effect.

Be careful in tracing, though, since the effect is frequently strong enough to lure the fingers of unwary tracers in toward the center of the configuration. We may simplify this pattern as we did the linear forms of the illusion in Figure 3.4. Figure 3.13B shows such a reduced pattern. Figure 3.13C shows a further simplification of the pattern. In this version, composed entirely of slanted lines, the spiral effect is considerably reduced but is sometimes still reported.

Subjective Contours

There is one set of shape illusions that is rather difficult to classify. They do not involve the distortion of elements, contours, or relationships within parts of the configuration but rather involve the perception of contours that are not physically present in the array. These are the so-called *subjective contour* illusions.

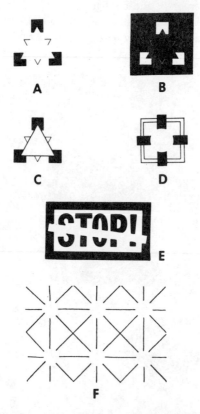

FIG. 3.14. Subjective contour illusions. (A) A central white triangle is seen where none is present in the stimulus; (B) reversing the brightnesses reverses the brightness of the triangle, which is now seen as black; (C) outlining the locus of the subjective contour eliminates the brightness differences; (D) a curved subjective contour; (E) a complex subjective contour in the form of an interposed white bar; (F) subjectively seen white circles appear where the lines would intersect.

The first report of such illusory percepts was by Schumann (1904). Since then, Coren (1972), Kanizsa (1955, 1974), and Ehrenstein (1954) have created a series of such figures. A typical configuration is shown in Figure 3-14A. In this configuration most observers report the presence of a white central triangle that is perceptually whiter than the background. The lines that bound the contour are not actually physically present. They are subjectively created, and hence illusory. If one reverses the brightness of this configuration, as is done in Figure 3.14B, the percept that results is that of a black triangle that is perceptually darker than the background. It is important to note that the illusion consists of both the creation of a contour and the creation of a brightness difference. Coren and Theodor (1975) have shown that overlaid boundary lines eliminate any perception of a brightness difference between the central and surrounding areas, as is shown in Figure 3.14C. Curved subjective contours can be created as well as the straight ones shown in Figure 3.14D.

A variety of more complex stimuli can be created that manifest subjective contours. For instance, in Figure 3.14E, one sees a subjectively bounded white bar interposed in front of the word STOP. In addition, Ehrenstein (1954) has shown that, in a simple interrupted grid pattern, subjective contours may be visible at the intersections. Thus in Figure 3.14F white circles are seen apparently overlying the points where the lines would intersect the grid.

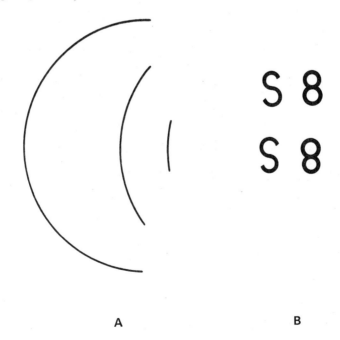

A   B

FIG. 3.15.   All the curves come from a circle with the same radius, although the smaller ones appear to be flatter; (B) the upper portion of both the *8* and the *S* appears to be equal to the lower portion in size, although it is actually much smaller as seen in the lower inverted figures.

These illusions are difficult to classify. However, it is obviously the case that the appearance of contours that are not present in the physical stimulation represents a novel and striking class of illusions.

Miscellaneous Shape Illusions

Some shape distortions do not depend on intersecting lines, shifted dark areas, or apparent contours. We will simply note two common illusions that seem to warrant inclusion. Consider the set of curves shown in Figure 3.15A. All these curves are part of a circle of the same radius. Perceptually, however, the shorter arcs seem to be much flatter than the longer ones and thus seem to belong to a circle with a much larger radius (Tolansky, 1964).

In Figure 3.15B, the *S* and the *8* on the top line look quite normal, with the top portion identical in size to the bottom portion. Actually, the upper portion of each figure is smaller than the lower portion. This is easily seen when we invert the figures as in the lower line (Luckiesh, 1922/1965). Inverting the page will also show the same effect.

Illusions of Direction, Location, and Shape
In the Environment

As in illusions of extent, there are many examples of illusions of shape and orientation that occur in situations other than on the printed page. For instance, the Poggendorff illusion (Figure 3.3) appears under a large number of guises in everyday life. In some of these situations, the resultant perceptual error is potentially dangerous; hence these illusions should be considered seriously, as has been pointed out by Fisher and Lucas (1969). For example, Figure 3.16A shows a radar screen similar to that used by air traffic control units in many large airports. Superimposed on the screen is a fixed pattern representing the flight paths under the operator's control. Approaching planes appear as streaks in the afterglow of the screen. Here we have depicted two planes, one approaching from the upper right and the other from the lower left. Looking at these flight paths, the radar operator might be apt to relax, since it appears that the plane on the left will fly well to the port side of the plane on the right. Unfortunately, the Poggendorff illusion is at work here and, as a ruler would show, the two planes are on a collision path.

Figure 3.16B shows how a Poggendorff illusion could interfere with a delicate operation. Suppose a surgeon, trying to extract a bullet located in the chest, looks at the fluoroscope image shown in Figure 3.16B in order to fix the position of his probe relative to the foreign body. At the moment, it seems clear that he should shift the direction of his probe since, if he continues in his present path, he will be low and to the right of the bullet. Unfortunately, this is another example of the Poggendorff illusion with the probe serving as the transversal and the rib

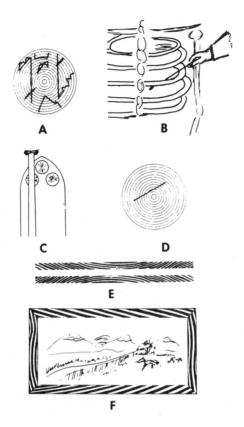

FIG. 3.16. Naturally occurring illusions. (A) The two flight paths, seen
as oblique streaks on this radar screen, appear as though they will not intersect, although they actually will; (B) The probe looks as though it will miss
the bullet on this fluoroscopic view, although it is correctly aligned; (C) the
line of the window seems to be discontinuous, due to the interposed pillar;
(D) the straight missile track on this radar screen appears to be bent;
(E) these boards look warped or bent, due to the end grain; (F) this picture
does not look square, due to the grain of the wood.

serving as the dividing bar. Actually, the probe is precisely aligned with the
foreign object in the picture and should not be moved laterally.

Architects seem to take the Poggendorff illusion into account without realizing
it. For example, you almost never see the situation depicted in Figure 3.16C in
which a column is placed in front of an arched portal or window. As can be
easily seen in the Figure, this configuration causes an apparent discontinuity and
distortion in the curve of the portal or window.

Radar screens can fool the unwary operator with other illusions besides the
Poggendorff. Figure 3.16D shows a radar screen with an overlay of concentric
circles used to enable the rapid calculation of speed and distance. The streak

running across the screen is a missile traveling at some 2,000 miles an hour. The task of the radar operator is to calculate the optimal course for an interceptor missile, based on the data given on the radar screen. Unfortunately, the concentric circles, which are of considerable help in estimating speed and distance, create an Orbison-like distortion (Figure 3.11) which causes the line representing the path of the missile to appear to be curved rather than straight. Visual estimates of its trajectory may therefore be in considerable error. Similar effects may occur in many measuring microscopes that employ concentric circular patterns super-imposed over the viewed surface.

When wood grain is pronounced and surfaces are unfinished or simply stained, the alternating streaks of light and dark can lead to shape distortions. Figure 3.16E shows how this effect can make straight boards appear to be warped when they are viewed endwise. An interesting complication of this effect may occur in furniture finished so that the bare wood grain is visible, causing table or chair legs to appear to be misaligned. Similarly, bare wood grain can make picture frames look out of square, as shown in Figure 3.16F. In this particular example, the picture appears to be narrower on the left than the right because of the grain of the frame. Again, we are looking at the same general variety of shape illusion that that has filled the preceding pages.

4 Structural Factors in Illusion Formation: Optical Contributions

Now that we have catalogued the major classes of visual illusion, it is time to turn to the problem of explaining these phenomena. In general, there are two classes of theoretical explanation, one of which we will call *structural theories* and the other *strategy theories.*

Structural theories propose that illusory distortions are based directly on the structural properties of the optical or neural systems. This type of theory proposes that the conscious experience strays from an accurate representation of the environment either because the image formed on the retina is inaccurate due to optical limitations of the eye or because the neural encoding of the information is distorted by physiological interactions occurring on the retina or at higher levels in the visual system. On the other hand, strategy theories propose that illusions arise during the course of cognitive processing of the visual information. This type of theory would attribute the perceptual distortions to biases introduced by judgmental and attentional processes that emphasize certain aspects of the array, or to processing plans, strategies, or assumptions that are inappropriate for the particular stimulus being viewed.

It is important to note that both structural and strategy theories assume a normal observer, who is processing all visual inputs, illusory and nonillusory, in a similar way. These distortions arise when the normal modes of processing, which are generally capable of producing accurate perceptual outcomes, interact with particular stimulus configurations to cause unexpected perceptual errors. In general, structural theories assume that these unexpected perceptual errors or illusions occur because the input is altered by the structural components of the visual system before any cognitive processing has had a chance to occur, whereas strategy theories assume that the input is a reasonably accurate representation of the stimulus and that illusions arise from transformations and interpretations of this input that occur at a relatively late stage of perceptual processing.

For the purposes of our discussion, structural mechanisms are concerned with the optical and neural system of the eye, up to and including the primary visual cortex. Strategy components include attentional factors and interpretive and learned aspects of information extraction, including any cognitive and heuristic techniques used by the observer in the evaluation of stimuli and the formation of the percept.

It is important to note that the general format of our treatment of the mechanisms resulting in visual illusions differs from the traditional procedure of looking at each pattern separately and trying to isolate its cause. Although some attempts at generality have occasionally been offered that extend the results from one configuration to several others, and intermittent bursts of theoretical enthusiasm have led a researcher to suggest that a single process can account for all visual geometric illusions, most explanations still seem bound to a particular pattern or set of illusion patterns. Our discussion reverses this usual process by dealing with a series of illusion-forming mechanisms and discussing their contributions to a number of effects. It seems likely that no one process can explain the myriad distortions we have already seen. In the next eight chapters we discuss and evaluate the various theories and mechanisms that have been proposed to account for visual illusions. Chapters 4, 5, and 6 describe possible structural mechanisms; Chapters 7 through 11 treat various cognitive strategies that have been suggested. We also consider how these processes interact. The general plan runs roughly from the most peripheral to the most central mechanisms. Thus Chapters 4 through 11 follow a pathway that takes us from the cornea to the cortex and beyond.

SOME BASIC OPTICAL CONSIDERATIONS

The first opportunity for the visual system to make contact with the external environment is through the dioptric system of the eye, which includes all the optically active components (the cornea and lens), which tend to bend or refract the light rays, as well as the optic media, which fill the chambers of the eye (aqueous and vitreous humours), through which the rays must pass. This is the image-forming system that focuses a pattern of light on the surface of the retina. Clearly, since all visual processes depend on this light input, the image projected on the retina is an important factor in determining the nature of our final percept. If the relationships depicted in the retinal image are distorted so that they no longer correspond to the relationships that exist in the environmental stimulus, our inferences about length or orientation of contours may be seriously in error. If the distortions are systematic, we may end up with a visual illusion.

There are certain implications of this line of reasoning that must be considered. The major one is that if we are to understand why our perception of a pattern differs from the actual physical stimulus in the environment, we must first ascertain whether there are any changes in the retinal image that might be responsible for the illusions we observe. This means that we must begin by investigating the manner in which images are formed in the eye and how such images may be distorted. Actually, the major consequence of passing the image of a pattern through the optics of the eye is reduction in sharpness or focus. In other words, images of clearly defined contours in the environment tend to be blurred on the retina. This blurring has important consequences and leads to a number of illusions; hence let us consider its sources and nature more closely.

Even a perfect optical instrument, in the shape of an eye, would take a theoretical point source of light and distribute it as a blur in the form of a normal distribution of light, bright in the center and fading out toward the edges, with a diameter of about 1.5 minutes of arc (Fry, 1953; Helmholtz, 1856, 1860, 1866/1962; Westheimer, 1963). Since the eye is not a perfect optical instrument, the resultant spread is considerably greater than 1.5 minutes of arc. There are several aspects of this imperfect optical instrument called the eye that cause this additional blur. The first is *spherical aberration*, which refers to the fact that the curvatures of the cornea and lens are not optically perfect. Instead of bending all the light rays so that they converge on a single point, the cornea and lens bend the peripheral rays somewhat too sharply so that they converge on a point in front of the point of focus of the more central rays. This optical effect is shown schematically in Figure 4.1A. One can see that when the image is in focus for the peripheral rays, as it would be if it were projected on a surface located at the dotted line marked I, the central rays would be out of focus. This means that there would be a halo of nonfocused light around the image. Bringing the central rays into focus by projecting the image on a surface at the dotted line marked II does not help either, since now the peripheral rays are out of focus. Thus, regardless of the state of accommodation of the eye, spherical aberration will tend to blur the image.

It is easy to demonstrate the way in which spherical aberration tends to spread out the pattern of light in the retinal image. Look at a point of light, such as a pin hole in a dark card illuminated from behind and viewed from a distance of a couple of meters, or a star viewed at night, and you will not see a clear, bright point. Rather, you will see a distribution of brightness with rays emanating from the center. These rays and the spreading of brightness in the center are primarily due to the existence of spherical aberrations. Clearly, such effects would serve to blur any pattern imaged on the retinal surface of the eye.

A second source of optical aberration arises from the fact that the optical system of the eye is not color corrected. This difficulty results in *chromatic aberration*. In many ways the eye acts optically as if it were completely composed of a single optical substance with the ability to bend light approximately equal to that of an eye-shaped vessel filled with water. To the extent that this is the case, the eye bends light differently depending on its wavelength. Short wavelengths of light are bent more sharply than long wavelengths, which means that the rays corresponding to the violet or blue hues will come to a focus in front of those rays corresponding to the red hues. This effect is shown schematically in Figure 4.1B. Notice that when the eye is accommodated so that the violet waves are focused, which would correspond to projecting the image on a surface at the distance of the dotted line marked I, the red waves would be spread out and thus not in focus. Exactly the opposite would occur if the eye were accommodated so that the longer wavelengths were in focus, as they would be if the image were projected at a distance corresponding to that of the dotted line marked II. Now the red rays come to a point and are in focus, but the blue rays are spread out and blurred.

You may easily demonstrate this effect for yourself by making a pinhole in an opaque dark card. Place a purple filter over the aperture and illuminate it from behind. The purple light transmitted through the filter contains both red and blue rays. If your eye has focused on the red rays, you will see a sharp red point of light with a violet haze around it. If your eye has accommodated for violet, you will see a violet point surrounded by a red haze. With intermediate focus the colors are seen fused as purple, but the edges of the point appear to be fuzzy or blurred, since such intermediate accommodation is appropriate for neither wavelength.

The magnitude of this effect is quite large. Byram (1944a, 1944b) and Sheard (1926) have shown that chromatic aberration leads to a refractive difference of better than two diopters between the ends of the visible spectrum. To the extent that most visual inputs contain a mixture of wavelengths, this source of image degradation may lead to considerable blurring of the image of any point or line imaged on the retina (Ivanoff, 1946).

Although chromatic and spherical aberrations are the major sources of image blurring in the eye; there is one other process that contributes to the degradation of the image. Light waves entering the eye are bent as they make contact with the edges of the pupillary aperture by the process of *diffraction*. This effect serves to spread out the image and, because of interactive and interference effects, results in a nonuniform distribution of light around the principal image of the stimulus. Figure 4.2A demonstrates diffraction. The input is represented by parallel rays entering a narrow circular aperture, such as the pupil. Notice that the diffraction effect transforms the light from a point source into a more spread out or blurred distribution like that shown in Figure 4.2B. The amount of diffraction interacts with pupil size. It is not very large when the pipillary aperture is reasonably wide; however, with a constricted pupil of 1 or 2 mm, such effects can become quite sizable.

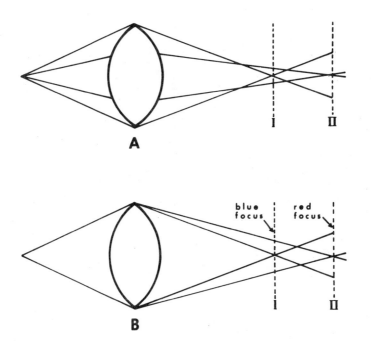

FIG. 4.1.   (A) A schematic diagram of the operation of spherical aberration, which shows how the peripheral rays come to a focus in front of the central rays; (B) a schematic diagram of the operation of chromatic aberration, which shows how the blue rays come to a focus in front of the red.

Considering all these sources of image degradation, plus some additional blurring of the image from light scattering in the optic media and from the uncorrected refractive error of about 0.0625 diopters found in most "normal eyes" (Ames & Proctor, 1921), it becomes clear that the retinal image is far from being a perfect copy of the input stimulus. It is spread out or smeared over a considerable portion of the retina, a fact as we will soon see, that leads to some interesting illusions of extent and direction.

IMAGE BLUR AND ILLUSION

Before we can make any precise predictions about how the optical blurring effects we have been discussing may produce illusory percepts, it is important to know what the retinal image of a contour actually looks like, given the fact that it is certainly degraded by these various optical processes. A number of investigators have directly measured the retinal image obtained from viewing a contour. They accomplish this measurement by having an observer view a bright luminous

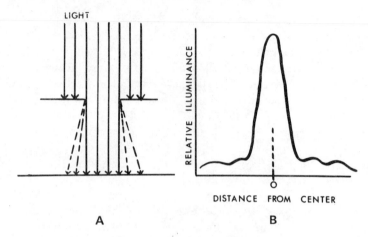

FIG. 4.2. (A) Parallel rays entering a narrow circular aperture are spread by the operation of diffraction; (B) the image of a theoretical point source of light operated on by diffraction.

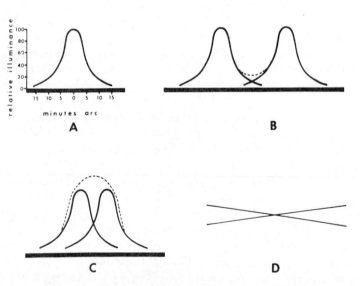

FIG. 4.3. (A) The spread of the retinal image of a bright line viewed through a 6 mm pupil; (B) the resultant light distribution of two separate points of light spatially separated; (C) the summation of the light distributions from two spatially proximal points; (D) an illusion in which the intersection of two lines meeting in an acute angle appears to be constricted.

line and then measuring the distribution of light reflected back along the input path, a process that should allow one to reconstruct the actual image (Campbell & Gubisch, 1966; Gubisch, 1967; Krauskopf, 1962; Westheimer & Campbell, 1962). Figure 4.3A shows one actual distribution of light in the retinal image of a line as measured by Krauskopf (1962). The line is viewed with the eye at best focus, and the pupil is 6 mm in diameter. Notice that the various sources of blur have distributed the light in the image. It now covers a sizable region of the retina and, rather than having sharp and well defined contours, is blurred at the edges.

Given that the retinal image is so blurred, why do lines usually appear so clear in the percept? A full answer to this question would be rather complex, involving several forms of neural interaction. Simply put, it seems as if the visual system assesses the retinal image and selects the peak of the light distribution as defining the location of the contour. If the blur is not too spread out, only this peak is represented in consciousness as the image of the line. The blur seems to be ignored or suppressed.

Up to now we have considered only the image of single points or lines. Most illusion patterns involve several contours and lines that are simultaneously in view. It is the presence of more than one stimulus contour in the retinal image that permits the interactions that result in illusory effects. Clearly, most opportunities for interaction occur when contours are close to one another, as when lines cross or converge to form angles. If we have several lines in close proximity, then their respective distributions of light, due to optical blurring, may well overlap. Consider Figure 4.3B, where we see two distributions corresponding to the images of two points of light (or two bright lines) on the retina. Since the brain assesses the locus of the contour by identifying the location of the ridge of maximal light intensity, this pattern of stimulation should result in the perception of two separate points of light. As indicated by the dashed line in Figure 4.3B, even in this situation, there may be some interaction between the two distributions on the retina. When the two points of light are moved close enough to each other, the light from the two images adds together to form a distribution of light that corresponds to what would be expected from a single point of light located somewhere between the original two points. This summed effect is shown as the dashed line in Figure 4.3C. Now consider what this type of interaction would do if we had a pattern consisting of two lines intersecting to form an angle. Far from the vertex, where the lines are far apart, the results should look like Figure 4.3B, and there should be no noticeable distortion. However, closer to the vertex, the distribution will begin to approximate Figure 4.3C. Hence the lines in the retinal image will merge and thus appear to intersect before the actual vertex of the angle. This should distort the perception of an angle in two ways. First, the vertex will appear to be shifted in the direction of the angle's interior; second, because of this shift in the apparent location of the vertex, the angle should appear to be more obtuse or "snub nosed" than it actually is.

These effects on the location of the vertex should be accentuated in acute angles. This fact allows us to predict a novel illusory effect. Figure 4.3D shows two lines that intersect to form two horizontally oriented acute angles. Notice that at the point of intersection there is an apparent constriction of the lines. The crossing lines almost seem to split into two separate acute angles, which seem to pull away from each other, so thin does the part that connects them appear. This is due to the predicted shifts in the apparent locus of the vertices into the body of the angle. If we consider some more complex patterns and merely add the individual effects of vertex shift and angle opening, we can explain a number of visual illusions that contain crossing or intersecting line elements, such as the Mueller-Lyer, the Poggendorff, the Zoellner, the Wundt, and the Hering figures (Chiang, 1968; Coren, 1969; Einthoven, 1898). Perhaps this is best seen in the Mueller-Lyer variant shown as Figure 4.4. The heavy lines represent the actual stimulus, whereas the dotted lines represent the resultant patterns on the retina. Notice that the vertices have moved into the angles, causing the distance between them to be enlarged in the right segment and contracted in the left. This is, of course, the pattern of spatial distortion usually obtained in this type of configuration.

To the extent that these illusory effects are caused by blurring of the image, anything that increases the amount of blur should increase the strength of the illusion. Ward and Coren (1976) did this optically by actually blurring the physical stimulus. They used the Brentano form of the Mueller-Lyer as shown in Figure 4.5A. When this image is defocused by two diopters, the pattern shown as Figure 4.5B results. Notice that in the optically blurred form the strength of the distortion is increased, with the apparently longer section appearing somewhat longer and the apparently shorter segment somewhat shorter. Ward and Coren reportedly doubled the magnitude of the usual distortion by means of such optical blurring. Although it is a somewhat heavy-handed technique, this demonstration does serve to indicate that blur can augment the magnitude of some illusory distortions.

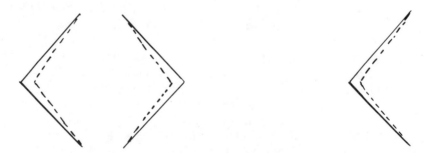

FIG. 4.4.   A demonstration of how blur interactions can lead to the Mueller–Lyer illusion (see text for explanation).

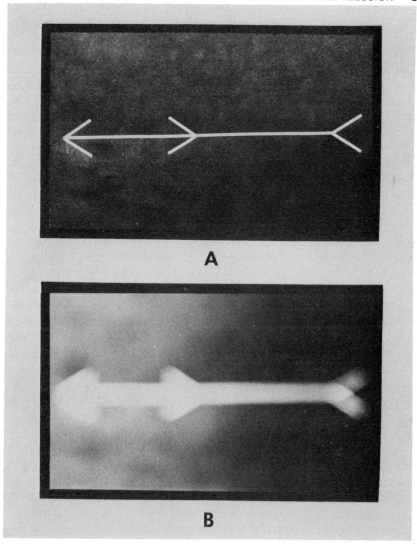

FIG. 4.5.   The effect of optical blur on the magnitude of the Mueller—
Lyer illusion (after Ward & Coren, 1976).

Coren (1969) utilized the reverse of the above procedure. He reasoned that if
he could reduce the blurring effects of the various optical contributions, thus
sharpening the image, he would reduce illusion magnitude caused by the sort of
image interactions we have been discussing. He used the Poggendorff illusion,
which contains several intersecting lines, as his stimulus. To understand how this
was accomplished, consider the first column of Table 4.1 which shows the
amount of blur that would be obtained in the retinal image of a normal eye

TABLE 4.1

Appropriate Computed Diameters of the Blur Disc Measured
in Seconds of Arc at the Nodal Point of the Eye

Sources of blur	4 mm pupil	1 mm pupil with 18 mm band with chromatic filter
Chromatic aberration	216	13
Spherical aberration	432	30
Diffraction	34	126
Assumed incorrected refractive error of 0.0625D	54	13
Total	736	182

Note: After "The Influence of Optical Aberrations on the magnitude of the Poggendorff Illusion" by S. Coren, *Perception and Psychophysics,* 1969, *6,* 185–186.

viewing a theoretical point of light, if we assume a 4 mm pupillary opening. Much of this image blur can be controlled. The amount of chromatic aberration can be reduced through the use of a narrow band interference filter. By limiting the wavelength of the light to a narrow range, the differential bending of the light is avoided. Thus all the rays come to a point of focus at the same place. Spherical aberrations may be reduced by use of a small artificial pupil that permits light to enter through only the center of the cornea and lens, thus reducing the size of the blur circle. This small artificial pupil will also correct the assumed refractive error in any normal eye (Ames & Proctor, 1921; Ludvigh, 1953). Unfortunately, a small artificial pupil also tends to increase the amount of diffraction somewhat, but this increase in blur is considerably smaller than the decrease that results from the control of other factors. The second column in Table 4.1 shows the amount of image blur for the specific interference filter and the 1 mm artificial pupil used by Coren (1969). Notice that much of the blurring has been reduced by this method of viewing. Coren then tested subjects under both normal and reduced blur conditions. He reports a reduction in the magnitude of the Poggendorff illusion under conditions of low blur, as would be predicted if interaction from blurred contours were a contributor to illusion magnitude. Unfortunately, the magnitude of the reduction in the illusion was considerably smaller than one would expect if image blur were the sole basis of the illusion. For example, if we assume any symmetrical distribution of blur on the retina and then reduce its spread by some percentage, the magnitude of the illusion should be reduced by the same percentage (Chiang, 1968; Pressey & den Heyer, 1968). When the illusion is viewed with a filter and artificial pupil, the blur is reduced by about 75% of its original amount if we assume that total blur is the determining factor, or by about 70% if we assume that the largest single blur circle is the determining factor. If the illusion were totally caused by blur effects, we would expect a reduction in illusion magnitude of at least 70%. Although it is true that the sharpening of the image reduced the size of the illusory effect, which seems to indicate that optical aberrations play some role in the formation of certain illusion patterns that contain intersecting line elements, the size of the reduction was only 15.6%. It becomes clear that, although the degrading of the retinal image by optical aberrations present in the eye may account for some illusory effects, it is only a partial answer.

PROJECTIVE GEOMETRY AND ILLUSIONS

There is one property of the eye that is frequently ignored but that has important optical consequences and seems to be responsible for an interesting class of illusions. It is the fact that the retina is not a flat screen on which the dioptric system of the eye focuses an image; rather, the retina is affixed to the inside of the eye, which itself is a hollow sphere. This means that different portions of the retinal surface are at different distances from the crystalline lens. To see how this affects the image, we can consider a physically hollow sphere with a small hole at one end. Let us mark a point in the center of this sphere opposite this aperture. If we were to coat the inner surface of the sphere with a photosensitive film, expose it to some light pattern projected through the hole, and later peel it off, we would find that any line not passing through the marked center point would seem to bow outward in the middle and inward in the periphery. This implies that straight parallel lines should not project curved nonparallel images on the retinal surface, since the eye can be seen as analogous to the hollow sphere, with the fovea analogous to the marked central point.

This distortion can be demonstrated fairly easily. Take a long strip of paper about 10 cm wide and place it on a table. When you view the middle of the strip, it will be clear that the ends of the strip (seen in indirect vision) seem to be narrower than the middle. The parallel edges of the paper now look like two concave arcs. Figure 4.6 shows another demonstration of this distortion. Adjust the page so that the checkerboard pattern is at a distance from your eye equivalent to the length of the line marked "viewing distance." Now fixate the center portion of the field. Under these viewing conditions, the physically parallel lines should appear to be barrel-shaped outward. By computing the appropriate hyperbolic curves, in a manner similar to that used by Helmholtz (1856, 1860, 1866/1962), we can construct a figure with curved lines (Figure 4.6B) that when viewed at the distance indicated, will appear with all lines straight and parallel. This is due to the fact that the distortion in the projected pattern within

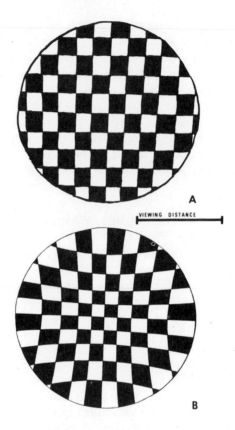

FIG. 4.6.   The barrel illusion. (A) When viewed at a distance equivalent to the length of the line marked "viewing distance," the checkerboard appears to be barrel-shaped outward; (B) when viewed at the "viewing distance," all contours appear to be straight.

the eye exactly compensates for the physical curvature in the pattern. Ames and Proctor (1921) showed that these distortions are simply due to the fact that the optics of the eye project the image on a curved retinal surface.

Although one might expect this distortion to be frequently reported, one virtually never hears it mentioned in normal discourse. This may be due to the fact that most of the lines in our field of view are too short to allow this illusory effect to manifest itself clearly. Alternatively, we may fail to notice this effect because we seldom make judgments based on indirect vision. Normally, the eye is continually moving so that images to be appraised fall on the fovea. Still, this is an ever-present aspect of the optical functioning of the eye that leads to systematic illusory distortions under appropriate viewing conditions.

In the preceding pages we have dealt with the way in which the optical properties of the eye distort the light pattern in the retinal image in a manner that leads to certain illusory distortions. The major effect associated with blurring of the image is to move the apparent location of the vertices of angles to a point further into the body of the angle, thus foreshortening the pattern and making acute angles seem to be slightly more obtuse. In addition we have seen how the projective geometry of the eye can make straight lines appear to be curved and curved lines appear to be straight. Even at a level so peripheral in the visual system that the stimulus information has not yet been encoded into a pattern of neural impulses, we find structural factors that can result in distortions leading to percepts that will differ from the actual physical stimulus in the environment. As we begin to encode the stimulus and pass it on to the higher centers, we will find that other mechanisms, leading to different illusory effects, will begin to manifest themselves.

5 Structural Factors in Illusion Formation: Retinal Components

As we saw in the previous chapter, the nature of the optical system of the eye causes some changes in the light input. This means that stimulus relations found in the retinal image may not be an exact copy of those in the environmental stimulus. Such changes in the pattern represented in the eye seem to contribute to some illusory distortions, especially when converging and intersecting lines are present. In addition to optical effects, there are a number of neural processes involving interactions between spatially adjacent cells in the retina that seem to contribute to some visual illusions. In this chapter we focus our attention on the way in which the percept may be distorted during the process of encoding the retinal image into a pattern of neural responses.

Before we consider the relationship between visual illusions and the physiology of the retina in any detail, a methodological comment is in order. Most of the research from which we have derived our knowledge of the nature of neural processing in the retina has been based on experiments with animals. Animal and human retinas often differ along many dimensions. If we wish to generalize from physiological data collected from such lower species, it is important to verify that animals are subject to the same patterns of visual illusions as humans.

To determine behaviorally whether an animal is perceiving a visual illusion is often quite tricky. However, a number of investigators have produced data that seem to indicate that many of the illusions found in humans are also present in infrahuman species. For example, Herter (1930) verified that the Mueller-Lyer illusion occurs in several species of fish. Winslow (1933) extended this work to chicks, and he was also able to show that these young birds seem to be affected by the horizontal-vertical illusion. Dominguez (1954) found that rhesus, mangabey, and cebus monkeys are susceptible to the horizontal-vertical illusion, as well as to the Helmholtz square distortion variant of the Oppel-Kundt illusion (Figure 2.1A). He reports that the size of the illusory distortion that he obtained in these animals was comparable to that normally obtained in humans. Duecker (1966) studied the Ebbinghaus and Zoellner illusions in a variety of species including fish, chicks, mistle thrushes, and guinea pigs. Although there was a good deal of variability in his data, animals that tended to respond consistently on illusion test trials tended to respond in the direction consistent with that expected if they were experiencing the illusion. Finally, Ducharme, Delorme, and Boulard (1967) have verified that the Oppel-Kundt illusion exists in the white rat. On the whole, then, these studies seem to indicate that nonhuman animals do experience illusions. Hence it seems reasonable to utilize animal physiological data in our exploration of structural factors that may be relevant to illusion formation.

PATTERNS OF RETINAL SPATIAL INTERACTIONS

Neural responses on the retina do not occur in isolation. There is much evidence to indicate that the way in which a region of the retina responds is often affected by the way in which neighboring regions are behaving. These interactions may be of two forms: summation and inhibition. Summation occurs when the activity of a given neural unit serves to increase the level of response of a nearby retinal region. An example of summation occurs when a light, too weak to be seen, is imaged on the retina. It has been demonstrated that the light will often become visible when a second point of light, also too weak to be seen alone, is imaged on an adjacent location (Graham, 1934). Under these circumstances, it seems that the two regions of activity generated by the spots of light are interacting in a facilitative manner, mutually increasing each other's response. Adrian and Matthews (1928) using the conger eel, Hartline (1940) using the frog, and Granit (1947), Kuffler (1952), and Barlow, Fitzhugh, and Kuffler (1957) using the cat, have shown that this neural pooling or summation of activity from adjacent regions originates in the retina. Their work demonstrates that a greater neural response from the retina is produced by a large patch of light than by a small one containing the same amount of light energy.

The effect of this summation or facilitation of activity over regions of the retina is very similar to the effects of blur that we considered earlier. Theoretically, this pattern of neural response should add to some of the distortions we illustrated in Figure 4.3, thus serving to shift vertices and open up angular patterns even more.

The other form of interaction occurring on the retina is inhibition. It is different in its method of action, and the nature of the illusory effects it produces are also quite distinct. Inhibition occurs whenever the activity of a neural unit is depressed by the presence of activity in another nearby region of the retina. Numerous experiments, most of which have used the horseshoe crab *limulus*, have shown that the action in a retinal receptor can be inhibited or reduced by activity in a nearby receptor and that the amount of inhibition seems to be directly related to the intensity of the firing of the adjacent receptor and inversely proportional to the distance between the two active units (Hartline, Wagner, & Ratliff, 1956; Ratliff, 1965). This process, usually called *lateral inhibition*, seems to play a part in some aspects of brightness perception and has been specifically related to simultaneous brightness contrast and the Mach band phenomenon (Ratliff, 1965). It also seems possible that lateral inhibition plays a part in certain illusions of shape and extent.

Given the fact that both summation and inhibition processes take place on the retina, their action must be taken into account whenever we have a pattern imaged on the retina, if we wish to predict the form of the final neural response. The composite effect of both these processes has been qualitatively and quantitatively specified on the basis of the available neurophysiological and physchophysical evidence by a large number of researchers including Bekesy (1960, 1967), Fry (1948), Huggins and Licklider (1961), Ratliff (1965), and Taylor (1956). Basically all these researchers propose that a point of light imaged on the retinal surface sets up a distribution of neural activity containing both excitatory and inhibitory components. A point of light produces a large neural response in the elements on which it falls. The summation effect causes some immediately adjacent neural units to be activated also, although somewhat more weakly. Beyond the range where the activity recruits responses from nearby receptors, there is a rapid change in the nature of the neural response. At these larger distances, neural interactions become inhibitory, thus reducing the activity in other retinal units. We may schematically depict this distribution of neural response to a point of light, as we have done in Figure 5.1A. The parts of the distribution above the horizontal base line represent regions of activity in which responses are excitatory and add to other ongoing neural action. The parts of the distribution below the horizontal line represent inhibitory activity that tends to subtract from, or depress, ongoing neural responses. Notice that summation responses are maximal at and around the point of stimulation. This activity is spatially adjacent to a region of intense inhibition which then diminishes as we move farther away. To get the composite pattern of activity for several points or contours imaged on the retina, we need only combine these distributions of activity. When areas of summation overlap, they add to each other, whereas when areas of inhibition overlap areas of summation, they tend to subtract, proportionally reducing the neural activity. To see how this process works, consider Figure 5.1B, which represents the activity set up by two points of light or two bright lines when they are imaged close together on the retinal surface. The major effect of combining these distributions is a summation of the two central regions of activity. Thus the composite response pattern is similar to that expected from the image of a single point of light located at a point between the two actual images, as shown by the dotted line. It should be clear that the process of summing neural activity and the resultant fusion of two points into one does not differ very much geometrically from our analysis of the effects of optical blur, which we described in the previous chapter. However, major differences do begin to appear when the two points of light are moved slightly farther apart, as shown in Figure 5.1C. Notice that with the two points more widely separated, the inhibitory spread of activity from one spot overlaps the excitatory spread of the other. Hence the rate of neural activity should diminish as the inhibition proportionally depresses the activity of neural units in its range. Since the strength of the inhibition is strongest near the point of stimulation and decreases as one moves farther away, the reduction in neural activity is assymetrical. As Figure 5.1C shows, the inhibition subtracts more activity from one side of the distribution of excitation than from the other. The resultant effect is shown as a dotted line. It should be clear that the peaks of activity in this combined distribution of activity are now farther apart than they were in the two original images, prior to the spatial interactions due to lateral inhibition. As we noted in the previous chapter, it seems reasonable to assume that the visual system assigns the spatial location of a contour to the position corresponding to the maximum or peak of activity in that region of the retina on which the image is falling. To the extent that this is so, the effect of these inhibitory interactions should be to move the apparent location of two closely spaced contours away from each other. Such a spatial repulsion effect could easily result in some illusory percepts.

RETINAL INTERACTIONS AND ILLUSIONS

Let us now see how these retinal interactions affect our phenomenal impressions of the location and extent of stimuli. Perhaps the most direct consequence of the operation of lateral inhibition is an illusory effect that is often called the *alignment illusion*. This distortion is shown as Figure 5.1D, in which the left-hand segment of the upper pair of lines is directly above and vertically aligned with the lower line. Notice, however, that it appears to be displaced slightly too far to the left. This displacement is easily predictable from the pattern of contour repulsion we discussed above and illustrated as Figure 5.1C. The effect is thus merely the consequence of having another contour in close spatial proximity. The magnitude of this distortion can be altered by moving the figure closer to or father away from the eye. This simple manipulation serves to change the visual angle of the separation between the upper pair of lines or more simply the location and relative proximity of the images of the lines on the retina. If the eye is close enough and the images are thus widely enough spaced so that the inhibitory flanks of one no longer overlap the region of excitation of the other, the illusion should disappear. The size of this illusion is small, with a typical dis-

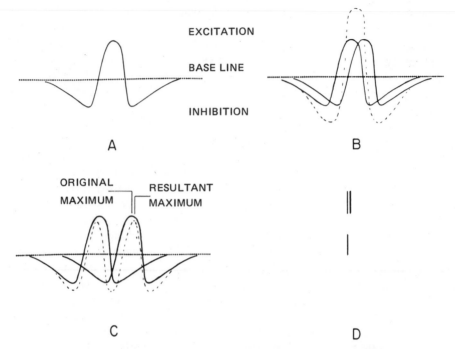

FIG. 5.1.   (A) Spatial distribution of the spread of neural excitation and
inhibition following stimulation by a single point of light; (B) summation
of excitatory peaks for two spatially proximal points imaged on the retina;
(C) Repulsion of excitatory peaks for two slightly separated points imaged
on the retina; (D) the alignment illusion in which the upper left line is
aligned with the lower line but appears to be displaced too far to the left.

placement of around 15 or 20 minutes of arc. This pattern has been systematically investigated by Day (1962b), Ganz (1964), and Pollack (1958).

There is a rather direct research technique that suggests itself as a method of
studying the effects of neural interactions on illusions. It would seem to be a
simple matter to image a classical illusion pattern on an animal retina and measure the resultant pattern of neural responses, mapped in a two-dimensional
manner across the surface. Certainly, this would directly assess the contribution
of neural interactions and produce clear indications of the nature and extent of
contour displacements, which could then be used as an indication that an illusion was present. Unfortunately, few such attempts have been made, and those
that have been made seem to have produced somewhat mixed results. For instance, Motokawa and Ogawa (1962) directly recorded the neural responses that
result from imaging the Delboeuf and Mueller-Lyer illusions on the carp retina.
For the Delboeuf illusion, they found the expected repulsion of the maxima of
neural responses for the half of the pattern that is phenomenally underestimated.

They also found an attraction of the maximum of neural response in the part of the pattern that usually results in overestimation of the test circle. Unfortunately, this result may be too consistent. Although it is easy to predict the contour repulsion effects from neural interactions, especially when the contours are separated by an appropriate distance, it is not at all clear how one could predict the displacement of two distributions of activity toward each other from consideration of neural summation and inhibition alone. The data from recording the retinal response pattern to the image of the Mueller-Lyer illusion are similarly suggestive and puzzling. The results do show a larger field of positive response for the apparently longer half of the illusion than for the apparently shorter half. Unfortunately, the field of positive response seems to reflect the maximum horizontal extent in the image of the apparently shorter half quite accurately. This means that one should be able to predict the overestimation of the wings-out half of the configuration but not the underestimation usually found in the wings-in half.

A number of investigators have attempted to use psychophysical data to explore the relationship between retinal interactions and visual illusions. They usually first attempt to compute the pattern of neural response from the retina for a specific illusion configuration, based on the known patterns of neural inhibitory and summation effects. Next they examine how well the phenomenology reflects the assumed underlying physiological response. Such an analysis typically begins by noting that lateral inhibitory interactions occur most strongly between points and contours that are imaged in close spatial proximity on the retina. This consideration leads to the conclusion that effects most likely to produce illusory distortions should be found in configurations containing intersecting or converging line elements, where contour elements are most likely to be close enough to interact. Bekesy (1967) and Ganz (1966a, 1966b) have provided detailed descriptions of some perceptual effects that may be predicted when contours intersect on the retina. They conclude that lateral inhibitory interactions can lead to a situation in which the activity peak corresponding to the vertex of the angle will be displaced inward toward the body of the angle due to the effects of blur (Figure 4.3) or neural summation (Figure 5.1B), while the sides will flare out slightly, due to the inhibitory repulsion effect. The composite pattern of activity is shown as Figure 5.2. The physical image of two intersecting lines on the retina is shown as solid lines in the figure, and the predicted ridges of maximum neural activity are shown as dotted lines. It is not very difficult, using this systematic distortion of intersecting line patterns as a building block, to predict a large number of illusions containing intersecting line elements. For instance, the displacement of the vertices is sufficient to explain the Mueller-Lyer illusion (cf. Figure 4.4), whereas the opening up of the angles could easily incline test contours resulting in illusions of direction, such as the Zoellner, the Wundt, the Hering, or the Poggendorff illusions.

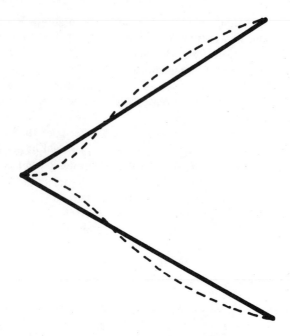

FIG. 5.2.   The displacement of the maxima of excitation for two converging lines, as a function of the action of lateral inhibition.

If such interactions actually occur on the retina, they should lead to a predictable set of contour distortions in the final percept. If we have a line that obliquely crosses a set of other lines, a displacement of the vertex might be expected to occur in the acute angle at each intersection. This should result in a set of apparent discontinuities or "breaks" in the test line, since the effect of the distortion is in the opposite direction on either side of the intersection. An example of this effect is shown in Figure 5.3A, which presents a herringbone variant of the Zoellner illusion. The two vertical lines appear to be made up of a series of small, steplike discontinuous segments. The apparent convergence of the two lines as they move up the page is easily predictable from the opening up of each acute angle, which should lead to a slight inclination of each line segment.

A quick glance back at Figure 5.2, however, reveals that there are other changes in the contour, besides a shift in the location of the vertex and an opening up of the angle, that should also be apparent. For instance, the sides of the angle (or, rather, the pattern of neural activity that represents the sides) is no longer a straight line but manifests clear curvature. Such curving of lines is not usually seen in intersecting line patterns, however. For instance, Figure 5.3B shows a standard Poggendorff configuration. Figure 5.3C shows an exaggerated version of the sort of local distortions, including curving of the lines near the point of intersection, that should be expected in this pattern, given the nature of the contour displacement effects supposedly resulting from retinal interactions. It is clear that these distortions do not appear in Figure 5.3B. Despite the fact that the curvature effects do not enter our conscious representation of the stimulus, there is an indirect way to show that such distortions may still be present and operating in the Poggendorff illusion. Figure 5.3D shows an exaggerated version of a Poggendorff configuration in which the transversals are bent to offset the predicted curvature from retinal interactions. If we scale this curvature down to the levels actually predicted, we obtain the figure shown as

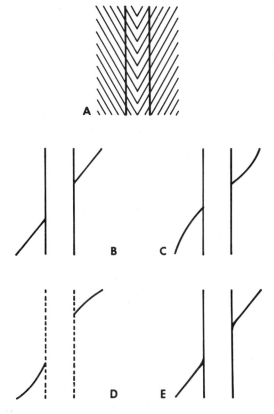

FIG. 5.3.   (A) A variant of the Zoellner illusion in which the two vertical lines appear to be made up of a series of small step-like discontinuous segments; (B) the standard Poggendorff configuration; (C) Exaggeration of the expected distortion based on contour interactions; (D) an exaggerated version in which the transversals are bent to offset the expected curvature; (E) the illusory displacement is offset by the slight curvature of the transversals.

Figure 5.3B, which was first investigated by Kobayashi (1956). Notice that curving the transversals in this way greatly reduces the illusory effect. This is the result we would expect if the curvature effects and the flaring out of the angle, as predicted by neural interactions, contributed to the distortion, since 5.3E was drawn to compensate exactly for these local effects.

EFFECTS OF STIMULUS CONTRAST

To the extent that retinal interactions account for some illusion effects, some additional predictions ought to be possible. For example, since the spread and intensity of lateral inhibition are related to the intensity of the retinal stimulation, reduction of the contrast of an illusion should result in a diminished illusion magnitude, since reducing the stimulus intensity difference between the contour and its background should reduce the spread and strength of the neural processes the image evokes on the retina. It is interesting that a number of investigators have shown that the Mueller-Lyer illusion (which contains the requisite intersecting line elements) is reduced when one reduces stimulus contrast (Bates, 1923; Dewar, 1967b; Wicklegren, 1965).

The overall effect of stimulus contrast on the magnitude of the illusion is much more complex, however. To begin with, it seems to interact with the duration of stimulus exposure. For brief stimulus exposures of approximately 500 milliseconds the results indicate that the higher the contrast of the stimulus, the greater the illusion magnitude (Ebert & Pollack, 1972, 1973a, 1973b; Pollack & Chaplin, 1964; Wicklegren, 1965). For relatively long stimulus durations, ranging from 9 through 18 seconds, one also finds that higher contrast stimuli produce greater illusion magnitudes in the Mueller-Lyer illusion (Pollack & Chaplin, 1964; Ebert & Pollack, 1973a, 1973b). At intermediate stimulus durations, however, ranging from about 1.5 through 4.5 seconds, there seems to be a breakdown in the relationship between contrast and illusion magnitude (Ebert & Pollack, 1973a, 1973b; Weintraub, Tong, & Smith, 1973). The reasons for this complex pattern of results are not at all clear, but in other modalities, such as the skin senses or the auditory system, Bekesy (1957, 1967) has shown that immediately following the onset of a stimulus there is a large burst of transient activity, proportional to the stimulus intensity. After this initial surge, it may take several seconds of continuous stimulation for the inhibitory effects to build up to their maximum level. It thus could be that the relationship between contrast and illusion magnitude for short exposures is due to the initial inhibitory response transient, and the correspondence for longer exposures may result when the inhibitory effects build up to their steady state intensities during prolonged stimulation. The middle range breakdown in the relationship between contrast and illusion magnitude may simply reflect the gradual transition of the retinal response from the onset activity to a steady state, which is associated with concomitant changes in the relative intensity of inhibitory processes. This must be viewed merely as a speculation until the actual details of the time course of retinal interactions are more clearly worked out.

There is another contrast manipulation that can also be used to explore the effects of lateral inhibition on the production of illusions. A low contrast stimulus produces both a diffuse center of excitation and less well-defined edges because of the shallowness of its inhibitory flanks. Thus, in low contrast stimuli, the point of maximum excitation is not as well defined as in higher contrast stimuli. This difference suggests that a given amount of inhibition should produce a larger shift in the apparent location of a low contrast stimulus. If such is the case, a high contrast including component and low contrast test element should produce greater illusion effects than if both the test and inducing elements were of either high or low contrast. This prediction has been verified by Oyama (1962) and Weintraub and Cooper (1972) for the Delboeuf illusion.

To the extent that anything that alters stimulus contrast should also alter illusion magnitude, it is interesting to consider the fact that there is a patch of yellow pigmentation called the *macula lutea*, which lies in front of the foveal region of the retina. Since this pigmentation lies between the incoming light rays and the retinal receptors, it should be clear that it might serve to alter the effective contrast of the stimulus by absorbing some of the light in the image. The denser the pigmentation, the less light will reach the receptors, and the lower will be both the initial excitatory response and the resultant inhibitory effect. Pollack and Silvar (1967b) and Ebert and Pollack (1973a, 1973b) have shown that individuals with denser macular pigmentation show a smaller Mueller-Lyer illusion, as might be expected from the contrast analysis. Bayer and Pressey (1972) have not been able to replicate these results; however, the variation in pigmentation of their sample was smaller than that used in Pollack's laboratory.

AGE TRENDS AND RETINAL FACTORS IN ILLUSIONS

It has long been known that many visual illusions vary in strength as a direct function of the age of the individual being tested. Some illusions seem to decrease in magnitude as the observer grows older, whereas a few increase or show only erratic patterns of change. Table 5.1 summarizes some of these results for seven common illusion patterns. The fact that illusion strength varies with age could indicate that there are structural changes in the optical or neural system of the aging individual and that these changes affect the way in which illusion patterns are processed. Such changes could also occur as a consequence of alterations in information-processing strategies as the individual becomes more experienced with his environment. A hint as to which of these alternatives is responsible may be suggested by carefully looking at Table 5.1 again.

Notice that the illusion configurations showing the most consistent age-related declines are the Mueller-Lyer and the Poggendorff. It is interesting that both these patterns contain converging and intersecting line elements that are the components most appropriate for neural and optical interactions. The Delboeuf, horizontal-vertical, Oppel-Hundt, Ebbinghaus, and Ponzo illusions contain fewer opportunities for contour interactions and also show less consistent age trends. A data pattern such as this suggests that chronological changes in the optical quality of the image formation system of the eye or in the efficiency of neural responses and interactions may be responsible for some of the age trends in illusion strength.

Pollack (1969) considered some of the structural changes in the aging eye that might affect illusion strength. He particularly singled out the fact that the crystalline lens in the human eye grows yellower with increasing age (Coren & Girgus, 1972a; Lakowski, 1962; Ruddock, 1965; Said & Weale, 1959; Stiles & Burch, 1959; Verriest, 1963). Because the major optical effect of this increased pigmentation in the lens is a reduction in the intensity of the retinal image, older individuals will have somewhat less bright images on the retinal surface. It is likely that this reduction in intensity reduces the spread and magnitude of the inhibitory processes, since the amount of lateral inhibition depends on the intensity of the initial excitation. Because anything that reduces the magnitude of neural interactive processes will also reduce the strength of any illusion caused by such interactions, it seems likely that the increased density of the crystalline lens in older observers would serve to support a reduction in illusion strength in some configurations. Notice that this effect works in much the same way as a reduction in stimulus contrast.

Unfortunately, the correlation between lens pigmentation and illusion strength has not been clearly established. Although Sjostrom and Pollack (1971) found a reduction in the Delboeuf illusion when a yellow filter designed to simulate the increased pigmentation of the lens with age is inserted in front of the eye, Weintraub, Tong, and Smith (1973) were unable to replicate this result for the Mueller-Lyer configuration.

Pollack (1963) offered an alternative structural explanation for the decreasing strength of intersecting line illusions with age by suggesting that there is an age-related decrease in neural efficiency. When he measured contour detectability thresholds in children varying in age from 8 to 12 years, he found this expected efficiency loss, which shows up as a decreased ability to detect contours in the older group. This difference is probably due to changes in the nature of inhibitory interactions on the retina, since there are no age-related differences in the detection of contours of different hues when brightness (on which the strength of the neural response depends) is held constant (Pollack, 1965; Pollack &

TABLE 5.1
Age Trends in Illusions

Configuration	Study	Age Trends[a]
Mueller–Lyer	Barclay & Comalli, 1970	−
	Binet, 1895	−
	Gaudreau, Lavoie, & Delorme, 1963	−
	Girgus, Coren, & Fraenkel, 1975	−
	Murray, 1967	−
	Noelting, 1960	−
	Piaget & von Albertini, 1950	−
	Piaget, & Marie, & Privat, 1954	−
	Pintner & Anderson, 1916	−
	Pollack, 1964	−
	Segall, Campbell, & Herskovits, 1966	−
	Sun, 1964	−
	van Biervliet, 1896	−
	Walters, 1942	−
Poggendorff	Girgus & Coren, 1976	−
	Leibowitz & Gwozdecki, 1967	−
	Pressey & Sweeney, 1970	−
	Vurpillot, 1957	−
Delboeuf	Giering, 1905	−
		0
	Piaget, Lambercier, Boesch, & von Albertini, 1942	−
	Piaget, Matalon, & Bang, 1961	−
	Ruessel, 1934	0
	Santastefano, 1963	0
Horizontal-vertical	Doyle, 1967	−
	Fraisse & Vautrey, 1956	0
	Hanley & Zerbolio, 1965	+
	Piaget, Matalon, & Bang, 1961	−
	Rivers, 1905	−
	Segall, Campbell, & Herskovits, 1966	0
	Walters, 1942	−
	Winch, 1907	−
	Wuersten, 1947	0
Oppel–Kundt	Gaudreau, Lavoie, & Delorme, 1963	−
	Piaget & Bang, 1961a	+
	Piaget & Osterrieth, 1953	−
Ebbinghaus	Ruessel, 1934	−
	Wapner & Werner, 1957	+
	Wapner, Werner, & Comalli, 1960	0
Ponzo	Leibowitz & Heisel, 1958	+
	Leibowitz & Judisch, 1967	+

[a] − = decreased; + = increased; 0 = no change/ambiguous.

Magerl, 1965). There is an impressive agreement reported by Pollack (1969) between the efficiency of contour detectability and the strength of the illusion
measured in the same observers, with both covarying with age.

There is an interesting manipulation that seems to verify the influence of
retinal neural interactions on age trends in illusion magnitude. Since lateral inhibition seems to require brightness differences on adjacent spatial loci of the
retina (Ercoles-Guzzoni & Fiorentini, 1958; Fry, 1948; Ratliff, 1965), one way
to reduce the effects of this mechanism would be to create configurations in
which the illusion pattern differs from the background in hue only, with brightnesses equated. When this is done, the usually reported age trends disappear
(Pollack, 1970).

Another piece of evidence that seems to lead to much the same conclusion
comes from Weintraub, Tong, and Smith (1973). If retinal efficiency is greater
for younger observers, then a unit increase in physical contrast should produce
a greater increment in lateral inhibition for younger observers than for older
ones. These investigators report that third-graders show a much larger increase in
illusion magnitude as a function of a given increase in contrast than do college
students.

Although these data are, at best, only suggestive, they do seem to indicate
that some age changes in illusion magnitude may be related to age changes of
a structural nature, involving changes in the efficiency of retinal neural interactions.

ILLUSIONS OF TOUCH

We have presented a series of arguments that seem to indicate that lateral inhibitory effects can cause certain visual illusions. If these distortions are caused
simply by lateral neural interactions, then any sense modality in which lateral
inhibition occurs should be subject to similar distortions. The easiest modality
with which to test this extension of the theory is touch. Mountcastle (1957)
and Bekesy (1960, 1967) have demonstrated that inhibitory interactions occur
between adjacent skin receptors, which are similar in nature to those found between adjacent elements in the retina.

The tactual analogue to a pattern imaged on the retina would be a pattern of
pressures passively impressed on the skin. Such an analogue is easily provided, at
least for illusion configurations, by using fairly large cardboard cut-oúts, which
are pressed against any broad, smooth expanse of skin.

As early as 1934, Revesz reported that a number of optical illusions could be
minicked in patterns of pressure on the skin and that they seemed to produce
the classically observed distortions. In a similar manner, Bekesy (1967), Hatwell,
(1960), Over (1966), and Rudel and Teuber (1963) have all found the expected
distortions for a tactual version of the Mueller-Lyer illusion. Bekesy (1967) has

even demonstrated that, if a simple angle is pressed on the skin surface, the vertex seems to be displaced into the body of the angle and the sides apparently flare outward, as we predicted from lateral inhibitory interactions and as illustrated in Figure 5.2. This distortion is the building block on which several illusory effects are based.

If these effects are predominantly due to mutual inhibition between nearby surface receptors, then as in the visual situation, one would expect illusions predominantly for configurations in which there are converging or intersecting ridges of pressure. A number of investigators have attempted to test for haptic illusions in configurations in which no such converging line elements are present. Bekesy (1967) reported that the Delboeuf illusion is found tactually although Hatwell (1960) could not replicate this. Similar inconsistencies are found with the Oppel-Kundt illusion. Although Bekesy (1960) reported that filled space is overestimated relative to unfilled space (as we find for the visual modality), Revesz (1934) found wide individual differences. Both Craig (1931) and Parrish (1895) reported that the divided extent is actually underestimated relative to the undivided extent. It is quite interesting that the Delboeuf and Oppel-Kundt illusions, which contain no converging or intersecting contours, do not reliably appear when patterns are pressed on the skin surface, whereas the Mueller-Lyer, which does contain such elements, does manifest itself tactually. Such a pattern of results seems to be consistent with the suggestion that lateral neural interactions can play a role in the formation of spatial distortions and by implication (since such lateral interactions are found upon the retina) may play a role in visual illusions.

6

Structural Components in Illusion Formation: Central Neural Mechanisms

Up to now we have been considering structural mechanisms that contribute to the formation of visual illusions. However, we have dealt only with the first stages of visual processing—the optical image forming mechanisms and the retina. It is quite clear that other levels of processing may also be involved in the creation of illusions. There is certainly ample opportunity for neural interactions to occur at higher levels, such as the lateral geniculate bodies or the primary visual cortex. Beyond the level of simple neural effects, illusions may arise from inappropriate information-processing strategies or cognitive judgmental processes. Complex methods are often needed to determine the contribution of such higher level structural or strategy mechanisms. Generally speaking, however, the most direct method involves removing the opportunities for optical and retinal neural interactions and testing the way this affects illusion strength. Presumably, any remaining distortion can be attributed to more central processing, once the peripheral structural mechanisms have been removed.

OPTICAL AND RETINAL INTERACTIONS REMOVED

In the previous two chapters we reviewed a number of optical and retinal mechanisms that can cause the displacement of the location of the vertex of an angle and open up acute angles, thus resulting in several illusions of extent, curvature, or direction. For both the optical mechanisms and the neural retinal mechanisms, the predictions depend on stimulus configurations that contain converging or intersecting line elements. There are a number of techniques that remove such stimulus components from the retinal image while still permitting reconstruction of the complete illusion configuration at a level of processing beyond the retina. Because these techniques bypass any possible optical contributions to illusions and also circumvent the effects of neural summation and inhibition effects between adjacent points of stimulation on the retinal surface, they are effective tools to study the effects of higher level processing on illusion formation.

Coren (1970a, 1970b) used a rather simple direct means to bypass retinal effects. He reasoned that the simple removal of all converging and intersecting contours from illusion figures would accomplish this end. To do this he took several standard configurations, removed the lines, and used dots to mark the ends of line segments and points of line intersection. Figure 6.1A shows a standard Brentano form of the Mueller-Lyer illusion. Figure 6.1B shows a dot form of this configuration, patterned after Coren. Notice that no converging or intersecting line elements exist in the dot pattern. Figure 6.1C and 6.1D show the Poggendorff illusion in standard and dot forms, and Figures 6.1E and 6.1F show the Wundt illusion. More recently, White (1972) performed a similar manipulation on the herringbone version of the Zoellner figure (Figures 6.1G and 6.1H).

Despite the fact that these dot forms do not contain continuous contours, acute angles, or contour elements in close enough spatial proximity to allow neural summation and lateral inhibitory effects to distort the shape of angles or the location of contours, we still find that all the standard illusion effects are still present, although the magnitude of the distortions is usually reduced. For instance, when one compares the size of the distortion obtained in the standard configuration with that obtained in the dot form for the Poggendorff and Mueller-Lyer configurations, the data reveal that the illusory distortion has been cut by about 40% (Coren, 1970b). This reduction in strength clearly indicates the removal of optical and retinal components and their contribution to the illusion, whereas the fact that significant distortion still remains indicates the existence of higher level components in the distortion.

Goldstein and Weintraub (1973) arrived at a similar conclusion using another technique to remove the physical contours from the retinal image. In effect, they used an illusion to create an illusion, by using a Poggendorff illusion partially made up of subjective contours, such as those we discussed in Chapter 3. Figure 6.2A shows a pattern similar to that used by these investigators. This manipulation allows the experimenter to provide the appearance of a line or contour without the usual physical brightness differences on the retina. In the absence of differences in brightness on adjacent portions of the retina, the possibility of optical or retinal interactions is effectively circumvented. As in Coren's dot form of the illusion, this manipulation reduces the magnitude of the distortion significantly, although a measurable residual effect in the usual direction is still found.

A number of other investigators have attempted to reproduce various illusion patterns using subjective contours. Figure 6.2B shows a subjective contour form of the Wundt illusion, suggested by Pastore (1971). Kanizsa (1974) has presented

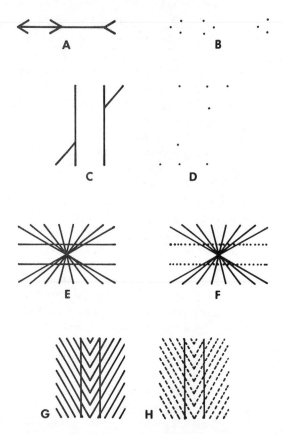

FIG. 6.1.   Standard illusion forms and Coren's dot forms. (A) Brentano
form of the Mueller–Lyer illusion; (B) dot form of the Mueller–Lyer
illusion; (C) standard form of the Poggendorff illusion; (D) dot form of the
Poggendorff illusion; (E) standard form of the Wundt illusion; (F) dot form
of the Wundt illusion; (G) standard form of the Zoellner illusion; (D) dot
form of Zoellner illusion.

variants of the Ponzo in which the inducing elements were subjective contours
and a variant of the Zoellner illusion in which the test elements were subjective
contours. Modified versions of these figures may be seen in Figures 6.2C and
6.2D. It is clear that the illusory distortions still exist in these configurations, although their strength relative to the standard forms of presentation has not as
yet been experimentally determined.

There is one major, potential difficulty with these procedures. Although they
effectively remove the possibility of optical and retinal interactions, they do so
by altering the stimulus pattern. It is possible that some of these alterations in
the configuration affect higher level processing in some manner, implying that
some of the reduction in illusion magnitude observed in these illusion variants

may not be due simply to the elimination of optical and retinal factors but may also reflect the disruption of processes operating on the array at a later site in the visual system. For instance, such stimuli may not be as effective in evoking the action of orientation-specific cortical cells that may play a role in illusion formation. At an even high level, such degraded stimuli may not elicit the same information-processing strategies that are usually used for objective and complete contours, thus reducing any distortions such processes might engender.

There is a technique that eliminates the contribution of optical and retinal mechanisms without any change in the nature of the stimulus reaching the higher centers. This technique involves the stereoscopic separation of elements in the illusion configuration. A stereoscope is a simple instrument for presenting any two pictures separately to the two eyes. Normally, these pictures or stereo-pairs are taken by a special pair of cameras separated by a distance equal to the distance between the two eyes. Alternatively, the pictures may consist of two line drawings, each of which represents the view from one eye. When viewed in the stereoscope, the two somewhat different images are synthesized into a single percept in which objects appear to be solid and spaces appear to be three-dimensional. Instead of presenting views that mimic real-life situations, one can use the stereoscope to present the separate components of an illusion configuration to each eye. Thus in Figure 6.3A we see a stereoscopic stimulus in which the par-

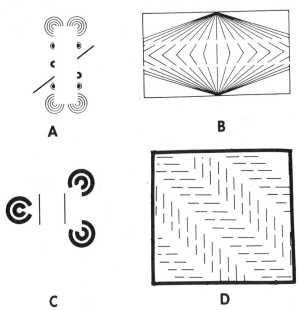

FIG. 6.2. Subjective contour variants of illusions. (A) The Poggendorff illusion; (B) the Wundt illusion; (C) the Ponzo illusion; (D) the Zoellner illusion.

allel lines of the Zoellner illusion are presented to the right eye, and the oblique inducing lines are presented to the left eye. If the observer has normal binocular vision and if there are adequate cues for binocular fusion, he melds to two monocular stimuli and reports seeing the fused array shown in the right-hand column. Notice that the final fused array contains exactly the same stimulus relationships and elements as the classical form of the illusion. Yet, since each eye contains only one of the monocular views shown, no one retina has been presented with the converging or intersecting line elements that could lead to distortions due to the operation of optical aberrations or neural interactions on the retina. Similar stereoscopic separation of test and inducing elements is possible for other patterns. Figure 6.3B shows the stereoscopic patterns that produce the Poggendorff illusion when fused, and Figure 6.3C shows a stereoscopic array that will produce the Ebbinghaus illusion (Schiller & Wiener, 1972).

Since it was first introduced by Witasek (1898), this method has been used to test a variety of illusion configurations (Day, 1961; Ohwaki, 1960; Springbett, 1961). In all cases, investigators have found a massive reduction in illusion magnitude when the stimulus was presented stereoscopically as opposed to normal viewing. It is important to note that this reduction in illusion magnitude may also reflect the distracting and disruptive effects of *binocular rivalry*, which is often reported in such arrays. Binocular rivalry is a phenomenon that occurs when the patterns presented to the two eyes are quite different and binocular fusion is difficult or impossible. Each eye in turn rejects its picture, or part of

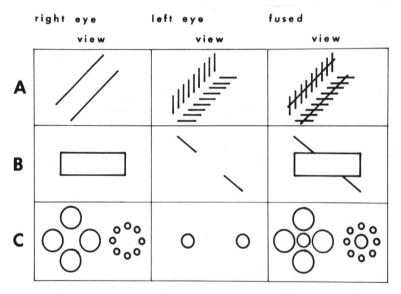

FIG. 6.3. Monocular views presented stereoscopically and their fused representations. (A) The Zoellner illusion; (B) the Poggendorff illusion; (C) the Ebbinghaus illusion.

its picture, so that continuous fluctuation of the stimulus elements seems to be taking place. In fact, if rivalry is severe enough, the test and inducing lines may seldom be seen simultaneously. Such continuous and alternating suppression is particularly likely to occur in figures containing many intersecting line elements. When complex arrays such as the Orbison or the Wundt-Hering figures are used, binocular rivalry probably makes it virtually impossible for the observer to fuse the images, implying that the stereoscopically combined array may be a very poor copy of the usual configuration. Schiller and Weiner (1962) managed to circumvent some of the problems of binocular rivalry by presenting the stereoscopic stimuli with very brief exposures. With brief tachistoscopic exposures, most observers do fuse the array. Like earlier investigators, Schiller and Wiener report that visual geometric illusions are still present when viewed in this fashion, although they are greatly reduced in strength.

The stereoscopic mode of presentation is a valid test of the contribution of optical and retinal factors *only* if the binocular rivalry problem is solved and *only* if there are no converging or intersecting lines imaged on either retina. It is, in fact, impossible to test the Brentano form of the Mueller-Lyer illusion by this method, despite earlier attempts to do so, because each retina must inevitably contain at least one pair of converging lines (cf. the figures in Fisher & Lucas, 1970).

Julesz (1971) and Papert (1961) introduced a significantly different variant of the basic stereoscopic technique that manages to avoid both peripheral interactions and instabilities in the fused representation. The stimuli for these experiments are constructed so that each monocular view presents a random texture of elements, containing no hint of the illusory configuration. Binocular disparity cues are, in fact, present in a subset of the textural units. In the resultant fused array, observers see the illusory configuration separated from the background in depth. An example of such a stimulus used by Coren and Girgus (1978) is seen in Figure 6.4B. When viewed stereoscopically, the Mueller-Lyer figure shown as Figure 6.1A is seen floating in front of the background. Since there are no monocular contours to interact and no rivaling elements to confuse normal fusion processes, this technique effectively removes many of the difficulties found in other modes of stereoscopic presentation. Using such random dot stereograms, Julesz (1971) found that observers still report many of the classical illusions. As might be expected, when Coren and Girgus (1978) measured the magnitude of the illusion obtained in configurations produced in this manner, they found that the Mueller-Lyer illusion is greatly weakened in its stereoscopic, interaction-free form as compared to the more usual form. It seems reasonable to suggest that these reductions in illusion strength represent the removal of retinal and optical interactions.

However, the existence of any illusion at all, when the configurations are presented in the form of a random dot stereogram, argues strongly for some central involvement in the formation of these distortions, since the first oppor-

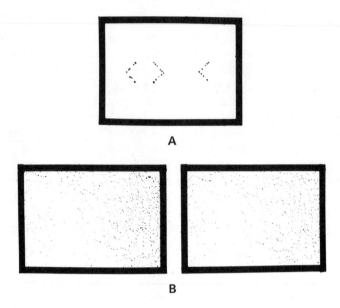

FIG. 6.4.   (A) The Mueller–Lyer configuration that is visible as a three-dimensional configuration when the two views in the random line stereogram shown in (B) are fused.

tunity for contour interactions must take place after binocular fusion has occurred and the pattern has been developed. Most evidence indicates that fusion occurs quite late, certainly beyond the lateral geniculate level and possibly even beyond area 17 of the cortex (Bishop, Burke, & Davis, 1959; De Valois, 1960; Hubel & Wiesel, 1961, 1962, 1968, 1970). Obviously, the central contributions that produce the illusion found under these viewing conditions may involve structural interactions among cortical neural units. In addition, higher level strategies based on cognitive processing may also play a part.

CORTICAL INTERACTIONS AND ILLUSION FORMATION

Koehler and Wallach's (1944) theory was probably the first to propose that visual illusions might be the direct result of cortical neural interactions. They offered a mass action theory proposing that there is an isomorphic (or relatively point-for-point) correspondence between the stimulation on the retina and the cortical response pattern. Furthermore, they assumed a similar isomorphism or direct correspondence between the cortical response pattern and the pattern represented in consciousness. According to their theory, prolonged stimulation causes the cortical neural tissue to become fatigued or satiated, with the cortical satiation then affecting the pattern of cortical excitation. Since the percept is isomorphic with the cortical response, this also should alter the conscious experience evoked by the stimulus. Koehler and Wallach used this process to predict several visual illusions.

Suppose we image a contour on a retinal region, resulting in an isomorphic ridge of cortical stimulation. Depending on the duration of the stimulus, the stimulated cortical cells would begin to be satiated, thus becoming less responsive to inputs. If we now present another contour imaged on a nearby retinal region, the distribution of response this new stimulus arouses in the cortex is affected by the reduced neural responsiveness. The manner in which this hypothesized process operates is shown in Figure 6.5. Notice that there is a region of lowered responsiveness centered around the place where a contour had been previously imaged. The distribution of neural response normally evoked in the cortex by a contour imaged at a nearby site is shown as the solid line. The region of lowered responsiveness that has resulted from prolonged viewing of the first contour, and the consequent satiation or fatigue of the stimulated cells, will create an assymetrical reduction in this second distribution of excitation simply because the fatigued units are less responsive. This causes the maximum of the second distribution to shift, which leads to an apparent shift in the location of the contour. Notice that this predicted shift in the perceived location of the contour is similar in nature to the displacement that was predicted by lateral inhibitory interactions on the retina. This means that similar distortions in angular patterns can be expected. Koehler and Wallach (1944) proposed that cortical interactions such as these could explain many visual illusions, provided that cortical regions were satiated or fatigued rapidly following the onset of a stimulus.

Koehler and Wallach (1944) originally proposed their cortical satiation theory to account for *figural aftereffects*, which are a set of perceptual effects in which the presentation of a stimulus affects the apparent locus of a subsequently pre-

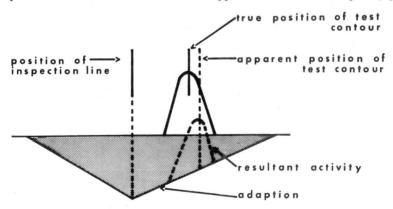

FIG. 6.5.   Contour repulsion as a function of cortical satiation, as proposed by Koehler and Wallach (1944).

sented stimulus imaged nearby even after the initial stimulus is no longer in view. Since these investigators have suggested that the processing of simultaneously and successively presented stimuli should be similar, one would expect the same illusory effect, regardless of whether the inducing and test elements in an illusion configuration are presented at the same time or in succession, since the fatigue or satiation effects would be expected to endure for some period of time after the actual activity aroused by the contour had ceased. Of course, the prediction that illusions will occur when the pattern elements are presented successively rather than simultaneously could have been derived just as easily from a theory based solely on retinal mechanisms by simply postulating that the requisite neural activity (such as lateral inhibition) persists over time. Some data indicate that these predictions are valid. Ellis (1969) tested successively presented versions of the Zoellner and Hering illusions, using intervals of up to 0.5 seconds between test and inducing elements and found the usual illusion effects. Wagner (1969) reported similar results for the Poggendorff and Ponzo illusions, and Robinson (1968) reported equivalent distortions for a number of angular distortions, regardless of whether the parts were presented sequentially or the entire pattern was simultaneously visible. Holt-Hansen (1961) reported that the illusory effect in the Hering illusion may actually be enhanced when the test and inducing elements are rapidly alternated.

However, not all the results from sequential presentations are as consistent with the expectations. There are some illusions that show effects opposite to the usual distortions when the test and inducing elements are presented successively. For instance, Ikeda and Obanai (1955) obtained the usual overestimation for the assimilation form of the Delboeuf illusion when the two circles were presented simultaneously. When the inducing circle and the test circle were successively presented, however, they always obtained the opposite effect—an underestimation of the test circle's size. This reversal is so reliable and powerful that it has often been classified as a separate illusion and is known in the literature as the *Usnadze illusion*. Figure 6.6 demonstrates the difference between simultaneous and successive presentations of the Delboeuf illusion. If you fixate the point marked "X" in Figure 6.6A, you will see that the inner circle of the right-hand configuration is apparently larger than the circle presented in isolation on the left. This is the usual assimilation version of the Delboeuf illusion. If you now fixate the "X" in Figure 6.6B for a few seconds and then quickly transfer your fixation to the point marked "X" in Figure 6.6C, the circle on the right will appear to be smaller than the circle on the left—the opposite of th classical effect. The reversal of the Delboeuf overestimation effect under successive presentation conditions has been demonstrated many times (Cooper & Weintraub, 1970; Seltzer & Sheridan, 1965; Spitz, 1967). Pollack (1964) has found a similar reversal for a sequentially presented Mueller-Lyer illusion. It seems likely that any theory using the same processes to account for both figural aftereffects and simultaneous illusions will have difficulty explaining these results.

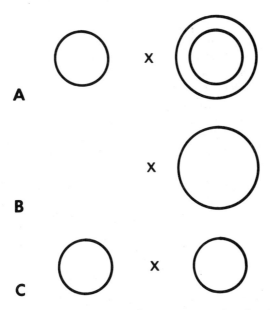

FIG. 6.6.   The Usnadze illusion. (A) The usual Delboeuf assimilation
effect in which the surrounded circle appears larger than the circle in isolation; (B) if you fixate the point marked "X" for a few moments and then
transfer your fixation to the point marked "X" in (C), the right-hand
circle appears to be smaller than the left, showing the reversed Delboeuf
illusion under sequential presentation conditions, which is called the
Usnadze illusion.

Koehler and Wallach's (1944) theory is predominantly of historical interest.
Although it does predict a number of illusion effects, it is based on a false physiological premise. Contemporary evidence seems to indicate that the cortex
does not act in a mass-action manner and does not produce patterns of stimulation isomorphic to the input array (Lashley, Chow, & Semmes, 1951; Sperry &
Milner, 1955). However, this theoretical position alerted investigators to the
possibility that structural interactions in the cortex might play a role in some
illusory distortions. In addition, it produced a body of data that indicated that
illusory effects could result from stimuli no longer present in the visual field.
Such distortions are presumably mediated by residual neural activity or are the
result of cognitive processing strategies that integrate visual information over
time.

INTERACTIONS OF CORTICAL FEATURE ANALYZERS

In an extensive program of research, Hubel and Wiesel (1959, 1962, 1968) have
demonstrated that many neural units in the visual cortex are selectively tuned to
respond to certain stimulus features, such as the orientation, length, and location

of contours in the visual field. The current belief is that each cortical neuron is tuned to a rather narrow band of stimulus values. A stimulus containing the appropriate features evokes a response from a given cortical unit, whereas a stimulus that does not contain the features does not elicit any responses from that unit and may actually inhibit ongoing activity. Some investigators have considered the possibility that such "feature analyzers" might interact with one another, thus altering the percept and causing some visual illusions (Coltheart, 1971).

Let us see how interactions among feature analyzers in the cortex can lead to visual illusions. Suppose we image a line on the retinal surface that has an orientation of $10°$ from the horizontal. For simplicity we will ignore the optical and neural interactions on the retina and consider only the effects that this stimulus elicits in the cortex. Neurophysiological evidence indicates that most neurons in the visual cortex are selectively responsive to lines within some range of orientation. Therefore, we would expect a neural response from those cells responsive to the region of the field in which the line appears, whose range of response includes orientations of $10°$. Of course, no one cell is so finely tuned that it responds to only a single line orientation. For the sake of argument we might propose that any given cortical unit will respond to lines that have an inclination within $5°$ of its preferred orientation. Thus some of the cells that will respond to this image may be preferentially tuned to $5°$, whereas others may be tuned to $15°$. We would expect, however, that the orientation signaled by the population of cortical units excited would simply be an average of the tuned orientations of the active visual units. Hence we would get a signal that the line is inclined $10°$. Suppose, however, that cortical feature analyzers interact with one another and that this interaction is inhibitory in nature. This suggested inhibition is somewhat different from the lateral spatial interactions that we talked about in the last chapter. This is orientation-specific inhibition, rather than location-specific inhibition. Each cell inhibits other neural units that respond to lines at the same retinal location but of a different orientation (within some range).

For the situation we have been considering we assumed that the line of $10°$ orientation will excite cortical neurons oriented between $5°$ and $15°$. Beyond this range, say for the next $5°$, there will be a range of inhibition. Thus cells responding to lines oriented between $0°$ and $5°$ or to lines oriented between $15°$ and $20°$ will be inhibited. This pattern of activity is diagrammed in Figure 6.7. Now let us add a second line to the retinal image. This line has an orientation of $20°$ from the horizontal. Its general pattern of excitation and inhibition will follow the same principles. Thus we might predict a composite response in which the $20°$ line excites units tuned to respond to orientations between $15°$ and $25°$, while inhibiting those cells tuned to respond to orientations between $10°$ and $15°$ or between $25°$ and $30°$. In Figure 6.7 we schematically indicate how these two distributions of cell activities will interact with each other. The $20°$ line will inhibit the cells signaling orientations between $10°$ and $15°$ that would normally

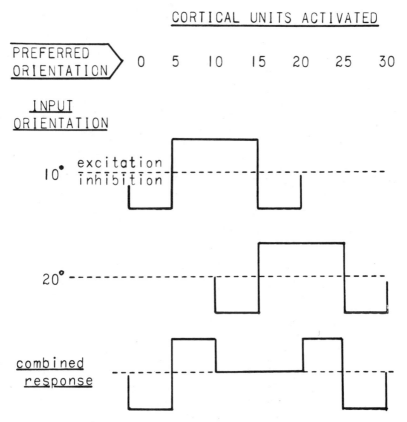

FIG. 6.7.   Interaction among orientation-specific cortical units can cause a shift in the mean signaled inclination of contours. (See text.)

fire strongly in response to the $10°$ line, and the $10°$ line will inhibit the cells signaling orientations between $15°$ and $20°$ that would normally fire strongly in response to the $20°$ line. If the inhibition is strong enough and if the resulting percept is simply the average of the response orientations of the active cells, instead of signaling two lines with orientations of $10°$ and $20°$ respectively, this pattern of activity will signal the presence of two lines, one with an inclination of $7.5°$ and the other with an inclination of $22.5°$. To the extent that the conscious percept reflects this signal, an acute angle made up of two such lines should be overestimated by several degrees. This process would be sufficient to produce the Poggendorff and Zoellner illusions. The resultant distortion is reminiscent of those we discussed in the preceding two chapters. It is important to notice, however, that this form of inhibition involves the mutual suppression of various feature analyzers, rather than point-by-point shifts in the locus of neural responses arising from lateral spatial interactions.

Burns and Pritchard (1971) directly measured cortical responses to illusion-relevant stimuli in the cat. Using an electrode inserted into the cat's brain, these investigators isolated 36 cells in the visual cortex, each of which showed a clearly definable maximum response to a specific line orientation and little or no positive response to lines that deviated by more than $15°$ from the preferred orientation. Burns and Pritchard then proceeded to measure the orientation preference of these same selectively tuned cortical cells when a second line was added to the retinal image. This added line intersected the test line at one end, forming an angle of $30°$. Their results indicated that the addition of the second line altered the orientation in the test line needed to produce a maximum response from these cortical units, as one would expect if populations of orientation-specific cortical feature analyzers interact as we have hypothesized. In Figure 6.8 the solid line represents the $30°$ angle, which served as the visual stimulus, and the dotted line represents the cortical image. Figure 6.8 is reconstructed from Burns and Pritchard's data. Notice that this composite cortical image shows a less acute angle than is actually present, with the vertex displaced into the body of the angle and the sides of the angle flared out. As we have noted several times before, such a distorted response to an angle can be used to construct a number of illusions.

Although Burns and Pritchard argued that their data indicated cortical involvement in visual illusions, it should be obvious that simply demonstrating the existence of a distorted pattern of cortical response does not necessarily indicate that the distortion actually depends on cortical interactions. The effect may have arisen much earlier. For instance, the image used to generate the cortical activity measured by Burns and Pritchard was projected on a screen in front of

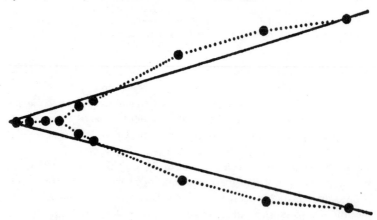

FIG. 6.8.   The solid line represents a 30° angle imaged on the retina, and the dotted line represents the cortical image of the same angle (after Burns & Pritchard, 1971).

the animal. Before reaching the cortex, it first passed through the optical system of the eye. Since the animal was maintained in a paralyzed state, it is unlikely that the crystalline lens was focused optimally for the image distance. Enough defocusing of the image may have occurred to produce a shift in the apparent locus of the vertex in the retinal image by means of the mechanisms we described in Chapter 4. In addition, there must have been ample opportunity for neural interactions to occur at the retinal level. If one considers the derived cortical pattern from Burns and Pritchard's data shown in Figure 6.8 and then flips back to Figure 5.2 and looks at the response patterns expected solely on the basis of lateral inhibition on the retina, the similarities are striking. The cortical response may thus be distorted because it accurately reproduces the image processed at lower levels, with distortion introduced at these earlier stages. Thus it should be clear that these data do not necessarily imply cortical interactions. This same possibility of the confounding of levels of processing arises in several psychophysical attempts to use cortical lateral inhibitory effects to explain visual illusions that pass the image through the normal optics of the eye and allow the usual retinal interactions to take place (Blakemore, Carpenter, and Georgeson, 1970). Much care must be taken to eliminate all earlier sources of distortion before assuming the existence of higher level interations.

HEMISPHERIC EFFECTS

Some sources of structural interactions in the formation of illusions are more global in nature. For instance, a number of investigators have recently shown that the two cerebral hemispheres are somewhat specialized in terms of their psychological functioning. Using subjects who have had the neural connective tissue that permits the exchange of information between the two cerebral lobes severed for clinical reasons, Gazzaniga, Bogan, and Sperry (1967), Levy-Agresti and Sperry (1968), and Bogen (1969) have all found that the left hemisphere seems to be more specialized for verbal and linguistic functions, whereas the right hemisphere seems to be better at analyzing geometric forms or performing tasks involving spatial relations. On the basis of data from subjects with cortical lesions, Milner (1971) indicated that the right hemisphere is superior at spatial functioning and the left at verbal functioning.

It is also possible to do purely behavioral experiments in this area, since the pathways from the right half of both retinas lead to the right cerebral hemisphere and the pathways from the left half of both retinas lead to the left cerebral hemisphere. Thus if you ask a subject to fixate a point and briefly flash a stimulus in the left half of the visual field, that stimulus will be initially processed in the right hemisphere. In a similar fashion, stimuli can be entered directly into the left hemisphere (Kimura, 1966, 1973; McKeever & Huling, 1971a, 1971b).

These investigations have shown that the perception and recognition of alphabetic material and words is better when the stimuli are projected to the left hemisphere (Kimura, 1966; 1973; McKeever & Huling, 1971a, 1971b) and that binocular depth perception and performance on spatial tasks is better when the stimuli are projected to the right hemisphere (Kimura, 1966, 1973).

Levy-Agresti and Sperry (1968), Bogen (1969), and Ornstein (1972) suggested that the right hemisphere seems to be specialized for a more global, Gestalt form of perception. On the other hand, the left hemisphere seems to be predominantly analytic, linear, and sequential in its mode of operation. If this is the case, certain patterns of visual distortions ought to be more apparent in one hemisphere than in the other. For example, a global or holistic approach to the apparently longer half of the Mueller-Lyer illusion might induce the observer to judge the length of the shaft in terms of the length of the entire figure. This approach would lead to a greater overestimation of shaft length than would a more analytic approach. A recent study by Clem and Pollack (1975) reported an increase in illusion magnitude for the standard form of the Mueller-Lyer illusion when it is projected to the right, or holistically-judging, hemisphere. On the other hand, this hemisphere shows reduced illusion magnitudes when the Mueller-Lyer is presented in sequential fashion.

Although the mechanisms underlying hemispheric differences are not yet known, this research may open up another avenue of investigation for possible structural factors in the perception of visual illusions.

GENETIC CORRELATIONS

Perhaps one of the more novel, although speculative, attempts to isolate structural components in illusion formation that are not readily accessible through more traditional techniques was attempted by Coren and Porac (1977). The rationale for their procedure stems from the fact that certain aspects of the structure of both the optical system and the retinal neural system seem to have genetic components (Francois, 1961; Waardenburg, Franceschetti, & Klein, 1961). To the extent that these systems are involved in illusion formation, one might expect to find correlations between illusion magnitudes measured in blood relatives.

Using a sample of 815 related pairs of individuals, Coren and Porac (1977) tested the standard Mueller-Lyer illusion, which contains converging line elements and for which there is fairly strong evidence for the existence of structural components, and the Ebbinghaus illusion, for which it is possible to use a structural explanation to predict the contrast portion (the underestimated central circle) but not the assimilation portion (the overestimated central circle). The results of this study must be viewed as being merely suggestive, since the sample size is relatively small for stable estimates of heritability. Nonetheless, they are quite interesting.

With the effect of age removed, Coren and Porac found a strong correlation between fathers and offspring for the apparently longer segment of the Mueller-Lyer illusion but no comparable correlation between mothers and offspring. This would seem to suggest that there is some inherited, presumably structural, component involved in the longer half of the Mueller-Lyer illusion and that this effect seems to be transmitted through the father. For the shorter segment of the Mueller-Lyer, Coren and Porac found only significant correlations between siblings. In the absence of any significant correlations between parents and offspring, a correlation in illusion magnitude among siblings would seem to imply some environmental or experiential effect on illusion magnitude, which probably stems from common strategies of viewing developed through the shared life style and common experiences of brothers and sisters in the same family.

For the Ebbinghaus illusion, Coren and Porac (1977) found strong cross-sex correlations between mother and son and between father and daughter for the underestimated portion. Such a pattern of correlations is usually interpreted as indicating the sex-linked transmission of a characteristic through the X-chromosome (See Bock & Kolakowski, 1973, who found similar patterns of correlation for human spatial ability). No significant family correlations were found for the overestimated portion of the Ebbinghaus illusion.

As we have noted earlier, it is fairly easy to predict the Mueller-Lyer illusion from structural mechanisms. However, when the horizontal shaft is present, as it was in this experiment, it tends to diminish the displacement of the vertex in the apparently shorter segment, since the added contour will somewhat offset the effect. Even when the horizontal shaft is present, this will not occur in the apparently longer segment, since the shaft is not in the path of the vertex displacement. With this in mind, the existence of genetic components in the apparr-apparently longer segment of the Mueller-Lyer illusion but not in the apparently shorter segment seems to be consistent with known processes of optical and neural interaction. The significant genetic effects found for the apparently smaller portion of the Ebbinghaus illusion are also interpretable, if the distortion arises from contour repulsion analogous to that already described for the Delboeuf illusion. The absence of family correlations for the apparently larger segment of the Ebbinghaus illusion may simply reflect the absence of structural mechanisms in this distortion.

It would be interesting to see this research extended, using much larger samples of subjects to stabilize the estimates of heritability and a much larger sample of illusion configurations, some of which can be predicted from structural components and some of which cannot. Nonetheless, the data from the present study are consistent with the hypothesis that structural components may play a part in the formation of some illusory distortions but not in others.

LIMITATIONS OF STRUCTURAL THEORIES

In this and the preceding two chapters, we have been able to specify a number of structural factors that seem to contribute to the formation of visual illusions. These have included optical factors, such as the blurring or degradation of the image as light passes through the dioptric system of the eye, facilitory and inhibitory neural interactions that may occur on the retina or at higher levels in the visual system, and some higher level processes associated with cerebral laterality and genetics.

Taken altogether, the data seem to indicate that a variety of visual distortions can arise from these sources. Unfortunately, the class of illusory effects produced by these mechanisms is somewhat limited. For the most part, all the structural mechanisms we have discussed lead to contour repulsion effects that are strongest when converging or intersecting segments are present in the visual array. Most of the perceptual errors presumably produced by these mechanisms depend on the opening up of acute angles and the relative displacement of the vertex into the body of the angle.

Although such a basic unit of distortion may be sufficient to explain some illusions of direction (such as the Zoellner and Poggendorff), some illusions of linear extent (such as the Mueller-Lyer), and some illusions of shape (such as the Wundt-Hering), it is exceedingly difficult to extend this type of analysis to a broader class of illusions. For some illusions, such as the Delboeuf, the Ebbinghaus, and the Ponzo, in which the distortion clearly depends on the relative proximity of contours, it is possible to use structural mechanisms to predict the contrast or apparently underestimated portion of the illusion by reference to inhibitory interactions that cause an apparent repulsion of the peaks of neural activity representing the contour locations. However, it is nearly impossible to find a structural mechanism that will predict the assimilation or overestimated portions of these illusions, in which contours are perceived as being too close to one another. For other illusions, such as the horizontal-vertical, the Oppel-Kundt, or subjective contours, one cannot at this point specify a predictive structural mechanism at all.

It is equally difficult to use our present knowledge of structural mechanisms to explain why many of the classical distortions still exist, although often reduced in magnitude, when all the converging and intersecting line elements necessary for optical and neural explanations have been removed (Coren, 1970a, 1970b; Goldstein & Weintraub, 1973; Julesz, 1971; Kanizsa, 1974; Papert, 1961). Such results seem to imply that either our knowledge of relevant structural interactions is incomplete or that a large percentage of most illusory effects is due to more cognitive factors involving complex information-processing mechanisms. To try to explain those illusory distortions that cannot be predicted from our present knowledge of structural mechanisms, we must turn to the consideration of these more complex cognitive mechanisms.

7

Illusions and Picture Processing Strategies

As we have seen in the preceding three chapters, there is a fair amount of evidence to suggest that structural components play a role in the formation of some visual illusions. However, it should also be clear that the mechanisms of optical and neural interaction cannot account for all the illusory phenomena described in Chapters 2 and 3. Because of this, we must now examine the second class of theories that has been proposed to account for visual illusions. We have called these *strategy* theories.

It is important to define what we mean by the perceptual strategies, as distinct from structural mechanisms, that are involved in the formation of illusions. Perhaps the easiest way to do this is to use an analogy. Suppose that the visual system is a computer. The stimulus input is equivalent to the data fed into the computer, and the percept is equivalent to the final computed result. If we have programmed the computer to add, and the inputs are a two and a three, the correct representation of the stimulus array is a five. Suppose that instead of this expected result, the computer output is six. This "error" which is equivalent to an illusion, could have arisen from two general classes of mechanisms. The first involves the actual structure of the computer and its registration equipment. If the card reader used to input our data is faulty, one would expect frequent computational errors since processing is then applied to distorted inputs. In a similar fashion, the error might arise from the miswiring of the apparatus, a nonfunctional or biased transistor, or a fault in the printing unit. All these sources of error depend on the actual construction of computing mechanisms; they are analogous to structural aspects of the visual system.

It is also possible for error to arise from sources quite independent of the mechanism itself. If an individual writes nonsense, the meaningfulness of the output is independent of whether he is using a fountain pen, pencil, typewriter, or quill. In the computer analogy, there are a number of ways in which errors may arise that are independent of structure. For instance, the computer may have been programmed to perform multiplication instead of addition. Although multiplication is a thoroughly reasonable mathematical operation, it is inappropriate for a situation in which addition is required. Multiplication and addition can be viewed as information-processing *strategies*. Illusion (here errors) may arise from the inappropriate use of a particular strategy. Another way in which strategies can produce errors involves the past history of the processor. For instance, the user may have previously input the number one and not cleared the register. Any new information would then be processed in conjunction with the stored traces previously laid down, which is analogous to the effects of past experience on the present percept. It also is a strategy mechanism, in that it is independent of the structural properties of the interpretive units. The memory traces may be stored on tape, on a disc, through the setting of relays, or even by the tripping of manual switches. The same illusion will arise regardless of the actual physical mechanism used.

Perceptual strategies are extremely important in the stabilization of our internal representation of external reality. The sensory information is processed by means of such strategies in order to ascertain the identity, size, and location of objects in the environment. A simple example of this occurs in *size constancy*. It is the case that the size of the retinal image varies as a function of the distance of the object. The farther away the object, the smaller the retinal image. Nonetheless, if we see an individual at a distance of 50 yards and he moves toward us, we perceive an approaching individual who is constant in size. If the percept directly covaried with the retinal image, we would see an individual apparently enlarging as he approached. Size constancy is thus a perceptual strategy whereby the distance of the individual is taken into account and the conscious representation is corrected so that it is in accord with objective reality. When the appropriate strategy is not applied, we are often tempted to call the resulting percept faulty or illusory. For instance, consider the situation in which a child points to a statue perched on a building high above the ground and asks, "Could I have one of those dolls?" When a 20-foot-high statue is seen as a small doll, it clearly constitutes a perceptual error. Yet this percept is consistent with an alternative interpretation of the retinal image. The final array of light could just as well have been reflected from a small figure (such as a doll) viewed at a much closer distance.

Many of the illusion effects we will be considering arise from plausible stimulus interpretations that happen to be inappropriate for the current viewing conditions but that in other contexts lead to accurate percepts. To some extent all perception involves assessing the current conditions and, on the basis of the available information, deducing what objects or conditions exist in the environment. Such deductions, or as Helmholtz (1856, 1860, 1866/1962) called them, *unconscious inferences*, account for much of the accuracy of perception but also for many visual illusions. It is these unconscious processes with which strategy theories are concerned.

PICTURE PERCEPTION AND ILLUSION PATTERNS

In a sense it is possible to interpret the process of perceiving as a search for meaning in the stimulus array. We are using the term *meaning* here to refer to the identity and location of the object or set of objects engendering the situation. Ames (1946) referred to these qualities as *thatness* and *thereness*. Helmholtz (1856, 1860, 1866/1962) described this search for meaning in two-dimensional representations in the following way: ". . .such objects are always imagined as being present in the field of vision as would have to be there in order to produce the same impression on the nervous system, the eyes being used under normal conditions."

Let us now consider a person looking at a simple illusion configuration. The source of stimulation is a pattern of lines drawn on the two-dimensional surface of a piece of paper. How does the observer go about assigning a referential meaning to this array? In part the answer to this question may lie in the area of picture perception, since we are posing a problem in which the lines drawn on a surface must be interpreted as representing more than mere lines. This tendency to view simple line configurations as if they were objects has often been documented (e.g., Gibson, 1951). The interpretation of simple line drawings as objects does not appear to be a learned skill, as was demonstrated by Hochberg and Brooks (1962) who carefully shielded a child from all pictorial representations until he was 19 months old. When the child was first exposed to two-dimensional representations, he easily recognized the objects shown as photographs or line drawings. Thus it seems that observers automatically attempt to interpret two-dimensional arrays as three-dimensional objects or, to use Ames' terminology, they attempt to ascribe a *thatness* to simple line drawings.

A larger problem arises when we consider how stimuli are localized and oriented in depth relative to the observer. Perhaps this will be clearer if we consider the most primitive of pictorial representations. This "picture" consists solely of one vertical line, as shown in Figure 7.1A. The conscious percept could, of course, simply represent the actual physical situation, which here is a thin layer of ink resting on a flat surface of paper. Yet if we occlude one eye and view this primitive pattern for a moment or two, alternative perceptual representations and meanings begin to appear. Our conscious interpretation fluctuates. The line may come to look like a used lollipop stick lying flat on a table or, alternatively, like a flagpole standing in a plane of snow. Other percepts may also

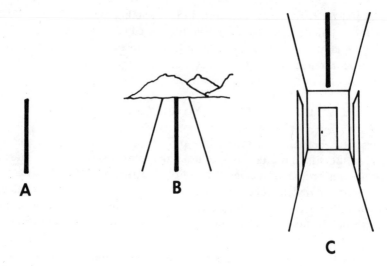

FIG. 7.1.   (A) A minimal configuration consisting of a single vertical line;
(B) an alternate configuration in which the vertical line is seen with the top
receding into the distance; (C) an alternate configuration in which the vertical line is seen with the bottom receding into the distance.

appear: Now we see it as an upright object located in the picture plane; now as a
line on a horizontal plane, receding into the distance, with either the lowest or
highest point closest to the observer. These alternative interpretations can be
more easily seen when the line is integrated into a more complex array, as we
have done in Figures 7.1B and 7.1C.

   This example makes it clear that it is possible to interpret even the simplest
two-dimensional array as a projection of a three-dimensional scene. To do this,
observers must interpret the depth cues in the pictorial array as if they were
depth cues in the real world. It has been shown that educated, adult observers
do, in fact, interpret pictorial depth cues in the same way that they interpret
real-world depth cues (Hudson, 1960, 1962, 1967). For example, Smith, Smith,
and Hubbard (1958) compared judgments of distance in a number of pictorial
representations of a corridor. As their stimuli, they used a black and white
photograph of the corridor, a line drawing of the corridor with great attention
to detail, a line drawing with less detail, and a line drawing containing no shading
or other additional cues. Regardless of the amount of detail or shading present,
all the stimuli produced equivalent distance judgments. It is clear that even
schematic pictures are treated as if they represent real world scenes or objects.
However, evidence seems to be accumulating to indicate that this ability, unlike
the identification of objects in a pictorial representation, does have learned components (Deregowski, 1973; Hudson, 1960, 1962, 1967). We will return to the
implications of this later in this chapter.

PICTORIAL DEPTH AND VISUAL ILLUSIONS

The tendency to view two-dimensional patterns of lines as representations of three-dimensional scenes can easily lead to percepts in which the apparent stimulus dimensions do not agree with the physical dimensions of the lines on the page. Figure 7.2A shows a picture representing a real-world scene of a road receding into the distance. Most observers see the two logs in the road as the same size, yet a ruler will quickly reveal that the upper log is considerably shorter than the lower log. This discrepancy between the perceived and physical sizes of the logs is apparently due to the fact that the observer has interpreted the depth cues in the picture to indicate that the upper log is farther away than

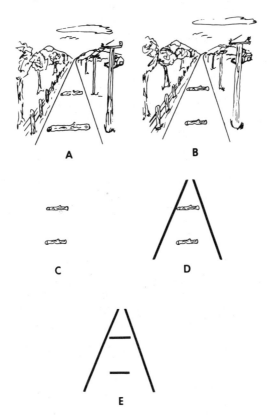

FIG. 7.2.   (A) A real-world scene in which two apparently equal size logs are seen at different distances; (B) a real-world scene in which two apparently unequal logs are seen at different distances; (C) the apparently unequal logs in (B) are physically the same size, as demonstrated when the depth cues are removed; (D) the illusory enlargement of the upper log occurs even when only the converging lines are present; (E) the Ponzo illusion.

the lower log. In the real world, the size of the retinal image (R) that is subtended by an object of a given physical size (S) varies inversely with the distance (D) of the object from the eye according to the equation $R = S/D$. Since there is little change in the phenomenal size of objects as a function of variations in distances from the observer, it must be the case that individuals take distance into account in assessing the size of targets. This is, of course, the familiar operation of *size constancy* that we discussed earlier. It seems clear that size constancy does not only depend on actual physical distance of targets but also may be triggered by *apparent* distance. Thus in Figure 7.2A the two objects are perceived as being the same size because the drawing incorporates a number of depth cues that alter the apparent distance of the logs. Size constancy is applied to this array as if it were a real-world scene. To the average observer, there is no question of an illusion being present in this configuration. This drawing is merely a "picture" of two equal size objects lying at different distances from the observer.

Now let us alter the scene slightly, so that it appears as in Figure 7.2B. Here again we have two logs lying on a road at apparently different distances. However, since the two logs are drawn so that they are physically equal on the page (thus projecting identical size retinal images), they are now represented in consciousness as being unequal in size. The apparently more distant log appears to be larger than the apparently nearer log. This percept is, again, a reasonable application of the size constancy mechanism. In the real world, the only way that two objects at different distances can subtend the same visual angle is if the farther object is actually physically larger than the nearer object.

When all the cues indicating an apparent difference in distance are removed (Figure 7.2C), the two logs from 7.2B are perceived as being equal in size. In Figure 7.2D, we have removed all the depth cues except the height in the picture plane and the perspective lines that converge along the sides. In this configuration, the upper log still looks longer. Many readers will notice that this configuration looks much like a variant of the Ponzo illusion (Figure 2.5); yet at the same time, it is a schematic representation of the real-world scene drawn as Figure 7.2B. The transition from Figure 7.2B to Figure 7.2D is slight indeed, yet we would not normally call Figure 7.2B an illusion, whereas we might very easily be tempted to call Figure 7.2D an illusion. It is certainly the case that we call the standard Ponzo configuration an illusion, and yet it is but one small step from Figure 7.2D to the illusion shown as Figure 7.2E.

What makes Figure 7.2E an illusion configuration? Perhaps it is the element of surprise, for in this primitive representation, most observers do not report that they are seeing a schematic drawing of objects at varying distances from the observer (Worrall, 1974). Thus we are surprised that two objects that are physically the same size, and hence project the same retinal image, manifest themselves in consciousness as being of different extents.

Apparently, despite the fact that the depth cues in Figure 7.2E are not sufficiently powerful to evoke an overt phenomenal impression of three-dimensionality, they are sufficiently strong to trigger the constancy scaling mechanism. A number of investigators have suggested that the inappropriate application of the size constancy mechanism to two-dimensional nonrepresentational stimuli is responsible for a large number of classical visual illusions (Coren & Girgus, 1977; Day, 1972; Girgus & Coren, 1975; Gregory, 1963, 1966, 1968a, 1968b, 1970; Kristopf, 1961; Tausch, 1954; Thiery, 1896).

In the Ponzo illusion, at least, there seems to be little doubt that size constancy plays some contributory role in the magnitude of the distortion. Leibowitz, Brislin, Perlmutter, and Hennessy (1969) supported this position with data showing that the strength of this illusion is considerably increased when it is displayed as part of a photograph rather than in its usual impoverished form. Since the photograph probably presents more convincing depth cues, the distance information should be more apparent and thus the constancy scaling mechanism should be more easily and efficiently evoked. This effect can be seen in Figures 7.2B and 7.2D, where the apparent size difference between the test elements is stronger for the version with the added pictorial depth cues. Similar results are reported by Newman and Newman (1974), who also found that increasing the depth cues increases the magnitude of the illusion in the pictorial array, although in their study, introducing conflicting depth cues did not produce a symmetrical reduction in the illusory magnitude. These studies make it clear that there is often only a fine line between an illusion and a picture.

SPECIFIC DEPTH CUES AND ILLUSION FORMATION

If the formation of certain illusions is due to the observer's implicit interpretation of the two-dimensional display as if it were a three-dimensional array, one useful strategy might be to look at the cues most frequently employed by artists attempting to represent the real world in pictorial arrays, in order to see if such cues appear in common illusion configurations.

Perspective

Lines that converge or slant tend to be seen as representing variations in distance. In general, regions in which the lines are closer together tend to be seen as farther away than regions in which the lines are farther apart. An example of this is shown in Figure 7.3A, where line A is seen as being farther away from the observer than line B. This is the distance cue that most likely causes the inappropriate triggering of the size constancy mechanism in the Ponzo illusion.

The first detailed treatment of the theory that pictorial depth cues and constancy scaling mechanisms might be responsible for some visual illusions proposed that the standard form of the Mueller-Lyer illusion (Figure 7.3B) contains perspective cues that lead to the components being interpreted as representatives of objects in depth (Thiery, 1896). For example, the apparently shorter half of

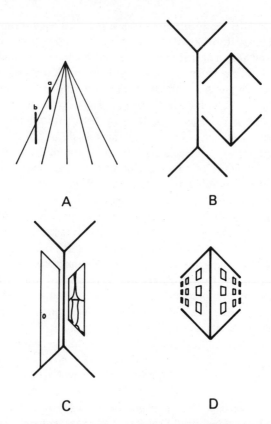

FIG. 7.3.   (A) Perspective as a depth cue, where line *a* is seen as being
more distant than line *b*; (B) the Mueller–Lyer illusion; (C) a depth interpretation of the apparently longer segment of the Mueller–Lyer illusion;
(D) a depth interpretation of the apparently shorter segment of the Mueller
–Lyer illusion.

the illusion may be seen as a sawhorse or trestle viewed from above, with the legs
(represented by the wings of the illusion) extending away from the observer. The
apparently longer half of the illusion may be seen as a similar sawhorse viewed
from below, so that the legs extend toward the observer.

A more familiar example of the perspective cues present in the Mueller-Lyer
illusion may be seen in the corners of rooms and buildings. Figure 7.3C shows
the interior corner of a room, with the lines of the ceiling and the floor describing the outward-pointing wings on the longer half of the Mueller-Lyer; Figure
7.3D shows the outer edge of a building in which the receding perspective lines
of the roof and the base make up the inward-pointing wings of the shorter half
of this illusion. If the observer assumes that the apparently closest part of the
figure is in the picture plane, the vertical line that represents the shaft of the
illusion must be farther away from the observer in Figure 7.3C than it is in

Figure 7.3D. Both lines produce equal-sized retinal images, yet they appear to be at different distances. This could occur only if they were physically different in size. Accordingly, the size constancy mechanism causes the apparently more distant line to be seen as being larger than the apparently closer line. Thus the Mueller-Lyer illusion may be interpreted as a schematic representation of the real-world scenes represented in Figures 7.3C and7.3D, in the same fashion that the Ponzo illusion can be interpreted as a schematic representation of the road-way with logs depicted in Figure 7.2B. In this example, the application of size constancy represents the use of an inappropriate strategy presumably evoked by the depth cues of simple linear perspective embodied in the converging line elements making up the wings of the figure, and this misapplication results in an illusory distortion (Thiery, 1896; Gregory, 1966).

Gregory (1966, 1970) supplied some direct evidence to support the existence of depth cues in the Mueller-Lyer illusion. He presented a luminous figure against a dark background. The figure was viewed monocularly to eliminate any depth cues from binocular disparity. In addition, it was only dimly luminous, so that textural cues for depth were eliminated as well. The observer was asked to set a binocularly viewed point of light so that it appeared to be at the same distance as various parts of the illusion configuration. The observers' settings indicated that they saw the shaft as being more distant than the wing tips for the apparently longer half of the illusion but as being closer than the wing tips for the apparently shorter half of the illusion. Given this difference in apparent depth, Gregory (1966, 1970) argued that simple evocation of size constancy is sufficient to explain the apparent difference in length between the two halves of the figure. Gregory (1966) also presented data that seem to show that the variations in apparent depth follow the same general trend as variations in the magnitude of the Mueller-Lyer illusion. Using a similar apparatus, Coren and Festinger (1967) found similar differences in apparent depth for a curved variant of the Ponzo illusion, which is consistent with a constancy explanation of this distortion.

Perspective cues that lead to differences in apparent depth have also been suggested as a possible cause for the Poggendorff illusion (Filehne, 1898; Gillam, 1971; Green & Hoyle, 1963, 1964). Figure 7.4A shows a double version of the Poggendorff illusion. In this figure, the segment of the transversal marked a is colinear with the segment of the transversal marked a', and the segment of the transversal marked b is colinear with the segment of the transversal marked b'. The fact that the transversal segment a seems to be closer to colinearity with the dotted segment shown as c indicates that the classical illusion is present in this configuration. Green and Hoyle (1963) suggested that these transversals could be seen as part of the representation of one end of a room, such as that depicted as Figure 7.4B. Line a', which represents the top of the baseboard, is colinear with line a, which represents the lower edge of the molding along the top of the wall. When seen in the context of a pictorial representation of a room, the illusion seems to be reduced.

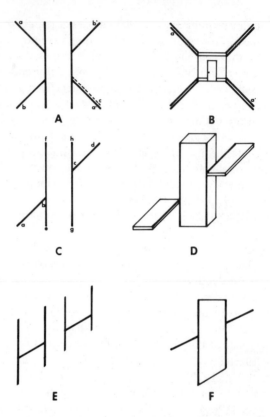

FIG. 7.4.   (A) A double version of the Poggendorff illusion; (B) a depth interpretation of the double Poggendorff; (C) the standard Poggendorff illusion; (D) Gillam's (1971) depth interpretation of the Poggendorff; (E) and (F) insertion of depth cues using relative height or linear perspective reduces the magnitude of the Poggendorff illusion.

Gillam (1971) clarified the predictions that might be made from such an interpretation and offered an alternative way of extracting perspective information from the standard Poggendorff configuration. She noted that, in accordance with classical perspective, oblique lines on the retina are normally processed as receding along the horizontal plane. Consider the Poggendorff illusion shown in Figure 7.4C. There are two oblique lines, *ab* and *cd*, which could be processed as if they were receding in space. Since the parallel lines *ef* and *gh* are equal in both length and height, they should be processed as if they were part of a plane parallel to the observer. Because of their position on the parallel lines, *b* and *c* should now be processed as equidistant points. Figure 7.4D illustrates this reasoning by deliberately introducing a strong impression of depth of the kind implied by the theory. Since points *b* and *c* are seen as being equidistant from the observer, their relative difference in height cannot be attributed to differences in depth in three-dimensional space but must be processed as a height difference along the two-dimensional plane implied by the two upright parallels. Thus the two transversals are not perceived as being colinear. Gillam showed that, if one alters the length of the parallels so that they are seen as receding in space to the same degree as the recession implied by the slant of the transversal, the illusion disappears. Figure 7.4E demonstrates how the illusion is attenuated when the parallels provide appropriate depth information. Similarly, Figure 7.4F shows how the illusion weakens when converging perspective lines are provided. Gillam argued that such demonstrations imply that the apparent distortion of direction in the classical Poggendorff configuration (Figure 7.4C) is due to the presence of the particular pattern of perspective cues for depth found in this figure.

Interposition

An object that partly blocks another object from view is seen as being closer than the partially obscured object, as shown in Figure 7.5A where the interposed square is clearly seen as being closer than the circle.

Coren and Girgus (1975) have shown that the interposition cues in minimal pictorial arrays, such as Figure 7.5B, can lead to size distortions based on depth processing. The configuration on the top in Figure 7.5B is drawn so that the line can be viewed as standing in front of the circle, and the configuration on the bottom is drawn so that the circle can be viewed as being interposed in front of the line. Thus this figure shows two circles which, through the depth cue of interposition, appear to be at different distances from the observer. Coren and

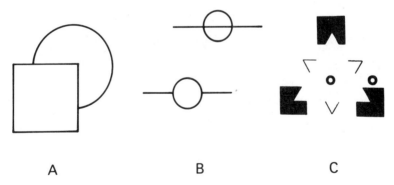

A   B   C

FIG. 7.5.   (A) Interposition as a depth cue, where the circle is seen as more distant than the square; (B) a minimal interposition illusion in which the upper circle appears to be larger than the lower circle (after Coren & Girgus, 1975); (C) the organization of subjective contours into different depth planes causes the circle on the white subjective contour to be seen as smaller than the circle on the background (after Coren, 1972).

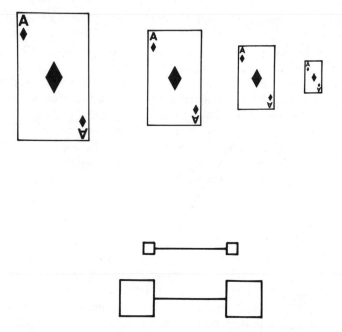

FIG. 7.6.   (A) Relative size as a depth cue, where the smaller cards are seen as being farther away than the larger; (B) a variant of the Baldwin illusion in which the upper line appears to be larger than the lower.

Girgus (1975) have shown that the apparently more distant circle (the one with the line in front of it) appears to be larger than the apparently nearer circle.

One of the most interesting forms of illusion that has been analyzed in terms of a depth-processing strategy explanation is the formation of subjective contours (Figure 3.14). Coren (1972) set out to create a series of subjective contour figures solely by the manipulation of apparent depth cues. The most powerful cue for this purpose seemed to be interposition. Figure 7.5C shows an array seen by most observers as a white triangle with its corners resting on black squares. The white triangle does not exist in the actual stimulus but is defined by subjectively created contours. According to Coren's analysis, this particular configuration is caused by interposition cues. This analysis is suppored by the fact that observers report seeing a white triangle *in front of* an outline inverted triangle, with its corners *resting on* three squares.

Coren (1972) extended this depth cue analysis to create a secondary illusory effect. He placed a small circle on the perceived white triangle and another small circle of identical size on the background. He reasoned that, if the triangle was seen as being interposed in front of the other objects on the page, it would also be seen as being closer than the background. The operation of size constancy should then cause the circle placed on the apparently more distant background to appear larger than the circle placed on the subjective contour triangle, through the operation of size constancy. This is, in fact, what occurs. The presence of this secondary distortion has been verified by Porac and Robertson-Mann (1976).

Relative Size

If two identical objects subtend different visual angles, the larger one is usually seen as being closer. This is illustrated in Figure 7.6 where one tends to see a row of playing cards receding into the distance, rather than a row of playing cards all at the same distance but varying in size.

In an impressive analysis of the possible role that pictorial depth cues might play in the formation of visual illusions, Day (1972) illustrated how many illusion effects could be interpreted in terms of the depth cue of relative size inappropriately evoking the size constancy mechanism. Figure 7.6 presents a variant of the Baldwin illusion in which the line flanked by small squares appears to be longer than the line flanked by larger squares. Day points out that, if large objects tend to be seen as being closer than small objects, the shaft between the small squares should be seen as being farther away than the shaft attached to the large squares. Since the shafts themselves subtend the same visual angle, the misapplication of size constancy in this situation could lead to the perceived overestimation of the apparently more distant target. It is interesting to note that, in both the Ebbinghaus illusion (Figure 2.7C) and the Delboeuf illusion (Figure 2.8A), the inducing stimuli surrounding the test element differ in size in such a way that Day's analysis of the possible role of relative size could be used to explain the direction of the perceived distortion for these arrays also.

Relative Height

In a configuration in which most objects are depicted as being below the horizon, objects higher on the picture plane tend to be seen as being farther away, as illustrated in Figure 7.7A where line a is seen as being closer than line b. With objects that are seen as above the horizon, targets lower on the picture plane tend to be seen as more distant. This is also illustrated in Figure 7.7A where line d appears to be closer than line c.

Girgus and Coren (1975) used this cue in an analysis of the horizontal-vertical illusion in which a vertical line is overestimated relative to a horizontal line of equal length. They pointed out that a horizontal line in a two-dimensional array offers little in the way of suggested depth cues. On the other hand, a vertical line frequently suggests a line receding into the third dimension, as we have illustrated in Figure 7.1. Suppose that the depth relationship is that depicted in Figure 7.7B. In this figure an eye is viewing a line lying on a surface perpendicular to the observer. Notice that point a along the line is farther away from the observer than is point b. Figure 7.7C shows the two-dimensional projection of this line

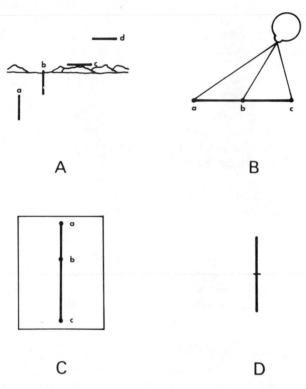

A   B

C   D

FIG. 7.7.   (A) Relative height as a depth cue, where lines *b* and *c* are seen as being most distant; (B) a schematic representation of an eye viewing a line that is lying on a surface perpendicular to the observer; (C) the two-dimensional retinal image of (B); (D) the hatch mark bisects the line although it appears to be too low.

as it would appear in the retinal image or in a photograph taken from the vantage point of the eye. Notice that point *a* is represented by a target higher on the picture plane than point *b*—another example of the depth cue of height in the picture plane. It is thus clear that this cue could serve to indicate that the top of the vertical line is more distant from the observer than is the bottom, especially if the observer treats the top edge of a piece of paper as if it were a horizon line. To the extent that observers encode vertical lines in this way, the horizontal-vertical illusion consists of a configuration in which a horizontal line and a vertical line subtend the same visual angle, but the vertical line appears to lie at a greater distance from the observer for most of its extent than does the horizontal line. Thus the vertical line is overestimated as a function of the mis-application of size constancy.

Girgus and Coren (1975) supported this notion by predicting a new illusion based on this depth analysis. They noted that the geometry of the situation indicates that a constant unit of retinal image length should represent a greater change in distance for the upper part of the vertical line than for the lower part of the line. In the scene diagrammed as Figure 7.7B, point *a*, point *b*, and point *c* are all equally spaced. It is clear, however, that in the two-dimensional projection of this configuration shown as Figure 7.7C, the images of the more distant points *a* and *b* are closer on the retina than are the images of the nearer points *b* and *c*. We might therefore expect that an observer asked to bisect a vertical line should overestimate the upper half of the line relative to the lower half. Figure 7.7D demonstrates that such an illusion does indeed exist. The hatch mark actually bisects the vertical line precisely, but it appears to be placed too low for most observers. Systematic trends in the perceived length of vertical lines, as a function of their length, can also be predicted from this analysis. Girgus and Coren demonstrated that, in general, lines differing from the horizontal tend to be overestimated as a function of the relative difference in height between the top and bottom of the line. This same mechanism may also explain the figure eight illusion in which the upper loop tends to look slightly larger than the lower, despite the fact that they are of equal size (Figure 3.15B).

Texture Gradient

Texture gradient as a cue for distance was first analyzed in detail by Gibson (1950). It combines some of the aspects of both relative size and perspective. Basically, it may be described by noting that regions in the field where objects or visual elements are more densely packed together seem to be farther away. Thus, as we look at Figures 7.8A and 7.8B, we see fields or planes receding into the distance. Clearly, if objects are depicted resting on these fields, they will appear to vary in distance from the observer, depending upon their location.

Gillam (1973) and Coren and Girgus (1977) have shown that texture gradients can be used to produce apparent size distortions, consistent with depicted depth. An example of such a distortion appears in Figure 7.8D, where the upper oval appears to be larger than the lower oval. One must ask if we are, in fact, dealing with an illusion in such an array. It is certainly the case that we are treading the thin line between a pictorial representation, where the evocation of the size constancy mechanism is an appropriate strategy, and an illusory distortion, where the evocation of such a scaling process is inappropriate. If Figure 7.8D had been designed to represent two different size objects on a textured or surrealistic plane, the resulting percept would have been labeled as "correct" rather than as "illusory."

As with several other depth cues, texture gradients may also be used to create subjective contour illusions (Coren, 1972). Figure 7.8C shows two different texture gradients composed of converging lines. Most observers report seeing two flat surfaces at different levels, with a "cliff" or "step" where the texture density shifts midway up the pattern. Virtually all observers report seeing a white line, which separates the two depth levels, at the point where the texture

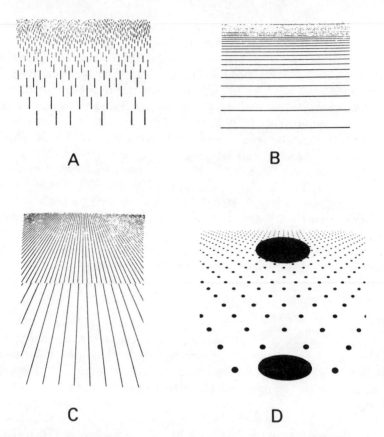

FIG. 7.8.   (A) and (B) Texture gradients as depth cues, where both arrays
appear to be plains or fields receding into the distance; (C) a subjective edge
produced by a sudden change in texture density (D) two ovals superimposed on a texture gradient, in which the upper appears to be larger than
the lower.

density shifts. Since this line is not present in the objective stimulation, it is a
subjective contour.

In this section, we have reviewed some of the major depth cues that are found
in pictorial representations. We have also shown that many of these cues can be
found to some extent in several visual illusion patterns. The distortions found in
these patterns seem to be consistent with a depth processing interpretation.
Some illusions, such as subjective contours, can apparently be generated by any
one of a number of different depth cues (Coren, 1972). Conversely, it appears
that some illusions may contain more than one kind of pictorial cue for depth
(Day, 1972). This analysis suggests that, if subjects view illusion configurations
as two-dimensional representations of three-dimensional scenes based on implicit
pictorial depth cues in the pattern, size constancy may be inappropriately
elicited, leading to a number of visual illusions.

EVALUATION OF THE CONTRIBUTION OF DEPTH CUES

If illusion magnitude is due to the triggering of constancy scaling by depth cues that are present in the illusion array, one might expect observers to report apparent depth spontaneously when viewing such arrays. Unfortunately, despite the obvious similarities between pictorial representations of depth and illusion configurations (cf. Figure 7.2), few such spontaneous reports of apparent depth are emitted by subjects either for the Ponzo configuration (Worrall, 1974; Worrall & Firth, 1971) or the standard form of the Mueller-Lyer (Hotopf, 1966; Pike & Stacey, 1968), even when a luminous figure is used to eliminate the possibility of conflicting flatness cues due to paper texture and accommodation.

Ward, Porac, Coren, and Girgus (1977) presented observers with 13 different illusion configurations and asked them to view them as if they were primitive pictures of objects or scenes. The observers were then asked to report what object or scene the configuration seemed to represent. The observer's responses were coded in terms of the presence or absence of depth and the appropriateness or inappropriateness of that depth to the illusory distortion. Overall, the data provided at best spotty support for depth processing theories of illusions. Nearly 60% of the responses indicated perception of the illusion configurations as if they depicted flat objects. There was no evocation of the expected perception of depth for the Delboeuf illusion, the Poggendorff illusion, the horizontal-vertical illusion, some variants of the Orbison illusion, the standard form of the Ponzo illusion, or the apparently shorter half of the Mueller-Lyer illusion. There was, on the other hand, some indication of appropriate phenomenal depth for the longer half of the Mueller-Lyer illusion, some Orbison variants, the Zoellner illusion, the Sander parallelogram, and the Ehrenfels version of the Ponzo illusion (which adds additional converging inducing lines to the interior of the standard inducing angle as was done in Figure 3.1D). Thus the data on phenomenal reports of depth from illusion arrays do not strongly support constancy scaling theories.

It should be noted that *registered* depth might be more important in these situations than *phenomenal* depth. There is some evidence that separate information-processing strategies are used to compute an object's phenomenal size as opposed to its phenomenal distance. For example, it is possible to insert prisms in a stereoscopic viewing apparatus that vary the degree of convergence of the eyes required to fuse the targets. Convergence is generally regarded as a cue for depth, since it covaries with the distance of targets. If we optically alter the convergence so that the eyes must rotate nasally, we would expect to find that the object appears to be closer and, to the extent that depth information is involved in constancy scaling for size, smaller. Under these circumstances, objects do in fact appear smaller but they do not appear closer (Heinemann, Tulving, & Nachmias, 1959; Rock & McDermott, 1962). Similarly, several investigators have reported that observers' estimates of the size of targets cannot be predicted from their estimates of the apparent distance of these targets (Gruber, 1954; Jenkin &

Hyman, 1959). These results seem to imply that phenomenal depth and phenomenal size are processed separately. It is possible that the depth information in two-dimensional arrays can be registered and utilized to evoke the apparent size distortions that are found in illusion configurations without ever appearing as a conscious impression of depth.

Other attempts to verify the role of depth cues in illusion formation have involved the addition of conflicting depth cues to the array to see if they will reduce or destroy the illusory effect. For example, Fisher (1968, 1970) used a configuration similar to Figure 7.9A which, because of ambiguous depth cues, tends to alternate in apparent depth. Sometimes it looks like a pyramid with its top pointed toward the observer and sometimes like a tunnel with its center pointed away from the observer. The two horizontal lines in the lower section of the figure create a form of the Ponzo illusion. The constancy scaling argument would predict that the usual illusion should be found when the figure looks like

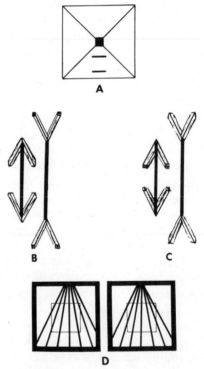

FIG. 7.9.   (A) A reversible figure in which the Ponzo distortion remains regardless of apparent depth; (B) and (C) the Mueller–Lyer illusion remains regardless of pictorial depth; (D) the Ehrenfels variant of the Ponzo illusion presented as a stereogram that removes the usual depth cues but does not destroy the illusion (after Pitblado & Kaufman, 1967).

a tunnel but a reversed illusion should be found when the figure looks like a pyramid. Unfortunately, the usual illusion always appears, regardless of the apparent depth. The line near the apex of the converging lines consistently appears longer than the lower line.

Fisher (1968, 1970) also altered the depth cues in the Mueller-Lyer illusion. Figure 7.9B shows a version of the standard form of the Mueller-Lyer that seems to be constructed of solid pieces of wood. Figure 7.9C shows this same configuration with the depth cues reversed so that the inward-pointing wings seem to point out toward the observer. If one looks at Figures 7.9B and 7.9C, it seems clear that the usual form of the illusion is present in both configurations, despite the difference in the phenomenal depth relations. Unfortunately, Fisher took no quantitative measurements to ascertain if the reversal in the depth cues led to a reduction in illusion magnitude.

Georgeson and Blakemore (1973) and Pitblado and Kaufman (1967) altered the apparent depth in the Mueller-Lyer and the Ponzo illusions by varying the binocular disparity in stereograms. As in Fisher's monocular manipulations, both illusions still persist, despite the changes in phenomenal depth. Figure 7.9D shows an Ehrenfels variant of the Ponzo illusion similar to that used by Pitblado and Kaufman (1967). When viewed stereoscopically, the fused array looks like an array of converging lines receding in depth within a vertical square, all of whose points are at a uniform distance from the observer. Despite the fact that the depth depicted in the array is no longer in accordance with that required by a constancy scaling explanation, the upper line continues to be seen as being longer than the lower line under these conditions. Unfortunately, as in Fisher's studies described above, observers were simply asked which of the two lines looked longer. If several mechanisms usually interact to produce a given distortion, a manipulation of one of the mechanisms should lead to a weakening rather than a complete disappearance of the illusion. In the absence of quantitative data, it is impossible to assess whether any reduction in illusion magnitude has occurred.

A stereoscopic depth manipulation has also been used to test the depth cue interpretation of subjective contours. Gregory and Harris (1974), Lawson, Cowan, Gibbs, and Whitmore (1974), and Whitmore, Lawson, and Kozora (1976) presented subjective contour figures such as Figure 7.5C in a stereoscope. They then varied the binocular disparity cue to depth so that the subjective figures were seen either in front of the pattern elements and thus in agreement with the interposition cues suggested by Coren (1972), or as part of the background and thus in opposition to the interposition cues. When the binocular disparity cues and interposition cues are in agreement, the subjective contour is clearly seen; however, when the disparity cues are pitted against the interposition cues, the subjective contour disappears, as might be expected from a depth interpretation.

Some investigators have varied basic illusion figures in order to look for a variety of secondary distortions that should be present if the basic effect is due to misapplied constancy scaling. Figure 7.10A shows a variant of the Ponzo illusion used by Humphrey and Morgan (1965), who argued that, if the converging lines suggest depth, figures closer to the apex of the angle ought to appear larger, regardless of shape or orientation. Most observers do not, however, report any perceived difference between the vertically oriented lines in Figure 7.10A, although all observers report the usual distortion for the horizontal lines in Figure 7.10B.

Several experiments have used the modified Mueller-Lyer figure shown as Figures 7.10C and 7.10D to test the implications of constancy scaling theory. Waite and Massaro (1970), Dengler (1972), Massaro (1973), and Griggs (1974) have all argued that, if the operation of size constancy is homogenous across the figure, the apparently longer half of the illusion shown as Figure 7.10C should also appear to have a wider central rectangle than the apparently shorter half of the illusion shown as Figure 7.10D. When subjects are tested on these figures, the usual length distortion is obtained; however, the widths are distorted in a direction opposite to that expected on the basis of constancy scaling. The reportedly more distant figure (Figure 7.10C) actually appears to be thinner than the reportedly nearer figure (Figure 7.10D). Such a result is somewhat embarrassing for picture-processing theories of illusions although, as Coren and Girgus (1977) have pointed out, similar assymetries in size constancy are often

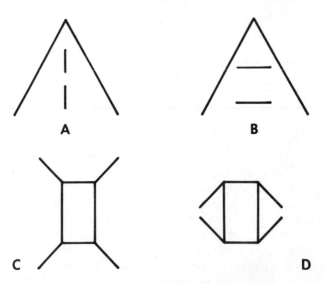

FIG. 7.10.   (A) A variant of the Ponzo illusion in which the obtained distortion is greatly reduced; (B) the normal Ponzo illusion; (C) and (D) rectangular variants of the Mueller–Lyer illusion in which the usual length distortion is obtained but a reverse width distortion appears.

found in actual pictorial arrays where the stimuli are meant to mimic the projection of a three-dimensional scene.

DIFFERENTIAL EXPERIENCE AND DEPTH CUE PROCESSING

Many investigators have examined the issue of constancy scaling in illusions by looking at individuals who have had different levels of experience with certain depth cues in the environment or with pictorial representations of depth. The data on the effect of experience on illusion magnitude are drawn primarily from developmental and cross-cultural studies. The developmental manipulation makes sense in that one would expect that older individuals will have had more experience with depth processing, constancy scaling, and pictorial representations than younger individuals will have had. The rationale behind cross-cultural studies rests on the fact that different cultures are exposed to different environments containing different patterns of depth cues. It is also the case that the use of pictures varies from one culture to another.

Let us begin by considering some of the developmental data. Leibowitz and Heisel (1958), Hanley and Zerbolio (1965), Leibowitz and Judisch (1967), and Farquar and Leibowitz (1971) have consistently shown that size constancy for distant objects increases as a function of chronological age. Given this consistent age trend, it would be reasonable to propose that illusions that seem to be based on the misapplication of size constancy would also increase in magnitude with age. The developmental trends are actually quite mixed, as we noted earlier in Table 5.1. For the Ponzo illusion, there does seem to be an increase in illusion magnitude with an increase in chronological age. One occasionally observes a decrease in the Ponzo in old age, however, although this decrease is not paralleled by a concomitant change in size constancy (Leibowitz & Judisch, 1967). For the Mueller-Lyer illusion, the vast majority of investigators report a decrease in illusion magnitude as a function of increasing age. Similar patterns of decrease are obtained for the horizontal-vertical illusion and the Poggendorff illusion. It seems somewhat difficult to reconcile a developmental increase in size constancy with a developmental decrease in illusion magnitude if one believes that misapplied constancy scaling is primarily responsible for these illusions. Of course, it is possible that these distortions are due to the operation of several mechanisms acting together. If this is the case, then there may be some process that changes with age in such a way as to offset the improvement in size constancy.

An interesting alternative way to look at the effect of experience on depth cue processing and illusions is to consider the percepts of adults who have been blind since birth (and hence deprived of the usual experience with depth cues and picture processing) and who have newly gained their vision. Gregory and Wallace (1963) tested a 52-year-old man who had been deprived of useful vision from an early age as a result of a corneal opacity. Two months after his vision was restored by a corneal transplant, Gregory and Wallace administered a number of visual tests, including the Hering, Zoellner, Poggendorff, and Mueller-Lyer figures. For this observer, who was visually naive and free from experience with visual depth cues, the usually observed distortions were either totally absent or greatly attenuated. On this basis, Gregory and Wallace concluded that experience and an ability to assess visual depth are integral parts of the perception of illusions.

Perhaps the most interesting alternative to developmental studies as a means of studying the effects of experience with depth cues on illusion formation involves the examination of the responses of various isolated cultural groups. By carefully selecting cultures, one may obtain populations in which there is little or no pictorial representation, as opposed to relatively equivalent cultures that do have pictorial arts. Alternatively, one can select cultures situated in environments where certain depth cues are more prevalent and others less available. When this is done, it is assumed that individuals should show greater illusions for patterns containing cues common in their environment and less illusion for patterns that contain less familiar, infrequently encountered cues.

The fact that pictorial depth cues do not universally elicit the perception of three-dimensionality has been systematically studied by Hudson (1960, 1962, 1967), who became aware of difficulties in spatial interpretation while testing South African Bantu workers in Johannesburg. He designed a pictorial perception test that utilized stimuli similar to Figure 7.11A. A three-dimensional interpretation of this line drawing based on utilization of the relative size and interposition cues results in the phenomenal impression that the hunter is trying to spear the antelope, which is closer to him than is the elephant. Alternatively, if the observer lacks any awareness of pictorial depth and simply responds on the basis of adjacency, the elephant will appear to be closer to the hunter and hence about to be speared. The general testing procedure employed by Hudson first assures that observers recognize all the elements before asking the critical questions: "What is closer to the man?" and "What is the man doing?" The replies to these questions serve to classify an observer as one who perceives pictorial depth or one who does not. The fact that many unsophisticated African observers have difficulty seeing pictorial depth in these pictures has been verified with subjects drawn from a variety of trival and linguistic groups (Deregowski, 1968; Deregowski, Muldrow, & Muldrow, 1973; Kilbride, Robbins, & Freeman, 1968).

Other kinds of two-dimensional pictorial displays have also been used to assess the perception of three-dimensionality. For instance, Deregowski (1968) presented line drawings such as Figure 7.11B to primary school boys and unskilled workers in Zambia, who were then asked to construct models based on the drawings. Most of the observers classified as three-dimensional perceivers on Hudson's test built three-dimensional models, whereas most of those classified as two-dimensional perceivers built flat models.

Another procedure that demonstrates cultural differences involves using an ambiguous figure shown as Figure 7.11C and often called the "two-pronged

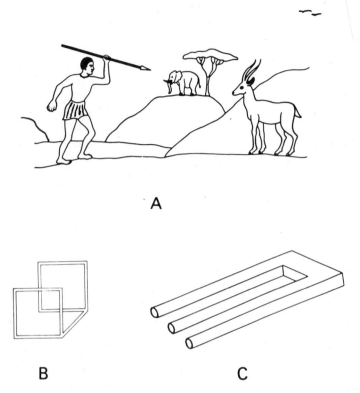

A

B   C

FIG. 7.11. (A) A line drawing, redrawn from Hudson (1960), used to test depth perception cross-culturally; (B) a drawing that served as a model for the construction of three-dimensional patterns in cross-cultural testing (after Deregowski, 1968); (C) an ambiguous figure called the "two-pronged trident."

trident." Many Western observers find this configuration difficult to view and interpret. This difficulty arises from the fact that, if the array is interpreted as representing a three-dimensional object, the local depth cues allow two conflicting percepts, which leads to instability in the phenomenal impression. If, on the other hand, the figure is seen merely as lines on paper, with no implied three-dimensionality, no such confusion should result. Using this picture and the perception tests discussed above, Deregowski (1969) classified Zambian students into three-dimensional and two-dimensional perceivers. He then asked both groups to view, memorize, and reproduce the ambiguous figure. As predicted, the individuals who ascribed three-dimensionality to pictorial representations had more difficulty reproducing the array than did the two-dimensional perceivers.

If these results indicate that there are cultural differences in the ascription of depth to two-dimensional pictorial arrays and if some visual illusions are caused by the misapplication of constancy scaling triggered by depth cues in two-dimensional illusion arrays, we ought to find cultural differences in the magnitude of some illusory distortions. With this in mind, let us review the data on illusion magnitude for various cultural groups.

Cross-cultural investigation of visual illusions began around the turn of the century with the work of Rivers (1901, 1905), who tested non-Western and Western individuals on both the Mueller-Lyer and the horizontal-vertical illusions. When compared to European samples, the non-Western groups showed considerably less susceptibility to the Mueller-Lyer illusion but greater susceptibility to the horizontal-vertical illusion. On the basis of these findings, Rivers suggested that these two illusions arise from different mechanisms. He proposed a physiological or structural basis for the horizontal-vertical illusion and a strategy explanation for the Mueller-Lyer illusion, based on differential experience with perspective cues. The general trends in Rivers' data have been replicated many times (Heuse, 1957; Jahoda, 1966a, 1966b; Morgan, 1959; Mundy-Castle & Nelson, 1962).

The most extensive cross-cultural study conducted to date is that of Segall, Campbell, and Herskovits (1963, 1966). These investigators prepared a field manual that included a set of illusion stimuli to test the magnitude of a variety of illusions, including the Mueller-Lyer, the horizontal-vertical, the Sander parallelogram, the Ponzo, and the Poggendorff illusions. A group of field-based anthropologists in Africa, the Philippines, and the United States collected data on a total of 28 sample societies. In addition, characteristics of the environment were rated to assess the presence or absence of certain kinds of depth information. Segall, Campbell, and Herskovits reported systematic differences in illusion magnitude in the various populations tested. They offered, in explanation, the *carpentered world hypothesis*, which suggests that susceptibility to illusions such as the Mueller-Lyer or the Ponzo is increased by experience in an industrialized or carpentered society in which rooms are square, buildings are rectangular, and roads are relatively straight. Subjects exposed to such environmental configurations on a daily basis should be more likely to interpret converging contours as implying depth, in the manner depicted in Figures 7.2 and 7.3. If an inappropriate application of size constancy is responsible for some illusion effects, it would be expected that subjects who live in European or urban environments would show larger Mueller-Lyer and Ponzo illusions than would subjects who live in less built-up environments. On the other hand, individuals who live in environments with long, uninterrupted expanses, where height in the plane would be a more salient depth cue, would be expected to be more susceptible to the horizontal-vertical illusion, in accord with the mechanism suggested by Girgus and Coren (1975).

Segall, Campbell, and Herskovits (1963, 1966) actually found that subjects who live in rural, more open environments tend to show larger horizontal-vertical illusions and reduced Mueller-Lyer and Ponzo illusions, as expected. In some respects, these interpretations follow the approach used by Brunswik (1956) and Tajfel (1969), who suggested that the ability of visual cues to trigger perceptual strategies is a function of their frequency and validity in the environment in which the individual lives. Overall the *carpentered world hypothesis* has received only sporadic experimental support. For instance, Leibowitz and Pick (1972) directly manipulated the number of pictorial depth cues in the Ponzo illusion by using a set of stimuli that ranged from a schematic representation of four lines to an enriched photograph of a road bed. They argued that, if constancy scaling strategies are involved in the formation of the Ponzo illusion, increasing the number of depth cues should increase the illusion magnitude. The samples tested included Ugandan villagers and college students from America, Guam, and Uganda. All the college students showed the basic Ponzo illusion and manifested larger illusions in the configurations that contained more depth cues. The Ugandan villagers, on the other hand, showed very little illusion for any of the Ponzo configurations.

Jahoda (1966a) tested two groups of Ghanaian subjects and a group of Europeans, using the stimulus set prepared by Segall, Campbell, and Herskovits. One of the Ghanaian groups was urban, and hence came from a Westernized or carpentered environment, whereas the other group was an isolated rural sample. One might expect that the Westernized Ghanaian group and the European group would respond similarly but in a different fashion from the non-Westernized Ghanain group. Unfortunately, the two Ghanaian groups responded alike, with both groups showing less susceptibility to the Mueller-Lyer illusion than the European group. These results are clearly contrary to the hypothesis. They are not, however, atypical. Similar results have been reported for studies in which carpenteredness and open vistas have been varied within other single societies (Berry, 1968; Gregor & McPherson, 1965).

Leibowitz (1971) suggested that educational factors rather than environmental factors can best account for these data. There is some evidence that the interpretation of depth in a two-dimensional array must be learned and that this ability is directly related to schooling (Dawson, 1963; Hudson, 1960, 1962, 1967; Kilbride & Robbins, 1968). Perhaps what is learned is not so much the response to three-dimensionality as the ability to ignore the conflicting depth cues that indicate the flatness of the page in a two-dimensional representation of a three-dimensional scene. After all, every picture contains not only cues that replicate projections of some three-dimensional arrays but also cues that indicate that all the pictorial elements lie on the same plane. Cues for flatness arise from information provided by binocular disparity, accommodation, convergence, and the lack of texture gradients, which serve to indicate that all the stimulus elements lie at the same distance from the observer. Learning to ignore these flatness cues probably requires the experience with pictorial stimuli that is usually provided in school, whereas learning to interpret specific depth cues may depend on the functional validity of those cues in the environment of the observer. Unfurtunately, the amount of schooling and the functional validity of various depth cues in the environment may often be confounded in many of the cross-cultural studies of illusions.

Kilbride and Leibowitz (1975) tried to avoid the problems associated with previous cross-cultural analyses. On the basis of responses to pictorial stimuli, they divided a group of Ugandan villagers into three-dimensional and two-dimensional perceivers. Culture and education were held constant, and the observers were divided solely on the basis of whether they saw depth in pictorial stimuli. The two groups were then tested on the Ponzo illusion, using configurations that varied as to the number of depth cues present. The three-dimensional perceivers showed the basic Ponzo distortion, which increased with an increasing number of depth cues. The two-dimensional perceivers showed little illusion. In addition, their responses were independent of the number of depth cues present in the configuration. These data suggest that differences in illusion magnitude are more a matter of individual predispositions toward the use of particular perceptual strategies than simply a function of schooling or environment, although these may play some role.

In addition, it is important to notice that data collected from a variety of societies may be confounded by structural factors. One such possibility arises from the fact that isolated tribal groups or relatively inaccessible rural communities may often have a relatively homogeneous genetic pool. Individuals within the same tribe or social group tend to grow up and marry within the community. As we have already noted in Chapter 6, Coren and Porac (1977) have presented data suggesting that there may be genetic components that affect the magnitude of some illusions. It is possible to imagine that in relatively inbred communities the average illusion magnitude may be artificially depressed or inflated due to the restricted range of genes present in the population.

An alternative structural explanation for some of the cross-cultural differences is based on the spurious correlation between pigmentation and degree of urbanization. As discussed in Chapter 5, Pollack (1963, 1970) and Pollack and Silvar (1967a, 1967b) have suggested that accuracy of contour detection and susceptibility to the Mueller-Lyer illusion both decrease with increasing chronological age. They contend that this reduction is due to a reduction in image contrast by virtue of the fact that the crystalline lens pigmentation grows denser as the organism ages (Coren & Girgus, 1972a). Any increase in lens density or in the density of the pigmentation overlying the marcula should serve to reduce illusion magnitude. To explain the cross-cultural differences that have been reported, one need only postulate that skin pigmentation and the density of pigmentation of lens and macula may be correlated. Berry (1971), who studied illusion susceptibility in Scottish, Eskimo, Australian aboriginal, and New Guinean samples, originally concluded that his results supported the carpentered world hypothesis. He later reanalyzed his data and found that the degree of pigmentation of the subjects was actually more highly correlated with illusion susceptibility than was an index of the carpenteredness of the environment.

Bornstein (1973) used the pigmentation hypothesis to predict how cultures tested in the Segall, Campbell, and Herskovits (1966) samples would rank on susceptibility to the Mueller-Lyer illusion. The rank ordering predicted by the pigmentation data provides a close fit to the magnitude of the illusion actually obtained for the various groups. Although the cross-cultural manipulation seems to provide an interesting technique for the assessment of environmental influences in illusion formation and, at face value, to provide some support for theories based on the evocation of perceptual strategies that inappropriately process illusion configurations as if they were projections of three-dimensional stimuli, it may be premature to conclude that environmental influences alone are responsible for the cross-cultural differences obtained.

Another set of studies that questions the underlying assumption of the cross-cultural manipulation and that also fails to support theories of illusions based on simple misapplication of size constancy scaling has emanated from the consideration of individual differences. Hamilton (1966) has demonstrated that there is no correlation between the magnitude of size constancy for real objects viewed at different distances and the magnitude of the Mueller-Lyer illusion for different observers. If the illusion were predominantly due to misapplication of constancy scaling strategies, one would expect that observers who show greater size constancy would also show greater illusion strength. Carlson (1966) has verified these results for the Mueller-Lyer illusion and extended them to the Sander parallelogram.

It may be the case that individuals who show good size constancy in three-dimensional displays are more sensitive to any available depth cues. This means that they might also be more responsive to the flatness cues in the illusion array, which would serve to attenuate the correlation between naturally occurring size constancy processes and those evoked in picture processing and possibly in illusion formation. It may also be the case that the range of size constancy abilities found in a given culture is too restricted; hence one must rely on the cross-cultural manipulation to obtain the range of variation necessary to produce significant correlations. Nonetheless, such results raise questions about theories based on a necessary relationship between size constancy strategies, pictorial perception, and illusion formation.

SUMMARY OF CONSTANCY SCALING AND ILLUSIONS

Constancy scaling theories of visual illusions have probably had more impact on the field than any other theory or set of theories. They have often provoked rather heated debates. Looking back across the data we have summarized in this chapter, it is clear that there is a large body of data that seems to be consistent with, and predicted by, such a theoriteical approach. It also is clear that there are many predictions made by such a theory that are not supported by the data. On the basis of the positive evidence, it is safe to suggest that depth processing plays a contributory role in the formation of some illusions. The existence of contradictory evidence leads us to temper this conclusion and suggests that constancy scaling processes are probably moderated by other mechanisms that may predominate in certain illusion patterns. It may well be that some investigators have asked too much of this theory. They have argued against it on the grounds that there are variants of some classical illusions that lack any apparent depth cue (Day, 1965; Hotopf, 1966; Zanforlin, 1967). Such arguments would be cogent only if one expects picture processing to provide the *sole* explanation for all varieties of visual illusions. As the preceding chapters have pointed out, however, there are many sources of visual distortion. To demonstrate that a configuration exists that cannot be explained by a particular mechanism does not invalidate the possibility that the same mechanism may contribute to illusory effects in other patterns. Such a result merely indicates that it is unlikely that any one mechanism can handle the entire universe of visual illusions. It seems somewhat unreasonable to require such scope from any one process. It is certainly the case that there are instances in which the presumption that the two-dimensional illusion configuration is treated as if it were the projection of a three-dimensional array leads to the prediction of some heretofore unsuspected illusions and often permits the explanation of some old ones. It is also the case that this mechanism does not provide the whole answer.

8

Global Impression and Averaging Strategies

One of the most important aspects of the perceptual process is its speed. The percept must be rapid and judgments made on the basis of the stimulus input must be immediate, so that the organism can adapt as rapidly as possible to a change in the environment. For instance, a driver glances through the windshield of his car and notices an individual crossing the road. On the basis of retinal image size, cues for distance, the other subsidiary cues, he must ascertain if the stimulus array emanates from an adult crossing the road at a comfortably safe distance ahead of his moving vehicle or from a small child who has wandered out a few yards away from the front of the vehicle. The driver instantly assesses the size and distance of the target and, on the basis of these judgments, reacts. Failure to judge size and/or distance correctly may be fatal for the pedestrian.

One consequence of a system designed for speed is an inevitable loss in accuracy. Overall features and general or global aspects of the stimulus may be encoded with much loss of detail. There are many instances when a global impression of a stimulus array will cause the distortion of individual elements. An interesting example of such a size distortion is found in judgments of the height of the American president, Abraham Lincoln. Most Americans would contend that he was an exceptionally tall individual, yet such was not the case. In most of the graphic depictions of Lincoln in the company of other individuals, he is seen wearing an unusually high top hat. Thus the total extent from the bottom of his feet to the top of the hat is quite large and the global impression of "tall" causes an overestimation of the man's height. It is not the case that we cannot differentiate where the man ends and the hat begins but rather that our impression of the size of the parts is affected by our impression of the size of the totality. A more contemporary example of this phenomenon may be found

145

when speaking to members of professional basketball teams. Many of these individuals have fairly commonplace heights of six feet, one or two inches. These athletes often report that people who meet them personally for the first time, after having seen them play, often express surprise at how "short" they are. It is almost as if being always viewed in a context of tall men had resulted in their height being perceptually assimilated toward the average of the group.

When we consider such instances of perceptual error based on global impressions, the analogy to visual illusions is an obvious one. Let us describe an illusion as a test element and a series of accessory lines. In general, the observer's task is to judge some aspect or property of the test element or extent. Since no illusion exists when the test element is presented alone, that is, without the inducing elements, it seems reasonable to assume that the accessory lines are responsible for the obtained distortion. A number of illusion theories have proposed that these distortions arise from the inappropriate inclusion of properties of the accessory elements into the judgment of the test elements. It is assumed either that the observer confuses the test element with the accessory lines (such as including the height of the hat in the judgment of Lincoln's height) or that he distorts his judgment in accordance with a global assessment of the properties of the accessory lines (such as averaging a particular player's height with that of the remainder of the team). Both of these positions, the confusion theory and the global impression theory, ultimately reduce to an information-processing strategy involving averaging, wherein the final percept reflects an extraction of the average size or direction of the accessory units in the array and the regression of all judgments of the properties of individual elements toward that mean value.

ASSIMILATION, CONFUSION, AND ILLUSIONS

One of the best configurations with which to demonstrate the operation of confusion and averaging theories is the Mueller-Lyer. In fact, Mueller-Lyer himself utilized a version of this theory to explain the illusion when he introduced it in 1889. The term he used, rather than *averaging,* roughly translates into *confluxtion,* meaning a "running together." Other investigators have used the term *assimilation.* Regardless of the term used, the strategy involved implies averaging. There are two general ways in which the averaging of elements may come about. The first implies an active strategy on the part of the observer, whereby he extracts the global impression of the array and biases his judgment toward this blanket assessment. This is a true averaging theory, since the observer actively seeks to extract the general features of the array, rather than segregating the individual elements. The second way in which averaging may come about involves a more passive process in which it is assumed that the observer has difficulty separating the test elements from the auxiliary lines. Perhaps, through inefficient information processing, he tends to confuse the test elements with some of the auxiliary lines. In the Mueller-Lyer configuration, for instance, the point where the shaft terminates and the wings begin is somewhat ambiguous, since all the contours run together. Theories based on this premise are usually called *confusion theories*.

Regardless of whether one adopts an active averaging theory or a more passive confusion theory, the assumption is made that, in the Mueller-Lyer configuration, the observer is attending not to the two horizontal lines alone but to the entire figure. In this context, it is important to note that physically the apparently longer segment with the turned-out wings does subtend a larger visual angle in the horizontal dimension than the apparently shorter segment with the turned-in wings. If the observer bases his judgment on the global impression of total length or if he fails to discriminate where the test shaft ends and the divergence of the wings begins, he will ascribe greater length to the portion of the configuration with the turned-out wings.

According to such a notion, the shape of the wings should not be particularly important in determining the presence or absence of the traditional Mueller-Lyer distortion. To some extent, this is in fact the case. For instance, in Figure 8.1A we see a variety of configurations, each of which contains elements that are attached to the ends of a horizontal shaft, thus increasing its global extent. Insofar as observers bias their judgment of the test element on the basis of their global estimation, all these lines should appear to be longer than the unadorned lines beside them, which are physically the same length. It is important to note that, although the shape of the wings seems to be generally unimportant for the presence of the illusory distortion in Figure 8.1A, as well as in the configurations we saw earlier in Figure 2.3, the wing shape does affect the overall magnitude of the illusion. Girgus, Coren, and Horowitz (1973) do show that, despite equal horizontal extents, converging line elements produce greater illusion magnitudes than do bowed or rounded accessory lines. In all these variants of the Mueller-Lyer illusion, however, it seems as if the surrounding elements form a context whose total extent is incorporated into the estimate of shaft length.

Pressey (1970, 1971) has made strides in quantifying the averaging notion, following a mode of analysis first advanced by Brunot (1893). To see how this more explicit formulation works, consider the Mueller-Lyer configuration shown as Figure 8.1B. The dotted horizontal lines indicate that there are a large number of lateral extents contained in this figure besides the test length itself. Notice that, with the exception of the test extent, these horizontal distances are longer for the wings-out segment than for the wings-in segment. Pressey (1967a, 1967b) suggested that our judgment of any one extent in such a figure containing many unequal horizontal distances is influenced by an average of all the lengths running parallel to the extent to be judged. He maintained that the test element is assimilated or regresses toward the average of the parallel extents in the field of view. Of course, the set of extents cannot include every possible distance in the field of view. Therefore, Pressey proposed that the averaging occurs only in a

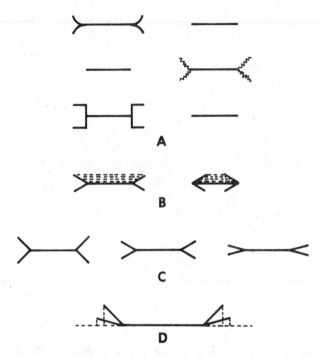

FIG. 8.1.   (A) Regardless of the wing shape, each of the apparently longer
segments of the Mueller–Lyer is overestimated relative to the lines without
wings; (B) the dotted horizontal lines represent the extents averaged together
in the Mueller–Lyer illusion; (C) the magnitude of overestimation increases
as the angle between the wings decreases; (D) this figure demonstrates how
the horizontal extent increases as the angle between the wings decreases.

limited area, defined by the boundaries of the observer's focal attention. He
called this area in which averaging takes place the *attentive field*. Despite the fact
that it has proved difficult to specify the boundaries of an attentive field precisely,
Pressey (1974) provided evidence for the occurrence of some sort of local
averaging process, showing that, by placing a comparison line above or below the
Ponzo configuration, such that the observer's attention is focused on either the
diverging or converging portion of the inducing lines, the observer can vary the
magnitude of the obtained illusory distortion. Although it may be too early to
resort to precise quantitative formulations, the idea of a general averaging mechanism in limited portions of the field seems to afford some promise.

    These global assessment, confusion, or averaging theories can handle a num-
ber of illusion phenomena more parsimoniously than some of their competitors.
Consider the well-established fact that, as one decreases the size of the angle
between the wings of the Mueller-Lyer, the magnitude of the illusion increases
(Dewar, 1967a; Heymans, 1896; Lewis, 1909). This effect is demonstrated in

Figure 8.1C with three variants of the apparently longer segment of the Mueller-Lyer illusion. A structural explanation of this effect would maintain that the critical variable in increasing the magnitude of the distortion in this situation is the relative proximity of the contours of the wings. As the angle grows smaller, theories based on optical aberrations or neural interactions predict that the locus of the vertex would move farther into the body of the angle, as discussed in Chapters 4 and 5. For an averaging theory, the critical part of the figure is its maximal and minimal extents. It is certainly the case that, as one varies the angle, one varies the total horizontal distance between the ends of the lines. This is shown in Figure 8.1D, where one can clearly see that smaller angles produce longer horizontal extents when wing length is held constant. Erlebacher and Sekuler (1969) simultaneously varied the size of the angle and the length of the oblique lines that make up the wings so that the distance between the wing tips was held constant. In other words, they clipped off portions of the wings for the smaller angle sizes so that the maximum horizontal extent remained unchhanged. They reported that, under these conditions where all horizontal extents in the field remain constant, the magnitude of the illusion remains constant, despite the variation of angle size.

Following a similar line of reasoning, an averaging theory should predict that increasing the length of the wings and holding angle size constant would increase the magnitude of the Mueller-Lyer illusion. Within limits, this result has been confirmed (Dewar, 1967a), although as the wings become inordinately long for the normally underestimated segment, they will cross, which limits the amount of stimulus variation possible for this configuration. Hence, most of this work has been done with the wings-out, normally overestimated portion of the figure. Lewis (1909) and Nakagawa (1958) both noted that, as wing length increases for the apparently longer segment, illusion magnitude increases up to a point, after which increases in wing length lead to decreases in the apparent length of the test extent. It may be argued that increasing the length of the appended wings beyond some point would not be an effective manipulation because the wings, when large enough, are no longer within the limits of the attentive field where the averaging would be expected to occur. Under such circumstances, the averaging mechanism might be abandoned or circumvented. Therefore, the proper range of values for an averaging theory would incorporate moderate wing length to shaft length ratios. In this range, the prediction seems to be verified. The apparent reversal of the illusion for extreme values will be dealt with in a later chapter.

Although the mechanisms controlling the elicitation of an averaging strategy are not clearly known, it seems likely that observers would be less apt to confuse the test elements with inducing elements or to rely on a global impression if the test extent were clearly differentiated from the inducing elements in some manner. Such differentiation would help to focus the attention of the observer and perhaps make it less likely that the properties of the accessory lines would be lumped together in the estimation of the test lines. There are a variety of ways to accomplish such differentiation. Benussi (1904) made the shaft and the wings of the Mueller-Lyer different brightnesses. Coren and Girgus (1972b) made the wings and shaft different colors while holding brightness constant and/or exploded the figures so that a small gap appeared between the vertex of the wing angle and the beginning of the shaft, thus making the point where the shaft ended and the wings began quite easily discriminable. The results of these studies indicate that the illusion is reduced when such differentiation between the shaft and the arrowheads is introduced. Coren and Girgus (1972b) further showed that the combination of two forms of differentiation, color separation and spatial separation, reduces the magnitude of the illusion even further. These data seem to imply that pointing out to the observer, through manipulation of stimulus properties, that the test extent is quite different from the extents embodied in the accessory lines leads to a less effective evocation of an averaging strategy.

PERCEPTUAL STYLE AND ILLUSIONS

There is a considerable evidence that there are systematic differences among individuals in their tendency to differentiate between the test element and context elements. In the framework of the theories we have been discussing, these individual differences may be viewed as a propensity toward or away from the use of an averaging or global impression strategy. The most systematic investigations of differences in habitual styles of viewing, encoding, and interpreting form stimuli have emanated from the laboratories of Witkin and his colleagues. Witkin (1967) has proposed that, in a variety of perceptual tasks, observers either characteristically respond in a global or *field-dependent* manner or in an articulated or *field-independent* fashion. Figure 8.2 shows an item from one of the tasks that Witkin has used to differentiate between these two types of observers. The observer is shown the hexagon on the left and asked to find it in the more complex figure depicted on the right. Whether he can ignore the complex context and find the hexagon, as well as how long it takes him to do this, is recorded. *Field-dependent* observers find this task considerably more difficult than *field-independent* observers.

According to Witkin, both socio-cultural and environmental factors may influence which perceptual style or strategy becomes dominant. Thus we might expect to find both cultural and individual differences and perhaps even developmental differences in the way in which observers respond to various stimulus configurations. In addition, if these holistic versus analytic viewing strategies reflect tendencies toward or away from the formation of global impressions, these differences in perceptual style should manifest themselves as differences in illusion magnitudes that correlate with measures of field dependence.

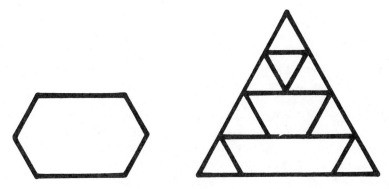

FIG. 8.2.   An example of an embedded figures test in which the simple figure on the left is embedded in the complex figure on the right.

It is interesting that Witkin, Dyk, Faterson, Goodenough, and Karp (1962) did in fact report a relationship between illusion magnitude for the Mueller-Lyer and field dependence as measured by the embedded figures test (an example of which we saw as Figure 8.2) or the Kohs Block Test (in which observers must synthesize a larger pattern through the use of small figural units painted on the sides of blocks). These results have been confirmed in part by some incidental reports from investigators conducting cross-cultural research projects in which a number of tests of cognitive skills are administered, including the embedded figures test, the Kohs Block Test, and several measures of visual illusions (Berry, 1966, 1968, 1971; Dawson, 1963, 1967, 1972; Wober, 1970). In general, these investigators report that more field-dependent (i.e., more holistic viewing) subjects tend to show larger illusion magnitudes on the Mueller-Lyer figure, the Sander parallelogram, and the Ponzo illusion. On the other hand, there appears to be no relationship between field dependence and susceptibility to the horizontal-vertical illusion, where the distortion cannot be predicted from an averaging model (Berry, 1968). Furthermore, the cross-cultural data seem to indicate that field dependence or field independence is probably characteristic of entire cultural groups. One isolated society might be highly field dependent whereas another might be highly field independent, suggesting that there is socio-environmental pressure on individuals in a given group that impresses upon them a specific perceptual style or reinforces the use of certain perceptual strategies. To the extent that these stylictic differences permeate cultural groups and further covary with illusion magnitude, one would expect cross-cultural differences in illusion strength, such as those which we discussed in the preceding chapter.

The studies described above, based on individual differences in perceptual style, have utilized observers with natural predispositions toward certain perceptual styles. Clearly, such results are difficult to interpret because other factors besides perceptual style may be covarying at the same time. Several investigators have attempted to avoid these methodological difficulties by systematically manipulating the perceptual style of observers through instructions given to the observer (Bates, 1923; Benussi, 1904; Coren & Girgus, 1972b). In general, these studies have attempted to vary viewing strategy through a voluntary restriction of attention, thus reducing the effect of the inducing elements. In Witkin's terms, this might be thought of as experimentally produced field independence, which would serve to offset an observer's natural tendency to view a figure globally or to average all the horizontal extents in the field. When observers are instructed to attend carefully to the test element in the Mueller-Lyer illusion and to ignore the wings, they show a significant reduction in illusion magnitude when compared with observers who view the illusion under the usual instructions (Coren & Girgus, 1972b).

The concept of different perceptual styles, incorporating differential tendencies to use averaging strategies, may also prove useful in understanding some of the observed changes in illusion magnitude that occur with age. To begin with a clinical line of research, there is some evidence from free responses to Rorschach ink blots that indicates that there is a shift from a global to a more analytic perceptual strategy with increasing age (Ames, Learned, Metraux, & Walker, 1953; Hemmendinger, 1953). In addition, one finds age-related improvement on embedded figure tests (Gollin, 1956; Heiss, 1930; Witkin, Goodenough, & Karp, 1962; Witkin, Lewis, Hertzman, Machover, Meissner, & Wapner, 1954) and the Kohs Block design test (Selinka, 1939), which suggests a similar developmental trend. Wapner and Werner (1957) suggested that these changes in perceptual strategies might explain the developmental decrease normally observed in the Mueller-Lyer illusion. In support of this point of view, Berry (1968) showed a correlation between field-dependence measures, illusion magnitude, and age in two different cultures. It may well be the case that the observed age trends in the Mueller-Lyer simply reflect the tendency in older individuals to restrict their attention to the test element, ignoring the inducing lines. It is interesting in this context that the horizontal-vertical illusion, which does not correlate with field dependence, also does not show any pronounced age trends.

Girgus, Coren, and Fraenkel (1975) have provided further evidence that indicates that the observed developmental trends in visual illusions may be due to an age-related decrease in holistic viewing and hence, perhaps, in the use of an averaging strategy. For the Brentano form of the Mueller-Lyer illusion (Figure 2.3B), these investigators found the usual decrease in illusion magnitude with age; however, for a disarticulated dot version of the illusion (Figure 6.1B), no sugh age trend was observed. They argued that, when the test element is clearly differentiable from the inducing elements, the child is less tempted to adopt a global strategy and more apt to utilize a judgmental procedure analogous to that habitually employed by the adult. This interpretation is further supported by the fact that, when children are instructed to scan the figure systematically, a procedure that might reinforce an analytic rather than an averaging strategy, the usually obtained age differences in the normal form of the illusion disappear after only 2.5 minutes of inspection.

Perhaps the most interesting study linking age trends and illusions with age trends in perceptual strategy was made by Parrish, Lundy, and Leibowitz (1968), who utilized a hypnotic age regression technique to try to get adults to adopt the perceptual strategy generally characteristic of children. Their subjects were regressed to an early age and then tested on the Poggendorff and Ponzo illusions. Under these conditions, subjects showed an increase in the Poggendorff illusion and a decrease in the Ponzo illusion, which is in accord with the normally obtained age trends. Certainly a shift from analytic to holistic viewing could explain this result. Although these findings have been difficult to replicate, they are extremely suggestive.

It is clear from the data presented above that a number of illusory effects, age trends, and cross-cultural results can be explained by a global impression or averaging mechanism. Unfortunately, there are a number of limitations to this approach. To begin with, a number of illusions do not appear to be susceptible to this kind of explanation. The Ebbinghaus illusion (Figure 2.7C), in which a test circle is surrounded by smaller circles, provides an example of a distortion that is not explicable in this fashion. An averaging or global impression theory would predict exactly the opposite distortion if the apparent size of the test element regresses toward the mean size of the configuration. It is, of course, unfair to require that a particular illusion theory be capable of explaining all possible illusory distortions. Rather, we should be content with the fact that some form of averaging principle may explain some of the classically observed illusory effects and may also serve as a secondary contributor in a number of others.

9 Contrast and Difference Extraction Strategies

In the preceding chapter we discussed a number of distortions that arise because of the use of an averaging strategy whereby the test element comes to appear to be more similar to other elements in the field. Thus in the context of large items, a given target may be overestimated. There is an equally common perceptual strategy that operates in exactly the opposite direction. This strategy emphasizes differences rather than similarities between judged and context items. For instance, if we observe a five-foot ten-inch sports announcer who is interviewing a team of basketball players, he may appear to be very short. If the same announcer is interviewing a group of jockeys, he may appear to be very tall. Notice that in this situation our estimation of the announcer's height does not regress toward the average of the group, but rather his relatively larger or smaller height is emphasized so that he looks very small in the context of large men and very large in the context of small men.

Such contrast effects are quite common. For instance, Helmholtz (1866/1962) described many instances of a general contrast strategy in which clearly perceived sensory differences tend to be exaggerated. He proposed that a variety of different types of cognitive contrast might exist including size contrast, directional contrast, and even shape contrast. This concept was elaborated by Wundt (1894), who called it the *law of perceptual relativity*. The generality of this process should not be underestimated. Consider the difference between your perception of a $20 a week raise when colleagues receive a $5 a week raise versus when colleagues receive a $50 a week raise. The feeling about the size of a pay increment varies as a function of the other pay increments against which it is contrasted, in the same way that the size of the central test circle in the Ebbinghaus illusion (Figure 2.7C) varies as a function of the size of the surrounding context circles.

Although contrast has been discussed for over a hundred years in the psychological literature, it has been referred to more as a description of a particular pattern of perceptual judgment than as a mechanism in its own right. It is certainly the case that contrast could be viewed as a perceptual strategy or style in much the same way that we viewed assimilation or averaging as a perceptual style. In this light, it involves feature extraction, where the features extracted reflect the relative differences between test and context elements. For example, in the Ebbinghaus illusion the observer notes that the test element is *smaller than* or *larger than* the surrounding elements. This notion of *smaller than* or *larger than* is then melded to the impression of the absolute size of the test element, in much the same way that the global impression of size in the averaging theories of the past chapter fuse with the judgments of the test item.

Numerous illusions have been dealt with in terms of contrast mechanisms. For instance, size contrast is usually invoked to explain the Ebbinghaus (Figure 2.7C) and Baldwin (Figure 2.4) illusions. To explain such figural distortions, Obanai (1954) has formulated a general judgmental principle that states that figures are seen as larger when adjacent to medium or small extents and smaller when adjacent to large extents. It is important to note that this statement is simply a description of the size contrast phenomenon and does not imply any particular information-processing mechanism.

Directional contrast has been used to explain the Zoellner illusion, in which it can be reasoned that the direction of the test elements is contrasted with the direction of the other lines in the field. Figure 9.1A shows a square filled with slanted lines. Although the short line in the center of the square is vertical, it appears to be twisted counter-clockwise in contrast with the inclination of the context elements. Exaggeration of the difference in inclination between the test line and the context lines, in the same way that one exaggerates the difference in size between test and context elements in the Ebbinghaus and Baldwin illusions, apparently produces the observed distortion.

Figure 9.1B shows a shape contrast effect that has been explored by Imai (1956a, 1956b). For the two arrays, the central curve is identical. However, the curve flanked by flatter curves appears to be more bent than the curve flanked by the more strongly curved lines. This is a contrast illusion of the same sort we have been discussing, since it may be interpreted as the exaggeration of a clearly perceived difference between test elements and context elements. Here the difference is one of shape rather than of orientation or size.

Let us now assess some of the predictions that might be made if we assume that contrast is a strategy of difference extraction that results in the formation of some illusions. For convenience, we will confine our discussion to illusions of size, because more data exist in this realm and parametric manipulations are more easily made. To begin with, if contrast simply involves accentuation of clearly perceived differences, then as the difference in size between test and inducing elements is increased, the magnitude of the illusion should increase. One

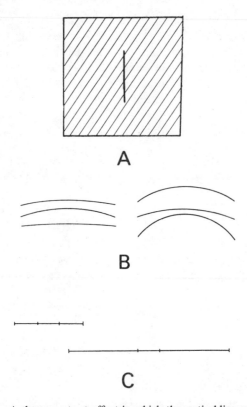

FIG. 9.1. A shape contrast effect in which the vertical line appears to be inclined in the direction opposite to the slanted lines of the field; (B) a shape contrast illusion in which a curve bounded by flat curves appears to be more bent than a curve bounded by sharp curves; (C) a linear size contrast illusion in which the central portion in the upper line appears to be larger than the central portion in the lower line.

would expect that the larger the difference between test and distorting elements, the larger the illusion. Massaro and Anderson (1971) and Girgus, Goren, and Agdern (1972) have shown that the apparent size of the central test elements in the Ebbinghaus illusion varies systematically with the size of the context elements. The larger the surrounding circles, the smaller the size of the central unit appears, with the reverse phenomenon occurring for smaller surrounding units. In the Baldwin illusion, Restle and Merryman (1968a) show similar variations in apparent line length as a function of the size of the squares placed at their ends. Unfortunately, neither the Ebbinghaus illusion nor the Baldwin illusion permits a very large range of variation before other extraneous effects begin to intrude.

A much more useful array for studying the effects of contrast is that shown in Figure 9.1C, in which a central segment of a line is judged in the presence of framing lines continuous with the judged segment. Notice that Figure 9.1C shows the expected size contrast effect, with the central segment appearing smaller when surrounded by large segments as opposed to when surrounded by small segments. The most systematic quantitative work on size contrast has been done by Obanai (1954) using this configuration. He reported that the central line is maximally overestimated when the size of the flanking lines are each half the size of the judged line. In other words, we find a nonmonotonic function as the lines get very small. Very small flanking units actually produce less effect than do intermediately small flanking elements. If we now increase the size of the flanking lines, one might expect that the judged length of the central segment would decrease, becoming veridical when the flanking segments are equal to the central segment. Strangely, veridical perception is not obtained until the flanking lines are made one and one-half times as long as the central segment. Maximal underestimation of the central segment is obtained when each of the flanking lines is twice the length of the central segment. Further increases in the size of the flanking lines do not lead to any change in the judged length of the central line until they become approximately four times the length of the central segment, at which time the effect begins to dissipate (Oyama, 1960). In other words, if the flanking elements are too large or too small, the illusory effect is actually diminished. In addition, there appears to be some difficulty in predicting the zero point, where the judgments change from overestimation to underestimation. In line with Obanai's (1954) data, Zigler (1960) found that the change from overestimation to underestimation in the central test circle of the Ebbinghaus illusion does not occur until the surrounding circles are larger than the central element, suggesting that size contrast might not be the only mechanism operating to distort the size of the test elements in these configurations. Of course, it should be clear that the line of argument we are considering here implies some quantification since we are attempting to predict a point of transition in size estimation. Perhaps this is an unfair demand to make of a contrast theory since in general we have not required such quantitative exactitude of any other position. Therefore, we will let the requirements for numerical exactitude pass by noting that even in the absence of a specifically supplied context, a "control" element is actually placed in a large but relatively ill-defined expanse. Thus the judgments of a test element in isolation may actually represent contrast against the larger overall expanse in the field and hence not be veridical in any absolute sense. If such were the case, it might considerably complicate the problem of the point of transition from overestimation to underestimation in contrast illusions. In addition, it would provide an incredible problem for any psychologist who wanted to establish a "true" baseline before making any parametric predictions.

It seems reasonable to assume that by emphasizing the context elements one might make them more salient and hence increase the magnitude of distortion. The simplest way of increasing the saliency of the context elements is to increase the number. Morinaga (1956) and Massaro and Anderson (1971) showed that increasing the number of context circles in the Ebbinghaus illusion increases the size of the illusion.

Another technique that seems to promise a manipulation of the salience of the context elements involves their proximity to the test component. One would expect that the closer the units that make up the context, the more easily the comparisons would be made and contrast would occur. Here the results are not quite so clear, thus providing a demonstration of the dangers inherent in testing theories of illusions by modification of figural components. For instance in Ebbinghaus illusion, one might expect that as one moves the larger circles away from the central test circle, one should see a gradual increase in circle size (diminution of the illusory effect). The opposite effect should occur for moving the smaller circles away, since the illusory effect in this half of the illusion is an overestimation of the central unit. When Girgus, Coren, and Agdern (1972) actually did this, they showed that for both halves of the illusion the apparent size of the central circle diminishes as the surrounding circles are moved farther away from the test component. This effect seems to be analogous to that observed in the Delboeuf illusion (Figure 2.8), in which the size of the central test unit apparently diminishes as the diameter of the concentric circle is increased.

Similar findings have been reported for the Baldwin illusion. When the flanking squares are moved outward from the test line, a gap is left between the test and the context elements (Restle and Merryman, 1968b). These investigators suggested that under these circumstances the extent of the gap between the test and the inducing elements may enter into the judgment of the test extent. If this occurs, large gaps, or inter-item distances, ought to produce underestimation of the test item. This idea is interesting since it predicts reversal in the contrast effect when the test items are extremely close, regardless of their size. Although such a reversal is not generally reported, there is some suggestion of it in the Girgus, Coren, and Agdern (1972) data. Hence it may well be the case that the spaces as well as the figures serve as components in size judgments. In addition, one should take the complexity of these results as an indication of the dangers inherent in assuming that simple changes in figural structure (such as the proximity of elements) create only the intended variations. Other factors may be varied as well.

An interesting use of perceptual contrast as an explanatory device was offered by Kuennapas (1955, 1957, 1959) in an attempt to explain the horizontal-vertical illusion. His argument was based on a principle similar to that offered by Restle and Merryman (1968b) that figures and spaces may contrast against each other. Kuennapas began with the simple observation that the shape of the visual fields is asymmetrical, with a much broader view in the horizontal extent than in the vertical extent. Thus a given length of contour covers a greater portion of the visual field in the vertical orientation than it does in the horizontal. To the extent that the perception of the contour is affected by contrasting the extent with the size of the space around it, one would expect systematic underestimation of the horizontal extent as compared to the vertical, simply because there is more space in the horizontal dimension between the ends of the line and the boundaries of the visual field. Kuennapas attempted to verify his hypothesis by placing artificial frames around figures. He found that surrounding an L-shaped variant of the horizontal-vertical figure (Figure 2.2A) with a rectangular frame in different orientations affects the magnitude of the distortion. The relative overestimation of the vertical line was considerably less when the long axis of the frame was vertical than when it was horizontal (Kuennapas, 1957). Kuennapas argued that this imposed frame mimics the framing effect of the visual field. In an attempt to make the artificial framing of contours more analogous to that obtained in natural viewing by the boundaries of the visual field, Kuennapas (1959) had observers wear goggles that varied the shape of their visual fields. This was accomplished by having the observers look through elliptical holes with various ratios of major to minor axes. As the long horizontal axis of the elliptical aperture was shortened, the overestimation of the vertical in an L-shaped version of the horizontal-vertical illusion was reduced. It is interesting, however, that even when the viewing field is circular, the illusion, although reduced, still does not disappear, which implies that, although the spaces surrounding the configuration in the visual field may contribute to the illusory effect, other processes are probably present as well.

An indirect line of evidence that also seems to support Kuennapas' hypothesis comes from a series of experiments that rotated the observer 90° so that the formerly vertical extent in the horizontal-vertical illusion becomes a horizontal extent in the observer's rotated visual field (Avery & Day, 1969; Kuennapas, 1958; Morinaga, Noguchi, & Ohishi, 1962; Rock, 1973). Under these circumstances, the environmentally horizontal line in an L-shaped Figure, which is now oriented vertically on the observer's retina, should appear to be longer than the environmentally vertical line, which is now oriented horizontally on the observer's retina. The results of these experiments supported this prediction; the illusion occurs as a function of retinal rather than environmental orientation. This seems to provide some support for Kuennapas' notion that the horizontal-vertical illusion arises as a function of the contrast between the target and the area around it in the visual field.

It is important to note that these observed contrast effects are not easily explicable in terms of structural interactions. It seems likely that they involve perceptual strategies utilized quite late in the sequence of information processing which eventually leads to the conscious percept. For instance, manipulations of attention seem to alter the magnitude of the illusion. For example, Restle (1971a, 1971b) reported that the magnitude of a size contrast illusion is reduced if the observer is instructed to ignore the surrounding context.

Further evidence indicating rather late application of contrast strategy in terms of levels of processing can be found in an experiment by Coren (1971), which used a stereogram of the Ebbinghaus illusion in which all the circles were physically the same size but appeared to be unequal (Figure 9.2E). When stereo-

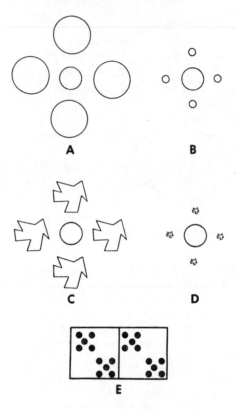

FIG. 9.2.   (A) and (B) The standard Ebbinghaus illusion; (C) and (D) the illusion is attenuated when the surrounding figures are dissimilar to the test figures; (E) a stereogram in which the Ebbinghaus illusion appears despite the physical equality of all the elements.

scopically fused, the top configuration appears as a central disc with four surrounding circles imaged some distance behind the plane of the test circle. The lower configuration has a central circle at the same stereoscopic distance as the test circle in the upper configuration, but the surrounding circles are seen as being relatively closer. As we pointed out in Chapter 7, where we discussed constancy scaling mechanism, when elements subtend the same visual angle but appear to be at different distances, the operation of size constancy causes the apparently more distant elements to be represented as being larger in consciousness. Thus we have created a situation in which, although all the figures in the array are physically the same size, the apparent size of the context circles in the upper array is larger than the test element, whereas the apparent size of the surrounding circles in the lower configuration is smaller than the central element. Coren (1971) reported that in this array the expected size contrast effect still occurs just as if the context circles had been physically varied in size. These data indicate that the contrast strategy is not imposed until after constancy sealing has occurred. This seems to imply that the information has passed through several levels of information processing before the contrast mechanism has the opportunity to operate.

Coren and Miller (1974) provided additional evidence that indicates that the size contrast strategy is not employed until a rather late stage in perceptual processing. They had observers scale a number of figures in terms of their apparent similarity to an outline circle. Using these scaled values, they then created a series of Ebbinghaus variants in which the central circles were flanked by inducing elements that differed along the dimension of perceived similarity. Their results indicated that the magnitude of the contrast illusion was reduced as the similarity between the test and inducing elements diminished. Figures 9.2A and 9.2B show typical Ebbinghaus configurations in which test and inducing figures are identical in form and hence are rated as maximally similar. Figures 8.2C and 9.2D show Ebbinghaus configurations in which the surrounding units are figures usually rated as highly dissimilar to the circle. Notice that the magnitude of the difference in apparent size of the two central circles is considerably less in Figures 9.2C and 9.2D. Coren and Miller pointed out that this seems to imply that the size contrast strategy is not applied until judgments of similarity have first been made.

In some respects, the data from this study simplify our task because they imply that the contrast strategy is selectively applied. This means that a researcher working on the Ebbinghaus illusion does not need to take into account the size of the walls of the room in which the experiment is conducted, which might otherwise provide a surrounding visual context of large elements, or the texture of the paper on which the illusion is printed, which might otherwise provide a surrounding visual context of small elements. Any stimulus in the visual field that is judged as being dissimilar to the test element will presumably be relatively discounted by the observer when making his judgments.

One of the major problems of contrast theories of illusions is the fact that they imply a mechanism without specifying when that mechanism applies or how it works. Because we have no way of discriminating on the basis of the stimulus array when we might expect a contrast effect as opposed to an assimilation or averaging effect, we tread dangerously close to restating the direction of our data without offering any theory at all. As yet, no one has adequately specified the antecedent conditions for obtaining contrast, as opposed to averaging effects. The best attempt to date is a suggestion by Wapner and Werner (1957) that contrast effects result: from an analytic or field-independent style as opposed to a global or field-dependent style. In support of this suggestion, they noted that the Ebbinghaus illusion, which shows a strong contrast effect, increases with increasing chronological age, thus covarying with the age-related increase in analytic perception, whereas the Mueller—Lyer illusion, which presumably is explicable in terms of an averaging or global impression effect, decreases with increasing chronological age. However, if this formulation were correct, one might expect that young children would manifest the reverse or averaging effect in the Ebbinghaus illusion since they are presumably utilizing a global perceptual style. This clearly does not occur; even very young children show contrast effects.

In many respects both averaging and contrast theories of illusion formation are predominantly descriptive. For limited sets of stimulus configurations, each seems to have some usefulness; yet, on the basis of the simple formulation of the theories themselves, one cannot predict the set of stimulus configurations to which they can be applied. Investigators describe elements as being averaged or contrasted only after a perceptual distortion has been reported for a given array. Thus it seems that until the mechanisms can be more clearly worked out, both these theoretical positions remain primarily descriptive in nature rather than explanatory.

10 Composite Strategies, Perceptual Fields, and Quantitative Theories

In the preceding two chapters we dealt with a set of complementary perceptual strategies. The first involves an averaging, or assimilative, process by which differences between a test element and its context are reduced. The second strategy is one of contrast, which augments the difference between the test element and the items that form its context. A number of theoretical systems have been offered that reportedly combine both processes under one theoretical rubric. For the most part, such models have tended to be quantitative in nature, attempting to describe systematic psychophysical relationships as various components in the array are altered. As the reader has probably noted, we have not presented much in the way of precise quantification in this volume, which reflects our judgment that neither the research nor the theoretical speculation about visual illusions has proceeded far enough to permit quantiification on anything but a descriptive level. In this chapter we will describe some of the quantitative formulations that have been proposed to account for assimilation and contrast phenomena, without discussing the mathematical structures that underlie these formulations. This is sufficient to allow us to assess the cogency of the theoretical argument, as well as the general trends predicted by the various models.

ADAPTATION LEVEL THEORIES

One of the most elaborate and general theories in the area of perception was offered by Helson (1964a, 1964b), whose model is one of the few basically quantitative models in perception. The major tenet of Helson's adaptation level theory is that an individual computes a weighted mean of three classes of stimuli to produce an adaptation level that serves as a reference, or base line, against which all new stimuli are compared.

The three classes of stimuli used in the computation of the adaptation level or reference level include both components of the array that are physically present and coded traces of past stimuli within the observer. The first set of stimuli, and probably the most important, are designated as *focal* stimuli. These are the stimuli presently in the focus of attention, or more simply, the stimuli actually being judged or estimated by the observer. The second class is designated as the *background* stimuli and includes all those stimuli that form the context against which the focal stimuli are observed or judged. In addition, there is a class of *residual* stimuli, which reflect stimuli previously observed. Residual stimuli include the observer's past experiences with similar perceptual situations and his physiological state, constitutional factors, and learned perceptual strategies or styles. It is significant that, although the focal and background stimuli are present in the array, the residual stimuli are present within the observer. All the stimulus values are weighted and then pooled together to form a weighted mean against which each new input is judged. The specific weightings for each stimulus class depend on situational factors, although generally the highest weight is given to focal stimuli and the lowest to residual stimuli.

Stimuli close to the adaptation level quantitatively tend to be seen as if they were at the adaptation level. Notice that this is an assimilation or averaging tendency, which minimizes the difference between a stimulus being judged and the mean of all the stimuli in the array. Stimuli far from the adaptation level tend to have this difference emphasized, thus causing a contrast-like effect. Notice then that both contrast and assimilation appear in this theoretical structure.

When actually applied to illusion configurations in a qualitative manner, this theoretical position seems to have some explanatory value. One of the illusions best handled by the set of strategies embodied in adaptation level theory is the Delboeuf illusion (Figure 2.8), in which the adaptation level may be seen as being the mean of the focal and background stimuli in the array. The focal stimulus here is the central test circle to be judged. The context stimulus is the outer concentric circle that is not directly judged but to which the focal stimulus is compared. It is quite clear that, when the two circles are similar in size, both will be near the adaptation level. Thus we might expect an averaging or assimilation effect, which should be manifested as an apparent increase in the size of the central circle. It should also manifest itself as an apparent decrease in the size of the context circle when its diameter is similar to that of the test circle. The first effect is simply the usual Delboeuf distortion; the altered perception in the size of the surrounding circle, although not usually measured, is also found with a high degree of regularity (Oyama, 1960). When the concentric circle is much larger than the central circle, a different situation holds. Now the focal stimulus is much more distant from the adaptation level, which is the pooled value of the test and surrounding circle. Under these circumstances, contrast, which would manifest itself as an underestimation of the central circle; may be expected.

There are several interesting aspects of Helson's theory. The first is that the theory is quantitatively stated and hence is susceptible to precise testing. The second is that the introduction of residual stimuli permits comparisons to take place over time and to change with experience. The existence of residual stimulus effects may be used to explain a large number of illusory distortions that occur when the test and the inducing elements are not shown to the observer at the same time. Cooper and Weintraub (1970) presented the context circles of the Ebbinghaus illusion (Figure 2.7C) followed (after an interval that ranged from zero to 7.5 seconds) by the center circle presented alone. As we have noted above, physically present stimuli, even when in the background, generally have a greater weight or effect than a remembered or residual stimulus. However, the existence of traces of the residual stimuli should still affect the perceived size of the test stimulus. Cooper and Weintraub reported that the illusion does exist under all the time intervals used and that, as the time interval between the context and the test element increases, the magnitude of the distortion decreases. Such a decrease can be interpreted as a decrease in the salience of the residual stimuli as they recede further into the past, thus becoming less effective. In the adaptation level model, this decrease would be quantitatively represented as a decrease in the weighting parameter for the context stimuli.

Helson (1964a) mentioned the fact that "spatial pooling," which is defined as the averaging across the field to form the adaptation level, could be used to explain some of the classically observed visual illusions. Unfortunately, he did not explicitly develop this application any further. The first direct application of the theory to illusory phenomena came from Green and Hoyle (1964), who attempted to explain the Zoellner illusion (Figure 3.2) by use of the adaptation level formulation. Since the Zoellner illusion is a directional effect, we are talking about the pooling or averaging of orientations rather than of sizes, as was the case with the Delboeuf illusion. Green and Hoyle argued that the many oblique lines in the Zoellner illusion serve as a context, which shifts the adaptation level in the direction of their mean value of inclination. If we now superimpose a vertical line over these oblique transversals, it would be seen as being some distance away from the adaptation level of inclination. This should result in an orientation contrast effect, which is consciously encoded as an inclination of the vertical line in the opposite direction. Because the usual Zoellner configurations involve several verticals with several sets of lines in different orientations, the implication is that the adaptation level is computed separately for varying regions of the field. Such a formulation can handle many of the parametric effects observed in the Zoellner illusion. For instance, it easily explains why the illusory effect grows stronger as more oblique lines are added to the array. It also explains why the effect increases as a function of increasing inclination of the oblique transversals. This approach may even be useful in explaining the reversal of the effect when the difference between the obliques and the transversal becomes quite small (Adam, 1964; Imai, 1962; Wallace & Crampin, 1969). The argument here is that, when the obliques are extremely tilted, they approximate the orientation of the vertical. Therefore, both the obliques and the vertical are close to the adaptation level. Under these circumstances, one would expect an assimilation or averaging of the inclinations rather than the usual contrast effect.

There is an interesting extension of adaptation level that is based on residual stimuli. Fisher (1969) showed that acute angles tend to be overestimated whereas obtuse angles tend to be underestimated. This very basic illusory effect has been used to explain a number of classical illusions such as the Poggendorff, although not always with great success (Hotopf & Ollereanshaw, 1972a, 1972b; Weintraub & Krantz, 1971; Day & Dickinson, 1975). Adaptation level theory suggests that this effect might be due to stored "norms" of right angles, which arise due to the ubiquity of perpendicular lines in the perceptual environment. Such ubiquitous stimuli should act as powerful residual stimuli to pull the perception of similar stimuli toward the stored "norm," which is serving as a sort of adaptation level. This process is thus a form of assimilation or averaging. Such effects, if they could be shown to exist, might be useful in explaining some of the crosscultural differences observed in some illusions as a function of the relative degree of urbanization, or carpenteredness, of the environment. Environments containing many square rooms should provide more residual stimuli to pull the adaptation level for angles toward 90°. This would imply that illusions explicable in terms of regression of angles toward 90° should be stronger in cultures with a high degree of carpenteredness.

In quantitative terms, the adaptation level is computed by taking the geometric mean of all the stimuli in the field, including the focal stimuli, background stimuli, and residual stimuli relevant to the judgment at hand. Each stimulus is weighted by an appropriate factor. Since the geometric mean is computed by summing the logarithm of all the individual stimulus values and dividing by the total number of stimuli in the array, there is a tendency to underestimate the contribution of larger stimuli and overestimate the contribution of small stimuli. Once computed, the adaptation level is then entered into an equation to predict the judged size of a stimulus. Merryman and Restle (1970), Restle (1971b), and Restle and Merryman (1968a, 1968b) have used the following general form of the equation to predict judged size:

judged size = physical size/adaptation level

These investigators have used this equation to test variations in the magnitude of the Baldwin illusion as a function of increasing box size or increasing size of the open space around the test element. They have also used this equation to test a series of line length comparisons in the presence of other context stimuli. In general, the judged magnitudes predicted by the equation fit reasonably well with the actual data, although some rather arbitrary determinations of the weighting functions were required to create this fit. Notice, however, that according to this equation the judged size of the test element will decrease as the size of the adaptation level increases, and the judged size of the test element will increase as the size of the adaptation level decreases. This implies that the equation reflects a contrast model in which the difference between the test element and the surrounding context is reflected in the judged size of the focal stimulus in an augmented fashion. Thus this quantitative formulation fails to predict any assimilation, including that which occurs when the size of the test element approaches the adaptation level. This is certainly a limitation since one of the main advantages of adaptation level theory was its ability to predict both types of distortion with a single framework.

A number of alternative mathematical formulations have been offered, based on the same general pattern of reasoning as that which underlies adaptation level theory (Anderson, 1970; Hake, Faust, McIntyre, & Murray, 1967; Massaro & Anderson, 1970; Rodwan, 1968; Waite & Massaro, 1970; Weintraub, 1971). The most clearly elaborated of these comparative judgmental models is based on Anderson's (1968) integration model. Its implications for illusions have been spelled out for the Ebbinghaus illusion by Massaro and Anderson (1971). The only major difference between this model and the adaptation level model is that Anderson's model incorporates a direct estimate of the relative size of the test elements and a single context element. This appears in the numerator of the equation and a weighted estimate of the size of the surrounding context elements appears as the denominator. Functionally, this model also only predicts contrast; it does not predict the occurrence of assimilation or regression toward an average value.

The adaptation level model is quite elegant in its conceptualization and should be capable of predicting a number of illusory effects. When we deal with the model in a qualitative fashion, it seems to be a fairly useful conceptualization. The quantitative formulations to date, however, seem capable only of dealing with contrast illusions. They clearly need some additional elaboration before they can quantitatively specify all the properties of the qualitative model.

FIELD THEORIES

There are a number of quantitative models that are not based on specific behavioral assumptions but that use mathematical analogs to electrical potential theory or electromagnetic fields. The rationale for selecting such an analog lies in the fact that illusions involve a two-dimensional space in which contours interact and apparently displace one another in the same way in which charged regions interact and displace or modify the locus of other charged regions.

Although such analogies are mathematically convenient, there are many difficulties associated with the field-theoretic concept when it is transferred from the realm of physics to the realm of psychology. To begin with, there is no evidence that any part of the nervous system operates by means of diffuse field interaction. Nonetheless, a number of investigators have found that analyzing stimulus interactions as if they were occurring in a force field yields reasonable perceptual descriptions and predictions of what happens when lines interact in the visual field. It is important in considering these theories to remember that they are only descriptive models. They attempt to find a single function or a small set of functions that can describe the phenomenal result. They should not be construed as theories that offer specific physiological or cognitive mechansims.

The first attempt to deal with illusory distortions in terms of field interactions was based on Brown and Voth's (1937) suggestion that the visual field is represented in the nervous system as a vector field. In this presumed field, each vector has a certain magnitude and direction. The vectors are of two general kinds — cohesive and restraining. The cohesive forces tend to attract stimulus points, whereas the restraining forces prevent such confluence. Orbison (1939a, 1939b) applied these force field concepts to static percepts, using stimuli with regularly spaced and repetitive geometrical backgrounds. He suggested that forces within a field seek a position of equilibrium, where cohesive and restraining forces are balanced. In geometric terms, this equilibrium point is represented by a situation in which contours in the field intersect at right angles. Where the intersection is different from a right angle, the locus of the contour is distorted in the direction of a position where the forces would be balanced. In this manner, Orbison easily predicted a number of distortions observed when geometric figures are superimposed on fields of concentric circles or radiating lines (Figure 3.11). These effects all involve an apparent opening up of acute angles, which would be equivalent to a regression toward the equilibrium position of perpendicularity, where all forces are in balance. Such reasoning can also be used to explain the effects observed in the Wundt—Hering illusion (Figures 3.9), the Zoellner illusion (Figure 3.2), and the herringbone illusions (Figure 3.10). It should be apparent that the basic judgmental principle embodied in this formal geometric mathematical formulation is simply the same tendency to overestimate acute angles and underestimate obtuse angles that we considered at some length in the chapters on structural factors. The sole difference here is that Orbison is describing the phenomenal effect without any reference to an underlying mechanism and without attempting to describe the obtained relationships quantitatively.

Unfortunately, Hofmann and Bielchowsky (1909) have shown that angles that intersect at 45° manifest little or no distortion, which cannot be easily reconciled with Orbison's formulation that there is a regression toward right angles. To accomodate these data and to specify Orbison's approach more precisely, Berliner and Berliner (1948) proposed a mathematical descriptive model. This model proposes that a geometrical figure superimposed on a geometrical field will be distorted at each intersection to a value that can be predicted from the following formula: C = sine 4a, where a is the size of the angle of intersection. This formula is, in fact, a useful one for illusions with intersecting lines. It should be remembered, however, that many of the classical intersecting line illusions, such as the Wundt—Hering, can be obtained in a dot form where there are no continuous contours or well-defined angles (Coren, 1970a), or even in a subjective contour form (Kanizsa, 1974; Pastore, 1971). In these configurations, no contour interaction of the kind required by Orbison or Berliner and Berliner is possible. It would be interesting to apply this mathematical formulation to these contourless stimuli to see how well it predicts the distortion in these configurations.

An alternative model, drawing much more heavily on an electrophysical analog, has been offered by Sickles (1942), who utilized a force field formulation based on electromagnetic theory in order to explain the Ponzo illusion. Sickles treated the area between the two converging lines as if it were an electromagnetic field distorted by the line within it. Since the forces within an electromagnetic field can be calculated, it is possible to compute the effects of such a line in a hypothetical field and predict changes in its apparent length as a function of its proximity to the sides of an angle. A similar attempt was made by Yokose (1954) and Yokose and Kawamura (1952), who applied Savar's law of electromagnetism to a number of different shapes, thus constructing equal force contours for the inside and the outside of the figures. The apparent displacement of points in the vicinity of various shapes could be predicted with considerable success on the basis of such equal force contours. This notion has been recently extended by Motokawa (1970), who attempted to take the crucial step of offering an actual mechanism for such electrical force interactions. He postulated local electrical fields on the retina, as we noted in Chapter 5. Unfortunately, as we discussed previously, once the mechansim is specified and one begins to extend the application of the model to a broader range of figures, its predictive ability seems to break down.

It is interesting that there is, in fact, no need to propose electromagnetic force fields when the same perceptual field effect can be produced by mapping a perceptual space in which the principles of assimilation (here attraction) and contrast (here repulsion) occur. Without specifying a general mathematical field notion but utilizing its principles implicity, Fisher (1968, 1969a, 1969b, 1971, 1973) and Quina and Pollack (1972, 1973) have suggested that gradients of distortion exist around contours. Their general formulations propose that close contours tend to attract each other, whereas more distant contours tend to repel each other. Very distant contours, of course, do not interact at all. In this way, Fisher (1968) was able to predict the Ponzo and the Mueller—Lyer illusion (the latter by pointing out that it may be viewed as a special case of the Ponzo illusion). Eriksson (1970) offered a similar formulation, using the openness of the space between two contours (i.e., whether or not it contains intervening elements), rather than proximity to determine whether contours will be attracted or repelled.

Unfortunately, there are problems with all the assimilation–contrast models of visual illusions, regardless of their degree of quantitative sophistication. Without exception, they have difficulty predicting the point at which no illusion will be obtained in the repulsion–attraction curve. Although adaptation level theory predicts both contrast and assimilation, the quantitative statements of the theory are capable only of predicting contrast, albeit with some precision. Fisher's contour proximity formulation works remarkably well for some configurations but predicts the opposite of the classically obtained distortion in some arrays, such as the Oppel–Kundt illusion, in which it would predict that the divided space would be seen as shorter because of the attraction of the spatially proximate contours. The electromagnetic analog of Yokose (1957) and Motokawa (1970) predicts an apparent rounding of corners and curvature of lines in straight-line figures, when they are presented in the visual field without any context elements. As is quite apparent from looking at such simple figures, such distortions are not obtained.

There is, however, a more serious problem with all these formulations. These theories, except for some speculation by Motokawa from the physiological realm and by Helson at the strategy level, are purely descriptive of the phenomenal outcome and do not suggest underlying mechanisms. As such, they are limited. They do not help us to understand *how* the raw visual input is transformed into the conscious percept in such a manner as to produce distortion. It is possible to hypothesize almost any number of underlying perceptual mechansims to fit any one of these descriptive models.

A TENTATIVE ASSIMILATION–CONTRAST MODEL

Given this state of affairs — that most composite models are primarily descriptive and lack specified perceptual mechanisms — one might wonder if it is possible to begin with a set of known perceptual strategies and from that basis evolve a theory that predicts both assimilation or averaging and contrast or differencing distortions. Actually, there are a number of indications in the literature that such is possible. We tentatively offer such a formulation that we call a *pool* and *store* model.

Let us first note that most visual arrays subtend a visual angle considerably larger than that of the foveal area of clear vision. This fact implies that only a small amount of the available visual information can be taken in a single glance. The perceptual inputs must be collected in multiple glances, and the stimulus input is distributed over time. This simple observation implies that information collected in former glimpses must be stored in some holding bank for use in the synthesis of the final percept. In other words, memoric processes must be involved in the perception.

Once we accept the fact that the stimulus input is temporally distributed, a number of interesting psychophysical studies become relevant. These studies involve visual judgments of line length and loudness. The data from these studies indicate that stimuli presented in close temporal proximity tend to be assimilated or averaged, whereas stimuli separated in time tend to manifest contrast or an accentuation of differences (Ward & Lockhead, 1970, 1971). On the basis of such findings it may be argued that information tends to be pooled in the immediate sensory register, which we might define roughly as the information coming in a single glance. The observer attempts to extract a global impression of that part of the stimulus array he is currently viewing by averaging all the extents in that view. Perceived sizes of extents that are available only through successive glances are a different matter. Under these circumstances, information from earlier glances must be held in storage for later use, implying that some encoding is necessary so that the observer can retrieve the information at a later point in the perceptual process. Thus he must be able to distinguish between each new piece of incoming stimulus information and those already held in storage. To do this, he may extract and emphasize the differences between new information and that already held in the sensory register. This process serves the function of making the most recent input easily discriminable from earlier stimulus samples. The resulting effect should be one of contrast.

To apply this mechanism to the illusion situation, it must be noted that, when parts of a stimulus that are to be compared are spatially proximal, they are presumably sampled in a single glance and hence should be pooled or assimilated. On the other hand, when the parts of the stimulus that are to be compared are far away from one another, they must be sampled with successive fixations. Because this implies use of a memory store, it should lead to an emphasis on differences, which would be manifested as contrast. Notice that this model provides a simple way for determining why certain illusions show assimilation and others show contrast. The critical variable is simply whether the stimuli are close enough to be glimpsed simultaneously and hence averaged, or whether they are distant enough to require successive sampling of the array.

To see how this might work, let us apply it to some classical configurations. Consider first the Dolboeuf illusion (Figure 2.8). If we look at the overestimated portion of the Delboeuf, which manifests assimilation or averaging, we find two circles that are spatially contiguous. The outer circle, which serves as an inducing element, is always in view when the observer is looking at the central test element. Thus its extent should be averaged or pooled with that of the judged element. Such an averaging would be expected to result in overestimation of the inner test circle. In the contrast or underestimated portion of the Delboeuf, the observer cannot view the test and inducing elements simultaneously because they are spatially separated by a considerable extent, which implies that he must compare them in memory. Since we are hypothesizing that such memoric storage emphasizes the differences between the elements, one should obtain a contrast effect under these circumstances, with the relative smallness of the central circle emphasized in comparison to the relative largeness of the surround.

A similar argument can be made for the Ponzo illusion (Figure 2.5A). It is likely that the test line near the apex of the angle cannot be viewed without some part of the converging sides of the angle also being present in the central field of view. Accordingly, under these circumstances, one would predict a pooling of the length of the test line with the total horizontal extent between the sides of the angle. The result of this, since the converging lines are beyond the ends of the test element, should be to pull the average outward, with a consequent overestimation of the test line. When the test line is placed farther down in the body of the angle, it becomes less likely that the test line and the outer converging contours are seen in a single glance in clear foveal vision. Thus we would expect the test line to be contrasted with the total horizontal extent between the sides of the angle and hence underestimated.

The model is also capable of explaining the Ebbinghaus illusion (Figure 2.7C). if one simply assumes that one of the critical parameters in this illusion is the distance between the central test circle and the center of each of the surrounding circles. This has been suggested by Cooper and Weintraub (1970) and Girgus, Coren, and Agdern (1972) to explain why the apparent size of the central test circle diminishes as one increases the distance between the test and surrounding inducing elements, regardless of the size of the inducers. It is but a small step to the Baldwin illusion (Figure 2.4A) and the similar results reported by Restle and Merryman (1968b).

It is interesting to consider a configuration such as the Mueller–Lyer illusion (Figure 2.3A) in this light. Since the ends of the shaft cannot be viewed without simultaneously viewing the wings, which meet and merge at the end of the shaft, one will always get assimilation of the length of the shaft to the average locus of the points that make up the wings. Thus the Mueller–Lyer illusion may be viewed as an assimilation effect due to pooling. It is possible to modify the basic configuration so that the shaft and wings cannot be seen in a single glance, by leaving a gap between the ends of the shaft and the wings. As the size of the gap increases, it should become less and less likely that the wings and the shaft end can be seen in a single glance, and the illusion should shift from one of averaging to one of contrast. Such results have been reported by Pollack and Chaplin (1964) and Fellows (1967, 1968). This effect is demonstrated in Figure 10.1, where all the shafts are the same size as the isolated line on the top.

Additional evidence for the *pool* and *store* model comes from an alteration of the usual paradigm of simultaneous presentation of test and inducing elements. By using successive presentation, we can force successive processing of elements usually seen together in a single glimpse. Under these circumstances, the model would predict that only contrast effects should be found, since the normally

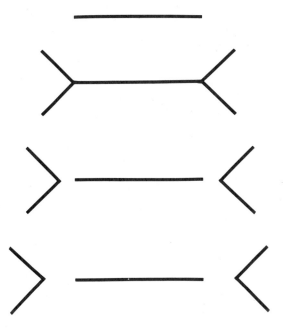

FIG. 10.1.   As the inducing wings are moved farther away from the shaft, the Mueller—Lyer illusion shifts from an assimilation illusion to a contrast illusion.

pooled components would no longer appear simultaneously in the sensory register. Data confirming this prediction have been found by Cooper and Weintraub (1970) for the Delboeuf illusion and by Pollack (1965) for the Mueller-Lyer illusion.

This brief description of a *pool* and *store* model for assimilation and contrast effects has much in common with the immediately preceding models. Its primary advantage lies in the fact that it proposes specific processing strategies and allows one to predict when contrast and assimilation effects will be obtained. It suggests that the information extracted from a single glance is global in nature, whereas the process of extracting information stored in some sort of short-term sensory memory emphasizes difference among the stimuli. In this fashion, assimilation or averaging and contrast or differencing may be viewed as resulting from a general process by which pattern information is extracted from the visual field and encoded for later use. Such a model must be viewed as being merely suggestive, although it does seem to offer more scope for research than do the purely descriptive models presented above. It should be noted that this model also suggests that the nature of the stimulus sampling may be an important variable in illusion formation.

Overall, one is left with the feeling that composite models capable of predicting both contrast and assimilation are in their infancy. It may be useful to quantify models as one creates them in order to work out their implications more clearly. However, given the fact that the underlying mechanisms themselves are not yet well specified, nor the critical variables yet isolated, quantification may be proceeding faster than is warranted. In general, success in incorporating averaging and differencing mechanisms in a single model has not yet been achieved and all these models remain useful in the descriptive, rather than the theoretical, realm.

11 Information Sampling in Illusion Formation and Destruction

In the preceding chapter, we suggested that, since the information from most visual arrays is distributed over time, the observer's search patterns might affect the forms of illusory distortion obtained. At a simplistic level, it should be clear that, if an observer fails to sample information for a particular part of the field, it is not likely that this unsampled information will enter into the final percept. In a similar manner, dwelling upon one part of the array may overweight that part of the configuration and thus influence any judgments made about the characteristics of the display. Notice that we are simply pointing out that the observer is not a passive receiver. He actively interacts with the stimuli, sequences the order of their input, stores information from them, and later synthesizes all these bits of data into his conscious representation of the stimulus. Information-sampling strategies involve the systematic direction of perceptual activities according to some complex cognitive plan.

PIAGET'S CENTRATION THEORY

One of the most elaborate information-sampling theories of the formation of visual illusions has been provided by Piaget (1969). In general, Piaget looks at the gathering of information from a visual display as an active search involving a series of *centrations*. A centration may be generally defined as a focusing or shift of attention. In Piaget's theory, the number of centrations on a part of the field determines the apparent size of the elements in that region. Objects receiving many centrations are overestimated in consciousness. When the observer views a configuration in which some of the elements are larger than the others, his attention or, in Piaget's terms, his centrations are first captured by the larger components.

Piaget uses this line of reasoning to account for contrast illusions. According to Piaget, each component in the visual field has an ability, which is some function of its size, to attract centrations. The larger the component, the more centerings it will elicit. When a large component is near a small component, it will attract even more than its usual share of centrations. Presumably, the size represented in consciousness incorporates the amount of time spent centered on a target. Contrast is thus a natural outcome of such a system.

Vurpillot (1959) defined the conditions under which assimilation, or averaging, will occur within Piaget's theoretical system. Suppose we had two lines differing only slightly in length. Under these circumstances, both lines should exert approximately the same pull on the observer as he systematically moves his attention from one part of the field to the other. Since the phenomenal representation of size is a function of the number of centrations, an even distribution of centrations across the array will lead to an underestimation of the difference between the two elements, which would manifest itself as the assimilation or averaging of the two extents.

Since receptor adjustments, particularly eye movements, are closely related to the distribution of attentional processes, Piaget has used them as an index of the pattern of centrations. Piaget and Bang (1961a, 1961b) recorded the distribution of eye movements across the horizontal-vertical illusion (Figure 2.2). Subjects tended to distribute their fixations so that there were more movements over the vertical line than over the horizontal line. These researchers argued that it is this centering of attention on the vertical line that accounts for its relative overestimation. Piaget (1969) has provided data that indicate that there are more fixations on the divided portion of the Oppel-Kundt illusion (Figure 7.7) than on the undivided portion. He argues that the dividing elements capture the attention of the observer, producing more fixations, or centrations, over that region of the field and hence leading to an overestimation of the divided portion of the illusion.

The core of Piaget's system is an active observer who is constantly exploring the visual environment. The act of fixating a target, or shifting one's attention to it, is only the beginning of the observer's interaction with the array. The observer is not only actively moving his eyes; he is actively making comparisons between the elements in different parts of the array. According to Piaget, relatively few of these comparisons, which he calls *couplings*, are made in the early stages of viewing a stimulus array. Thus, the percept is initially characterized by centration or focusing of attention. As the observer continues to scan the array, however, he increases the number of couplings as he actively compares the extents in the stimulus. When all possible comparisons between the elements have been made, one might expect that the original illusory effects would be somewhat reduced, since the asymmetries in centrations and couplings have been reduced.

According to this hypothesis, one would predict that illusions should decrease with prolonged inspection. It is interesting that such a decrease has been noted for many illusion configurations, including the Zoellner, the Poggendorff, the Mueller-Lyer, the Wundt-Hering, and the Oppel-Kundt illusions (Coren & Girgus, 1972c; Coren & Hoenig, 1972). On the other hand, since coupling involves a comparative judgmental strategy, illusions involving cognitive contrast should be increased as more time is available to explore the figure and make such comparisons. Examples of such increases are fairly rare, although they are reported in some studies that show that certain illusions increase in magnitude as exposure time is increased from very brief tachistoscopic presentations to free or continuous viewing (Piaget, Bang, and Matalon, 1958).

Piaget has also argued that the differences in eye movement patterns between adults and children reflect differences in their centrations. He has proposed that children are less able to make comparative couplings between relevant areas of the stimulus array and thus do not actively distribute their attention across the array. In some respects, he is arguing that a child's attention tends to be caught and fixed by one portion of the field, whereas the adult utilizes a strategy that allows isolation and comparison of various elements. Within the framework of this position, differences in the deployment of attention could account for the age-related decreases that have been reported for most illusions, such as the Mueller-Lyer (see Table 5.1).

In some respects, Piaget seems to be offering a kind of cognitive style explanation for developmental changes in illusions that is quite similar to that offered by Witkin (1967). Witkin's perceptual style explanation and Piaget's decentration explanation both involve an age-related shift from global viewing to analytic viewing. Apparently their differences in terminology have prevented researchers from recognizing the common basis of these two formulations. The major difference between them seems to be that Piaget requires that the observer actively sample from the array, whereas Witkin sees the observer as a much more passive agent. The critical aspect of both of these theories is that they attribute illusory distortions to the way in which attention is deployed across the visual field and to the way information is sampled and encoded.

An interesting set of implications emanates from Piaget's notion of an active observer distributing his attention across the visual field. Clearly, anything that would alter the distribution of attention should alter the magnitude of the illusion. As we have already noted in an earlier chapter, there have been some indications that such attentional manipulations do have an effect. For instance, Coren and Girgus (1972b) were able to reduce the measured magnitude of the Mueller-Lyer illusion by around 20% by simply asking observers to pay special

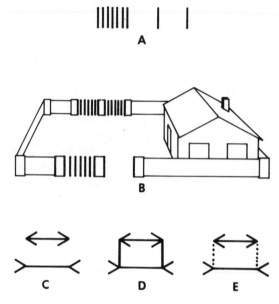

FIG. 11.1. (A) The Oppel–Kundt illusion in which the divided space appears to be longer than the open space; (B) the illusion is reduced when it is integrated into a meaningful context; (C) the Mueller–Lyer illusion is reduced when it is integrated into a regular geometric figure (D), or if the integration is merely suggested. (E).

attention to the test element and to ignore the wings of the figure. To the extent that it is the wings of the figure that cause the distribution of attentional centrations to be asymmetric, this result is quite predictable from Piaget's theory.

Using a somewhat more covert manipulations, Vurpillot (1963) integrated a number of classical illusion figures into familiar pictorial representations. Consider Figure 11.1A, which simply shows the Oppel-Kundt illusion with the usual overestimation of the divided extent. Following Vurpillot's lead, one can integrate the Oppel-Kundt illusion into a familiar configuration. In Figure 11.1B, we have altered the illusion array so that the two halves of the configuration now appear to be part of a gardengate. It should be clear that the distortion is noticeably diminished in this situation. It might well be argued that this dimination results from the fact that both halves of the illusion configuration are now interpreted as being similar units having similar identities. To the degree that this is the case, the number of centrations elicited by each component may well be equalized; after all, one half of a simple gate should not warrant more attentional focusing than the other. In the absence of a differential distribution of attention, the usually obtained illusion of extent should not manifest itself.

A somewhat similar manipulation was used by Piaget, Maire, and Privat (1954), who found that the Mueller-Lyer illusion is greatly attenuated when it is made part of the sides of a square. Actually, the figure does not have to be square in order to obtain this reduction of the illusion, but some connection between the two halves of the illusion configuration must be suggested (Girgus & Coren, 1973b), as can be seen in Figures 11.1D and 11.1E in which the magnitude of the Mueller-Lyer illusion is greatly reduced as compared to the magnitude in the usual form in Figure 11.1C. Piaget and his colleagues reasoned that reduction in illusion magnitude occurs because the suggestion that both halves of the distortion are part of the same figure evens out the distribution of attention to the various segments of the configuration.

An interesting distortion that is also predictable in terms of Piaget's theoretical position is the *error of the standard*, a term apparently first used by Wuerston (1947) to refer to an often observed psychophysical error. Suppose we are constantly comparing a set of variable lines to a common linear extent, which we will call the standard. Generally speaking, there is a tendency for observers to overestimate this standard length. According to Piaget, this extent is overestimated simply because it receives a greater amount of attention than do other portions of the field.

Fraisse, Ehrlich, and Vurpillot (1956) used this standard psychophysical situation and instructed observers to fixate one part of the field but to give maximum attention to another part. The part of the field given maximum attention was overestimated, whereas the fixated part was not. These data make it clear that the process with which Piaget is concerned is an attentional one, under central control. Although eye movements and fixations may frequently serve as an index of the part of the field being attended to, they are not necessary for the deployment of attention and thus are not critical as an explanatory device. Taken all together, the data seem to support Piaget's position that the way in which information is sampled interacts with illusion formation.

EYE MOVEMENTS AND ILLUSIONS

As we noted above, Piaget has frequently used eye movements to indicate the distribution of attention during the viewing of the visual stimulus. A number of other investigators have suggested a much more intimate connection between eye movements and the resulting percept. These investigators have suggested that some information from the eye movements themselves might enter into the final percept. Because, as we move our eyes around the visual field in order to fixate various targets, our pattern of movements (or to be more precise the vectors describing our sequential directions of gaze) provide a sort of map localizing points in space. These theorists have suggested that this map might be encoded at some level, either in the form of muscular memories or intended movement patterns. Such a map could then be used as an aid in computing the direction of targets or the size of the extent between points in the field. To the extent that this map is in error, we might expect illusions to result.

The first systematic theory of eye movement involvement in visual illusions is probably that of Wundt (1898). He noted the not very surprising fact that it takes a longer eye movement to traverse a longer line than it takes to traverse a shorter line. If there is information from each eye movement about the amount of effort required to move the eye across a given extent, this information might then be available as an additional input into the observer's perceptual calculation about the extent of the figure. The elegance of this proposal lies in the fact that presumably anything that alters the degree of effort needed to make an eye movement should then alter the estimate of the size of the target.

Wundt applied this concept to the horizontal-vertical illusion (Figure 2.2) in the following way. He observed that horizontal movements of the eyes seem to be "more easily made" than vertical movements. He argued that, in this illusion, since the vertical line is the same length as the horizontal line but requires more effort to scan, it will be perceived as being longer.

The notion of effort expended in eye movements may be extended to deal with other illusory configurations. Thus Wundt suggested that the interposed elements in the divided extent of the Oppel-Kundt illusion (Figure 7.7) induce a tendency in the eye to stop on some of the included divisions. This stopping and starting of the eye requires more effort than does the single movement emitted across the undivided space. Because of this additional effort required to traverse it, the filled space is intepreted as being longer than the unfilled space.

Some of Wundt's contemporaries proposed that direct proprioceptive feedback from the emitted eye movements rather than the effort expended determines the resulting percept. Thus van Biervliet (1896), Binet (1895), and Lipps (1897) proposed that the Mueller-Lyer illusion (Figure 2.3) could be explained by the fact that the eyes tend to be drawn outward into the wings of the apparently longer segment of the figure, whereas they tend to be arrested, or stopped short, by the inwardly turned wings of the apparently shorter segment. If proprioception from such eye movements is entered into the computation of the shaft length, it could easily affect the perception of length in this figure, thus causing over- and underestimations in the predicted directions.

Unfortunately, theories based on actually emitted eye movements over illusion figures have often run into empirical trouble. Many investigators have tested illusions under conditions in which subjects are unable to make overt eye movements. In the absence of such eye movements, there is no proprioceptive feedback or feelings of effort from the eye. If the eye movement theorists are correct, no illusions should exist in the absence of eye movements.

A number of techniques have been used to obviate eye movements. The oldest of these involves using a tachistoscope to flash illusions at exposure durations too brief for the occurrence of eye movements. Lewis (1908), working with the Mueller-Lyer illusion, and Hicks and Rivers (1908), working with the horizontal-vertical illusion, reported that these illusions still occur under such exposure conditions where effective eye movements cannot occur over the stimulus. In fact, there is even some suggestion that illusion magnitudes may be elevated under brief tachistoscopic exposures.

Recently, more sophisticated attempts have been made to eliminate the effects of eye movements over illusion figures. This newer technique involves the stabilization of the retinal image, using a contact lens arrangement patterned after that of Ditchburn and Ginsborg (1952). With this system, despite any attempted rotation of the eye, the retinal image remains fixed on the retina. Eye movements do not shift the retinal image and hence are not correlated with the stimulus array. Pritchard (1958) showed that both the Zoellner illusion and a variant of the Ponzo illusion continue to exist under these conditions.

Evans and Marsden (1966) used a bright flash to place afterimages of many classical illusion configurations on the retina, thus stabilizing the retinal image and rendering eye movements ineffective. Despite the stabilization of the illusion image, most observers still report distortions in the classically observed directions.

It should be noted that none of these studies that remove the normal relationship between eye movements and retinal image changes actually stop the eye from moving. They merely eliminate the normal visual effect of such movements. Eye movements may still occur in the same directions and to the same extent as they would occur under normal scanning conditions. One could argue that, as long as the movements occurred, whether or not they were effective in the actual scanning of the stimulus, their extent could be entered into the final computation of perceived distance. However, Smith has served as a subject in an experiment in which he was administered curare, a drug that blocks neural transmission across the muscular junction, thus preventing any kind of eye movement. Even under these conditions, he found that he could report the locus and size of targets, which implies that his spatial perception was not impaired (Smith, Brown, Toman & Goodman, 1947). In addition, there is as yet no definitive evidence that proprioceptive feedback from eye movements is available to consciousness (Brindley & Merton, 1960). Taken altogether, the data suggest that eye movements do not play a vital role in the perception of direction or extent.

Even given such evidence, psychologists have been reluctant to give up the notion that eye movements and eye movement information play a role in determining the conscious percept beyond the selection of targets to be viewed. To maintain this position, in light of the negative evidence, an alternate theoretical formulation has been offered, which proposes that eye movements are computed and held in readiness to be emitted across the array and that it is these eye movement tendencies, not the actual eye movements, that are used in the synthesis of the conscious percept. Such a formulation avoids all the problems associated with the eye movement theories described above.

The eye movement readiness theory is actually quite old. It was originally suggested by Wundt (1898) in a rather speculative form and later was modified by Heymans (1896) and Muensterberg (1897). Festinger, Burnham, Ono, and

Bamber (1967) elaborated on this theoretical approach and extended it to account for a number of perceptual effects. Eye movements held in readiness have been used to explain several illusory distortions, including the Mueller-Lyer (Burnham, 1968; Festinger, White, & Allyn, 1968), a curvature illusion (Coren & Festinger, 1967), and several illusions of direction (Virsu, 1971).

One difficulty with this theoretical position is that it is virtually impossible to tell which eye movements are held in readiness for any given array. Generally speaking, investigators have used the actual pattern of emitted eye movements as the best index of the eye movements waiting for release. When they have found patterns of eye movements made in response to some configuration that correlate in direction and magnitude with the direction and magnitude of the perceived illusory distortion, they have suggested that such results support the theory. Since 1897, when Delabarre performed a heroic experiment in which a plaster cap was fitted across his eye, attached to a set of levers that mechanically recorded his eye movements when viewing the Mueller-Lyer illusion, researchers have been able to relate eye movement patterns to illusions. For the Mueller-Lyer illusion, for instance, observers usually make longer eye movements when scanning the shaft in the apparently longer segment than when viewing the apparently shorter component, and the magnitude of these eye movement errors seems to be related to the magnitude of the illusory effect (Delabarre, 1897; DeSisto & Moses, 1968; Festinger, White & Allyn, 1968; Judd, 1905; Stratton, 1906; Yarbus, 1967).

Unfortunately, evidence that the length of the actual eye movements and the apparent size estimation in certain illusion configurations are correlated does not tell us very much. The extent may be over- or underestimated because the eye movement computation is erroneous or an eye movement may be too long or short because it is based on an erroneously perceived extent. Alternatively, both the eye movement and the conscious representation may be based on information extracted from the array. It should seem, in fact, to be somewhat more efficient if the same information were used to compute both the eye movement and the percept. There seems to be no particular functional benefit to the organism to compute the eye movements first and then base all further analyses on this preprocessed information. The data obtained so far seem only to show that eye movements are related to perceived distortions in some correlational manner. To date, there is little evidence to suggest that they play a causal role in illusion formation.

EYE MOVEMENTS AND THE DESTRUCTION OF ILLUSIONS

Up to now we have dealt with illusions as if they were static, unchanging phenomena. Actually, this is not the case. Around the turn of the century, a number of investigators began to notice that the strength of the Mueller-Lyer illusion seemed to diminish with continued inspection (Heymans, 1896; Judd, 1902, 1905; Lewis, 1908). Since that time, a large number of investigators have confirmed the fact that the Mueller-Lyer illusion reduces in magnitude with continued free viewing (Coren & Girgus, 1972b, 1972c; Crosland, Taylor, & Newsom, 1929; Day, 1962a; Dewar, 1968; Koehler & Fishback, 1950a, 1950b; Moed, 1959; Mountjoy, 1958; Parker & Newbigging, 1963). This phenomenon has been termed *illusion decrement.*

Decrement in illusion magnitude following inspection is not confined to the Mueller-Lyer configuration. Many other illusions, including the Poggendorff, the Zoellner, the Wundt-Hering, and the Oppel-Kundt illusions, also show a reduction in strength after periods of prolonged viewing (Cameron & Steele, 1905; Coren & Girgus, 1972c; Coren & Hoenig, 1972). Although the specific mechanisms involved in illusion decrement are not fully known, there is considerable evidence that they involve changes in information sampling strategies that rely on eye movement information.

The manner in which eye movements are utilized in order to correct illusory distortions apparently depends on the fact that the purpose of a saccadic eye movement is to place the image of a target on the fovea, where the clearest vision is available. In a general sense, it might be said that the loci of targets in the visual field are extracted, and these computed positions are used to guide a coordinated pattern of contractions of the extraocular muscles so as to center the fovea on any point selected for viewing. In some respects, one may view the pattern of motor commands issued to the eye muscles as a sort of hypothesis. One is hypothesizing that the target actually lies at the coordinates estimated. If, following the actual emission of an eye movement, the target image is on the fovea, the hypothesis has been confirmed whereas if the target has been missed, then the hypothesis needs to be amended. If the fovea is directed on the basis of an illusory percept, errors will occur following actual eye movements. When attempting to fixate a vertex in the apparently longer segment of the Mueller-Lyer illusion, the fovea should overshoot, and when attempting to fixate a vertex in the apparently shorter segment, the fovea should undershoot, stopping short before reaching the vertex. As noted above, such systematic errors are usually reported by investigators who have recorded eye movements over illusion figures. For example, Festinger, White, and Allyn (1968) recorded eye movements emitted during the scanning of the Mueller-Lyer figure and found that the eye movements are erroneous in the manner predicted. However, confirming an observation originally made by Judd (1905), they also noted that immediately following an erroneously long or short saccadic eye movement, a small corrective flick of the eye is made to center the vertex on the fovea. They hypothesized that these corrective eye movements provide the observer with information about the direction and extent of the distortion and that, on this basis, the observer reprograms both the saccadic eye movements and his percept so that they are more veridical. This process is partially confirmed by the fact that, following a period of inspection, during which time the usually reported diminution in illusion strength has occurred, observers tend to make more accurate eye movements.

If eye movements and their subsequent corrections are necessary for illusion decrement, illusions should not diminish during inspection if the eye does not freely move over the figure. A number of studies have been conducted in which one group of observers was allowed to scan the figure while other groups of observers were required to fixate a portion of the array. Day (1962a), Festinger, White, and Allyn (1968), and Hoenig (1972) all report that little or no decrement of the Mueller-Lyer illusion occurs under conditions of fixation, as opposed to a marked weakening of the illusion when systematic eye movements are permitted over the figure. Coren and Hoenig (1972) have verified this finding for the Oppel-Kundt illusion.

A number of other techniques have been used to prevent error feedback from eye movements while viewing illusions. Lewis (1908) briefly flashed a Mueller-Lyer stimulus and found that even after thousands of presentations spaced over several days little diminution or decrement of the illusory magnitude occurs. Burnham (1968) arranged a situation in which observers smoothly tracked a spot of light moving over the Mueller-Lyer figure. Since the eye was tracking the spot of light rather than making free saccades, no opportunity for erroneous eye movements was present. Consequently, this group of observers showed no illusion decrement. Hoenig (1972) used an illusion stimulus of diminished size, with a visual angle smaller than that of the fovea. Given such a small stimulus, effective eye movements over its extent are not possible; hence error feedback is again restricted. Under these circumstances, illusion decrement also does not occur.

The process by which an illusory distortion is destroyed is extremely interesting in that it provides a change in the perception of the illusion without necessitating any change in the physical stimulus itself. The important variable seems to be the observer's history of interaction with the illusory configuration. As he systematically samples information from the array by moving his eyes across it, he somehow garners information about the nature and extent of the illusion. The conscious percept is then altered toward veridicality. It becomes clear that patterns of information sampling may result in either the formation or destruction of illusions. In the following chapter, we show how illusion decrement may prove to be a powerful tool in our attempt to understand the mechanisms underlying illusions and the relative contribution of varying levels of processing to illusion magnitude.

12

The Psychoanatomy
of Visual Illusions

In the preceding eight chapters we have been confronted with a multitude of mechanisms, structural processes, and judgmental and information processing strategies, all of which have been proposed to explain visual illusions. In some respects, their number and diversity is almost overwhelming. It is clear that these distorting agents may introduce themselves in any stage in the perceptual process. Some of them seem to act as early as the initial formation of the optical image on the retinal surface, whereas others wait almost until the final formation of the conscious representation of the stimulus (Girgus & Coren, 1973a). In addition, many of the illusion configurations we have discussed seem to offer the opportunity for more than one mechanism to operate. For instance, when the stimulus array contains converging lines that intersect to form an angle, contributions to the resulting distortion may arise from factors associated with optical blur, lateral neural interactions on the retina, lateral interactions in the cortex, or judgmental strategies that treat the angle as if it were a perspective cue or an enclosing frame. It is possible that all these mechanisms play a role whenever such an array is present or that one particular source of distortion predominates in a given configuration, depending on the nature of the accessory lines and their relationship to the test elements.

It is, however, possible to bring some order to this exceedingly complex situation if we begin by accepting the notion that many different mechanisms may interact to form any given illusory distortion. Once having accepted this premise, it is appropriate to shift the focus of our inquiry so that we no longer try to find one lone causal agent for any given distortion. Rather, we must try to determine what contribution each mechanism and processing level makes to the final illusory percept. In some ways, our task is similar to that of the biologist or physiologist who wishes to determine how several mechanisms interrelate to sustain some life process. Since most bodily functions are sequential, biologists and physiologists frequently use a research paradigm whereby the process is interrupted or stimulated at varying stages in order to ascertain what functions take place before or after the point of intervention. In many respects, when considering the formation of visual illusions, we are engaged in an analogous task. It is certainly the case that we are looking at a visual system that processes information sequentially, beginning with the peripheral optics and moving on through the retinal neural substrate and visual pathways up to the visual cortex. Unfortunately, beyond the primary visual cortex, the strict sequential nature of the system seems to disappear. Our task differs from that of the biologist, moreover, since we wish to dissect a phenomenal experience rather than a physical entity. All indications about the nature of the system must come solely through behavioral indices that indicate changes in the conscious experience. We may be said to be engaged in a form of *psychoanatomy* in that we are using behavioral techniques to isolate the contributions of various physiological and cognitive processes to the final form of a psychological entity—the illusory percept.

THE PRIMARY DIVISION

The initial phases of information processing in the visual system are serial in nature. Information is first processed by the peripheral optical image-forming components, proceeds to the retina, moves up he visual pathways, through the lateral geniculate, and then to the striate cortex. Beyond the first set of cortical connections, neural physiology fails us and we can no longer track the information flow accurately, probably because the manner of information processing shifts from a serial, sequential mode, in which each successive stage operates on the transformed information from preceding levels, to a parallel processing mode, in which many interpretative activities take place simultaneously, perhaps all converging on a common final point. Since the visual system is composed of a series of stages, the first step in our psychanatomical dissection of visual illusions must be to decide where to enter the system in order to begin the analysis.

Conceptually, there is a kind of natural dividing point at the juncture where the optical neural structure can no longer predict the final percept and cognitive processing or judgmental strategies must be taken into account. Traditionally, psychologists have called this the division between *psysiological mechanisms* and *cognitive mechanisms*. This choice of terminology may merely reflect the fact that those researchers who call themselves physiological psychologists tend to study the earlier levels of processing, whereas cognitive psychologists tend to focus on the later. Unfortunately, this terminology seems to ignore the fact that all behaviors have an underlying physiological base. An alternate, popular way of representing this primary division is to call the neural and optical components *peripheral* and the judgmental strategy components *central* processes. However, this set of labels lacks a certain degree of specificity, since it is not immediately clear whether Area 17 of the primary visual cortex should then be considered central or peripheral. To avoid the difficulties inherent in these traditional labels, we will continue to use the functional terms *structure* and *strategy*. By the term *structure* we refer to all the neural and optical processes that form the basis of the operation of the visual system. Structural components are potentially measurable using direct physiological procedures. By *strategy*, we refer to information-processing strategies that may vary as a function of experience, expectations, or test requirements. The reader will note that we have already used this terminology in Chapters 4 through 11, where we have attempted to specify the implications and limitations of these labels. Perhaps their main asset is that they are somewhat new terms and hence are not fraught with a long history of misinterpretation.

If we are to begin to dissect an illusion, we first must develop a "surgical" technique that allows us to separate structural from strategy mechanisms in a fairly direct fashion. There is a procedure that seems quite promising in this endeavor, which is based on a set of observations described in the preceding chapter. As we noted there, beginning with Heymans (1896), who reported that the magnitude of the Mueller-Lyer illusion seems to diminish during a period of continuous free inspection of the configuration, many experiments have shown that this *decrement* in illusion magnitude is quite reliable for the Mueller-Lyer (Burnham, 1968; Coren & Girgus, 1973; Dewar, 1968; Festinger, White, & Allyn, 1968; Judd, 1902; Koehler & Fishback, 1950a, 1950b; Mountjoy, 1958; Parker & Newbigging, 1963). This diminution of an illusory distortion during a period of free viewing is not specific to the Mueller-Lyer configuration. As noted earlier, Coren and Girgus (1972c) found a similar decrease in illusion strength in the Poggendorff, Zoellner, and Wundt-Hering illusions, and Coren and Hoenig (1972) reported a similar reduction in the Oppel-Kundt illusion.

There has been some debate about whether illusion decrement represents the removal of the strategy components involved in the formation of visual illusions or whether, instead, structural mechanisms, usually proposed in the form of cortical fatigue or satiation, might account for the diminution of illusion magnitude during inspection (Coltheart, 1971; Koehler & Fishback, 1950a, 1950b). The bulk of the evidence clearly indicates, however, that illusion decrement functions by eliminating the strategy components, leaving the structural substrate clearly exposed.

First of all, on purely logical grounds, it seems highly unlikely that lower level structural mechanisms could account for illusion decrement. There is no reason to think that a few minutes of free inspection of a pattern of lines could lead to a modification of the amount of blur resulting from the crystalline lens or the optic media. Furthermore, there is no evidence that the gain or distribution of lateral inhibition will be affected through simple viewing of a stimulus. Ascription of decrement to a higher level of processing is further supported by a study by Porac and Coren (1977), who allowed observers to view the Mueller-Lyer illusion with one eye and obtained the usual decrement in the illusion's magnitude. They then tested illusion magnitude in the other eye and found that the decrement had, in fact, transferred from one eye to the other. This result implies that the processes involved in decrement must occur beyond the first point of binocular interactions, at least in Area 17 of the cortex or beyond.

If cortical structural mechanisms in the form of fatigue or satiation were responsible for illusion decrement, steady fixation of the stimulus should lead to more decrement than free inspection, simply because the locus of stimulation would be more constrained, leading to more satiation. However, as we pointed out in Chapter 11, Festinger, White, and Allyn (1968) and Hoenig (1972) found more decrement in the Mueller-Lyer illusion when the eye moves systematically from vertex to vertex and little decrement when there is steady fixation, a result that has been verified by Coren and Hoenig (1972) for the Oppel-Kundt illusion. Converging on the same general conclusion are studies by Lewis (1908) that indicated that repeated presentations of the Mueller-Lyer illusion at exposure intervals too short to permit functional eye movements results in little decrement, even when practice sessions are extended over several days.

Furthermore, because all the structural explanations of illusions depend on the interaction of converging or intersecting line elements should show more decrement than variations of the same illusion containing no such elements, if illusion decrement is caused by structural mechanisms. However, Girgus, Coren, and Horowitz (1973) have shown that the same rate and amount of illusion decrement is obtained for seven different variants of the Mueller-Lyer illusion, including both variants that contain many converging lines and variants that contain no converging line elements at all.

In addition, satiation and fatigue explanations predict that the magnitude of transfer of illusion decrement from one configuration to another should depend on their structural similarity—that is, the number of common elements or features in the two stimuli. Strategy explanations, on the other hand, would contend that the amount of decrement that transferred to a new variant of the illusion would depend on the observer's cognitive assessment of the similarity between the practice configuration and the test configuration, regardless of the number of elements in common. Coren and Girgus (1974) exposed observers to the standard form of the Mueller-Lyer illusion and obtained the usual amount of decrement. They then tested the transfer of the diminution of the illusion to a series of variants of this configuration. They reported that the amount of illusion decrement that transferred, or generalized, to other variants of the figure was predicted almost perfectly by subjective ratings of the similarity between the standard form of the Mueller-Lyer used as the practice figure and the variants used as test figures in this study. When they attempted to analyze the data on the basis of the number of common features or elements in the illusion configurations, they found that these did not predict the transfer of decrement nearly as well as the ratings of perceived similarity.

Taken together, the data clearly imply that illusion decrement represents a reduction in the information-processing or strategy components of an illusion and that structural mechanisms do not seem to be directly involved. Additional evidence implies that this diminution in illusion magnitude represents a form of perceptual learning in which the observer alters his information-processing strategy in order to correct the discrepancy between his percept and the external physical relationships in the stimulus. Mountjoy (1958) and Dewar (1968) provided data that indicate that the rate of illusion decrement varies as a function of traditional learning variables, such as the spacing of trials. Furthermore, illusion decrement persists and even accumulates over days and weeks of practice as would be expected if it were a kind of perceptual learning (Girgus, Coren, Durant, and Porac, 1975; Judd, 1902).

As discussed in the preceding chapter, the basis of this learning seems to be a knowledge of processing errors gleaned from the exploration of the figure by means of eye movements. Using the Mueller-Lyer illusion, a number of investigators have indicated that observers make systematic eye movement errors while initially scanning the figure (Delabarre, 1897; Festinger, White, & Allyn, 1968; Judd, 1905; Stratton, 1906). These eye movement errors, which are clearly correlated with the direction and extent of the illusion, are immediately followed by small corrective eye movements (Festinger, White, & Allyn, 1968; Judd, 1905). As the observers continue to inspect the figure, the eye movements become more and more veridical (Festinger, White, & Allyn, 1968). It seems likely that the observer uses his eye movements to probe the stimulus and test his conscious representation of it. When he finds that the percept is in error, he systematically begins to modify the information-processing strategies that led to the error. As he does so, he can confirm the appropriateness of his strategy modification and the increased veridicality of his percept by basing his eye movements on his newly modified strategies. This is reflected in the increasing accuracy of the eye movements. It seems likely that illusion decrement is the result of the modification of the information-processing or strategy components of illusion formation, based on error feedback from the eye movements used to scan the illusion figure.

This process implies that we can use illusion decrement as a tool to estimate the relative contributions of structural and strategy components in any given illusion. Presumably, the initial illusion magnitude contains both structural and strategy components. However, after the observer has modified his inappropriate strategies and the consequent reduction in illusion magnitude has fully occurred, only the structural components of the illusion should remain. The residual level of distortion that remains after illusion decrement should thus serve as a measure of the relative structural contribution to the initial illusion magnitude.

To see how this process works, consider an experiment by Girgus, Coren, Durant, and Porac (1975), who used two forms of the Mueller-Lyer configuration, the Brentano form (Figure 12.1A) and Coren's dot form (Figure 12.1B). The many converging and intersecting line elements in the Brentano form of the figure would lead us to expect that a considerable portion of the distortion obtained for this configuration is due to structural interactions associated with optical blur, lateral neural interactions on the retina, or interactions among cortical orientation-specific units, as discussed in Chapters 4, 5, and 6. On the other hand, the lack of such converging or spatially adjacent contour elements in the dot form would lead us to expect that very little, if any, of the distortion in this configuration is due to structural mechanisms. With this in mind, Girgus, Coren, Durant, and Porac (1975) had observers view one of these configurations for 10 minutes a day, for a total of five consecutive days. The results are shown in Figure 12.2. Notice that in each day's inspection the magnitude of the illusion diminishes. This is the decrement usually obtained. In addition, the initial illusion magnitude, measured when the observer first entered the testing room on each successive day, shows a gradual reduction. Presumably, this decrease in illusory effect represents a gradual change in the observer's information-processing strategies as he views these configurations. Notice, however, that the minimum asymptotic level for each figure is virtually unchanged over the course of the five days. That is, the minimum amount of illusion at the end of the first day of practice represents something of a floor, below which the size of the illusion never falls. This asymptote presumably represents that part of the illusory effect due to optical and neural factors, since these factors are unchanged by simple inspection of the pattern. As predicted, the Brentano form shows a considerably

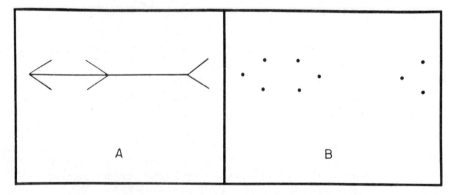

FIG. 12.1. The stimuli used by Girgus, Coren, Durant, and Porac (1975). (A) The Brentano form of the Mueller–Lyer illusion and (B) Coren's dot form.

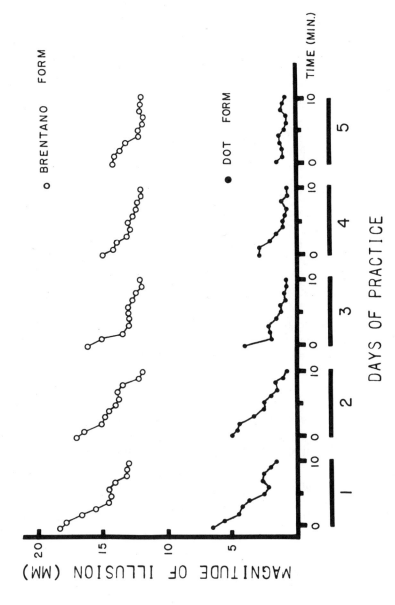

FIG. 12.2.   The magnitude of two forms of the Mueller–Lyer as a function of continued inspection over a period of five days (Girgus, Coren, Durant, and Porac, 1975).

higher asymptote than the dot form. In fact, 65% of the initial illusion magnitude is still present in the Brentano form after five days of inspection, whereas only 12% of the initial magnitude remains in the dot form, and this 12% is not statistically different from zero.

One last point that is noteworthy is the fact that, if both forms of the Mueller-Lyer illusion are supported by the same erroneous perceptual strategies, which come to be corrected during the course of viewing the configuration with active eye movements, we ought to find a similar amount of reduction in the two arrays. If we look at the absolute amount of decrement in millimeters rather than in percentage of initial illusion, it becomes clear that we find the same size reduction of about seven millimeters in the two configurations. This finding implies that the information-processing strategies being corrected are relatively equivalent for the two arrays.

We can not use these data to assess the relative contributions of structural and strategy components to these two variants of the Mueller-Lyer. Given the fact that the available evidence clearly indicates that illusion decrement is due to changes in information-processing strategies, the 35% of the Brentano form of the illusion that disappeared during inspection should represent the strategy components of this configuration and the 65% of the illusion that remained throughout the five days of practice should represent the structural components. In the dot form, the 88% of the distortion that disappeared during decrement would be attributed to information-processing strategies whereas only the residual 12% would be ascribed to the various possible structural mechanisms. Of course, it is possible that there are some immutable strategy factors that are not subject to recalibration during inspection. These factors would manifest themselves as additional residual illusion magnitude, thus causing us to overestimate the amount of distortion contributed by structural sources. Nevertheless, these data clearly show how illusion decrement can be used to separate the structural from the strategy components in a particular illusion.

SUBDIVISION OF STRUCTURAL COMPONENTS

Once the primary division into structural and strategy components has been made, it is useful to subdivide each of these classes of mechanisms into their respective components. There are several procedures we have already encountered that can be used to eliminate some structural components in order to assess their contribution to the final illusion magnitude. Let us review some of these techniques.

Coren (1969) used an artificial pupil and narrow band chromatic filters to decrease the blurring of the retinal image, while leaving all other mechanisms unaltered. This technique serves as a direct means of assessing the contribution to illusion magnitude produced by the degradation of the image as it passes through the ocular dioptrics.

Several techniques have been used to eliminate any possibility of optical and neural interactions on the retina. Day (1961), Ohwaki (1960), Schiller and Weiner (1962), and Springbett (1961) have done this by presenting in a stereoscope some of the line elements from a given configuration to one eye and the remaining elements to the other eye. By so doing, one can arrange the stimulation so that no converging or intersecting lines appear on a single retina. In the fused image, however, the complete configuration is seen. Since binocular fusion presumably occurs after Area 17 of the primary visual cortex (DeValois, 1960; Hubel & Wiesel, 1961, 1962), this technique can be used to prevent any interaction between adjacent contours from occurring prior to the cortex. Unfortunately, there are methodological problems with this technique. In the fused view, at points where the elements from one eye's input make contact or intersect with those presented to the other, rivalry or instability of the fused percept is apt to occur, so that the test and inducing elements are not seen simultaneously in fused vision. This may lead to a reduction in illusion magnitude that has nothing to do with optical or neural interactions on the retina.

Julesz's (1971) random dot stereograms, in which each binocular view presents a random texture of elements containing no hint of the illusory configuration, provide an elegant solution to the problem of instability in illusion stereograms, while still bypassing retinal levels of processing. When binocular disparity cues are introduced into a subset of the textural units, observers see the illusory configurations separated from the background in depth, with no rivalrous elements to confuse the perception. Unfortunately, this technique is not free of all technical problems. The lines used in constructing the configurations must have sufficient bredth to be visible in the stereogram and thus may be considerably wider than those normally used in classical configurations. In addition, although the configurations have the general shape of the illusion forms, they look more like cardboard texture cutouts suspended above a textured background than like lines on paper. Thus, when Julesz (1971) reported that the Zoellner illusion does not appear in random dot stereo presentations, one does not know whether this is because the Zoellner illusion depends solely on peripheral structural interactions or because the stereogram must use nonoptimal line widths and spacings in order to be visible to the observer, thus interfering with the information-processing strategies from which the illusion normally arises.

It is also significant that, although these procedures rule out the possibility of optical and retinal neural interactions, they do not rule out the possibility of higher level structural interactions that might occur at Area 17 of the cortex or beyond. Since the fused view is available in the primary visual cortex, it is possible that orientation-specific or disparity-specific receptors, which have been shown to be present at this level, may interact to cause some of the observed distortions.

Coren's (1970a, 1970b) procedure, in which all the line elements are eliminated from the configuration and the line ends and vertices are replaced with dots, also clearly avoids the possibility of optical aberrations and lateral inhibitory interactions by removing the converging line elements necessary for their evocation. However, even this technique does not avoid the possibility of neural interactions between orientation-specific receptors that may occur in the cortex. It is possible that two dots separated by some distance may be a sufficient stimulus to trigger some cortical feature extractors as suggested by Harris and Gibson (1968). In addition, phenomenologically, the test figures Coren uses are not perceptually equivalent to the original configuration that the experimenter set out to investigate. Extrapolated connections between two dots, provided by the observer, may evoke different perceptual strategies from those used for real contours. It may well be the case that these arrays affect strategy as well as structural components.

The final means or bypassing optical and neural interactions utilizes illusion configurations in which the inducing or test contours are replaced by apparent subjective contours that have no physical brightness gradients (Goldstein & Weintraub, 1973; Kanizsa, 1974; Pastore, 1971). These configurations look much more like the standard figures than do Coren's dot forms and hence are less likely to evoke different information-processing strategies. However, it is possible that even these figures are capable of triggering orientation-specific receptors in the cortex, and thus all structural interactions at this higher level cannot be ruled out.

This brief methodological review should make it clear that some subdivision and isolation of mechanisms grouped under the structural rubric is possible, although some conservatism in interpreting the results is probably still warranted.

SUBDIVISION OF STRATEGY COMPONENTS

In many respects, subdivision of the contributions to illusion formation that arise from the various information-processing strategies is a more difficult task than subdivision of the structural mechanisms. This may be because structural processes tend to occur in a fixed defineable sequence as one ascends the visual system. Contrast this to strategy mechanisms, where several judgmental processes may be operating simultaneously. Certainly there is no evidence to allow us to assume a strict sequential model for these higher level processes. This fact puts a greater strain on the techniques that can be used to separate possible strategy components. Nonetheless, a few experiments have attempted a further partitioning of strategy contributions to illusion magnitude.

Gogel (1975) provided evidence that the illusion-producing computations take place after the relative depth of the test and inducing elements has been assessed. He presented the inducing angles from two Ponzo configurations stereoscopically, so that they were seen at different depths and facing in different directions. He then presented a pair of test lines that could be manipulated so that they were seen at the apparent depth of either one of the two inducing angles. He reports that under these conditions the matnitude and direction of the illusion depends on which inducing angle appears to be coplanar with the test lines. Similarly, Julesz (1971) manipulated random dot stereograms so that the test and inducing elements were at different apparent depths. Under these conditions, the illusion magnitude was greatly reduced. Such demonstrations clearly suggest that the processing responsible for the illusion takes place after the relative depth of the components of the figure has been assessed.

Other experiments indicate that relative size judgments take place some time after the operation of the size constancy mechanism and after the apparent similarity of the components in the configuration has been assessed. Coren (1971) has shown that the Ebbinghaus configuration can be found in configurations where all the elements are physically the same size. In this experiment, the apparent size of the surrounding stimuli is manipulated through the mechanism of size constancy. Thus the illusion-producing mechanism must be applied after the operation of size constancy. Coren and Miller (1974) have shown that the magnitude of this same illusion depends on the apparent similarity between the test and inducing stimuli. Hence the size contrast operation must occur after figural similarities have been cognitively assessed.

All these experiments tell us something about the order of processing involved in illusion formation at the strategy level. Unfortunately, this approach has not been used extensively to explore the contributions of various strategy components to final visual distortions. It does, however, provide an interesting approach for the future.

THE ANATOMY OF AN ILLUSION

It is obvious from the discussions and data we have already presented that illusions may be caused by a multiplicity of mechanisms. We have seen how illusions may arise from optical factors associated with dioptric limitations of the eye, from neural interactions on the retina and perhaps the cortex, and from a complex of cognitive judgmental strategies. More important, we have seen that removal of one, and sometimes even several, levels of processing usually reduces the magnitude of classical illusion configurations but rarely totally destroys the illusory effect, implying that other distorting agents still remain operative. If we are to understand any illusion completely, we must be prepared to partition the contributions that arise from each of the levels of processing.

As an example of how this partitioning may be done, let us now attempt to dissect the Poggendorff illusion (Figure 3.3), using data generated by the various techniques we have described above. The Poggendorff illusion has several qualities that make it a useful demonstration case. It contains converging and intersecting line elements and thus should have some structural contributions.

Furthermore, a fair amount of quantitative data, pertaining to both structural and strategy components, exist for this configuration.

Let us begin our analysis with the most peripheral structural level. In an experiment we described in Chapter 4 in some detail, Coren (1969) used artificial pupils and narrow band chromatic filters to reduce the amount of the blur in the retinal image stemming from optical aberrations in the eye. He managed to diminish the amount of blur in the image by 70% using these techniques. He reported a concomitant reduction in the magnitude of the illusion of 15.6%. If we extrapolate from this result to a situation where 100% of the blur has been eliminated, we would expect that the illusion magnitude would be attenuated by approximately 22%. Thus it would appear that about 22% of the magnitude of the Poggendorff illusion is due to optical contributions.

To assess the contribution of lateral inhibition on the retina, we must be rather indirect. Coren (1970a, 1970b) used a dot form of the Poggendorff, eliminating all continuous contour elements. Goldstein and Weintraub (1973) constructed forms of the Poggendorff in which the vertical lines intersected by the transversal exist only in the form of subjective contours. Since neither of these variants of the Poggendorff illusion place converging lines through the dioptrics of the eye or in the image on any retina, they effectively eliminate both optical and neural retinal interactions. When we compare the magnitude of the illusion obtained with these configurations with that obtained in the control configurations, in which the contours are actually present, we find a 40% reduction in illusion magnitude. Since we have already ascertained that optical factors account for 22% of the effect, we may assume that neural interactive effects account for the remaining 18% of the accumulated 40%. It should be remembered that, although it is certainly the case that these manipulations eliminate retinal interactions, they may also eliminate the possibility of cortical interactions among higher level orientation-specific receptors, which would also manifest itself as a reduction in distortion. This possibility implies that lateral inhibitory effects on the retina do not account for more than 18% of the usual illusory distortion in the Poggendorff. If the dot and subjective contour forms of the configuration do not successfully bypass cortical as well as retinal neural interactions, lateral inhibitory interactions on the retina may account for somewhat less than 18%.

Up to now, we have dealt with only the major structural sources of illusory distortion. We may now assess the percentage of distortion that arises from processing strategies by using the illusion decrement procedure. Coren and Girgus (1972c) found that 39% of the initial illusion magnitude in the Poggendorff had disappeared after a five-minute inspection period. Since a five-minute inspection period is probably not long enough for the illusion decrement to have reached asymptote, the amount of the Poggendorff that is due to information-processing strategy components may, in fact, be somewhat greater than 39%.

If we now consider all the components of illusory distortion we have isolated for the Poggendorff thus far, we find that 22% of the illusion is due to optical aberrations, 18% is due to neural interactive effects, probably at the retinal level, and at least 39% is due to information-processing strategies. This leaves 21% of the usually observed distortion unaccounted for. Some of this residual magnitude might represent strategy components, which might have disappeared if a longer period of decrement had been utilized by Coren and Girgus (1972c). In addition, some of this residual magnitude may contain nonplastic cognitive judgmental strategies, which are not susceptible to modification with simple inspection. It is also possible that a proportion of this remainder consists of higher level structural factors involving the interaction of orientation-specific receptors in the cortex.

The above analysis should make it clear that, despite that apparent simplicity of the classical Poggendorff configuration, the perceptual effect is actually a compound distortion, resulting from several levels of processing within the visual system. It should also be apparent that, if we are to understand any illusory distortion completely, we are going to be forced to engage in some kind of psychoanatomical dissection such as the one just demonstrated.

ADDITIVITY IN ILLUSION MAGNITUDE

In the preceding section, we attempted a dissection of a single illusion configuration so that we could see how the distortion manifested in consciousness was actually an amalgam of a number of different mechanisms, all acting in consort to produce the illusory effect. In many respects, this dissection was meant to be didactic in nature, rather than a complete description of this simple array, since the specific numerical results are limited to the specific variant of the illusion used. In contemporary psychology, there is some pressure toward the development of formal models to describe behavioral phenomena. Although we have not attempted more than a suggestive mode of analysis, it is important to note that we have already made a certain set of assumptions that may serve to limit the generality of our analysis. In general, we have been assuming that the illusory effects from each level add to the effects of the preceding levels. In this kind of simple additive model, the final illusory magnitude is assumed to be the sum of all sources of distortion. It is, of course, equally possible that illusory effects add in a nonlinear fashion. There may even be complex interactive loops that cause an attenuation of the distortion from one source in the presence of information from a second source. However, since an additive model is the simplest kind, it seems reasonable to begin with it and to reject it only when and if the data make it no longer tenable.

For those who wish to embark on formal model building, it is interesting to note that it is possible to assess the adequacy of an additive model directly by combining several illusory effects. If the various sources of distortion simply add, then the combined illusion should reflect the sum of each of the distortions taken separately. Ni (1934) looked at combinations of the horizontal-vertical illusion, the Mueller-Lyer illusion, and the Oppel-Kundt illusion and created configurations that combined pairs of these illusions arranged so that the total illusion strength should add. Figure 12.3A shows the combination of the horizontal-vertical and Mueller-Lyer illusions, Figure 12.3B shows the combination of the horizontal-vertical and Oppel-Kundt illusions, and Figure 12.3C shows the Mueller-Lyer combined with the Oppel-Kundt illusion. Ni's data indicate that, for Figures 12.3A and 12.3B, the combined illusory effect is greater than it is for either of the two illusions measured alone, although the composite effect is somewhat smaller than the simple sum of the individual effects. However, for Figure 12.3C, the magnitude of the illusory effect seems to lie somewhere between the two individual effects, as if the observer had taken the average value of the two simple distortions. These data seem to indicate that the interaction of processes occurring at various levels may decrease, as well as increase, the magnitude of any single distortion.

It is possible to interpret these data in terms of successive versus simultaneous processing of visual information. If the processing involved in the horizontal-vertical illusion occurs either before or after the processing strategies involved in the formation of the Mueller-Lyer and the Oppel-Kundt illusions, there might be successive processing of the information from the two illusions that make up

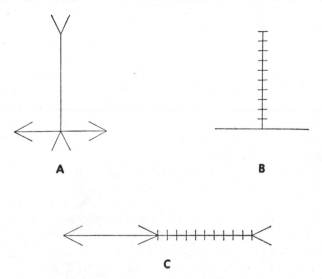

FIG. 12.3.   Three composite illusion figures. (A) The horizontal-vertical and the Mueller–Lyer; (B) the horizontal-vertical and the Oppel–Kundt; (C) the Mueller–Lyer and the Oppel–Kundt (redrawn from Ni, 1934).

the combined figure. Such successive processing might allow each illusion to contribute to the total effect in a summative manner. Under these circumstances, one ought to find additivity in Figures 12.3A and 12.3B. If the processes involved in the Oppel-Kundt and the Mueller-Lyer figures occur at the same time (that is, in parallel), discrepant estimates might be passed on to a final evaluation center. Under these circumstances, it might be reasonable to expect the averaging of the two effects found in Figure 12.3C. It may be argued that addition is more likely to occur when each of the distortions operates successively rather than simultaneously. It should be remembered, however, that, despite the fact that Ni's figures are a combination of classical configurations, they look phenomenally different from any of the component elements presented alone. Observers may process these figures as essentially new configurations, using strategies that are not usually applied to any of the classical configurations by themselves. It is interesting that these deviations from simple additivity hold the promise of providing a new set of tools whereby one may tease apart the levels of processing in illusion formation. To the extent that we get simple summation effects, we may assume serial processing; whereas, to the extent that we get simple averaging effects, we may assume parallel processing.

In summary, then, we may look at most illusory percepts as representing the combined effects of many levels of information extraction in the visual system. These levels include both structural and strategy components. It is important to realize that this mode of dealing with illusions involves a significant shift in point of view relative to that usually found in the literature. To begin with, illusions are no longer dealt with simply in terms of the direction or form of distortion obtained phenomenologically. Nor are we talking about illusory effects solely in terms of the parameters of the stimulus. Rather, we have begun to speak of these distortions as if they were the final product of an amalgamation of interacting mechanisms. One no longer speaks of a single *theory* or *cause,* but now of the *relative contribution* of a number of causes and levels of information processing. It is hoped that this kind of eclecticism will provide new insight about the nature of illusory processes. It at least breaks the historical chains that bind us to the ideal of a single unified theory of illusions.

13 Toward a Taxonomy of Visual Illusions

In the preceding discussion, we emphasized that illusions are phenomena with multiple causes. They arise from no one single source. Rather, the final distortion represented in consciousness may contain contributions from many levels of processing and may represent the operation of many mechanisms, all of which combine to produce a conscious representation at variance with the physical reality. In considering any illusion as the result of a number of independent contributing mechanisms, we have been forced to offer a more complex model of illusions to researchers. This model requires assessing the relative contribution of many factors to each illusory distortion. If an accurate picture is desired, investigators can no longer look for a single, universal illusion-causing process but must look on all levels of the visual system as interacting in the process of illusion formation.

This shift in viewpoint from the traditional single-theory position to one of multiple causation suggests alternative research strategies that may be useful in solving some of the long-standing problems associated with visual illusions. Let us deal with one such example of a problem that is soluble if one accepts the idea that many levels and many mechanisms may all contribute to a single illusory percept.

In the past 120 years of research on visual illusions, a number of structural mechanisms and cognitive strategies have been isolated. Hundreds of new illusion variants have been created. It is distressing that, despite a literature containing over a thousand papers, we are apparently still unable to find a simple way to classify the set of visual phenomena that we call illusions. This is a troubling state of affairs because almost all sciences began by *first* establishing a typology that allowed a mass of data to be sorted and organized. It is true that classification does not in and of itself provide us with explanations. Nonetheless, many advances in the sciences have been triggered by the creation of a meaningful classification system that organizes the subject matter and hence simplifies the thinking about the phenomena under study. The most successful classification schemes in science, such as Ray and Willugby's (1676-1704) and Linnaeus' (1735-1738) taxonomies of living things, Thompson's (1832) classification of archeological finds, and Mendeleyev's (1869) organization of chemical elements, have been basically descriptive in nature. The pattern of organization that resulted from such attempts, however, did serve to suggest new hypotheses. Several gaps in Mendeleyev's periodic table of elements suggested that new elements were yet to be found and indicated their chemical properties. The repetitive nature of the pattern in each grouping later served to suggest and support the notion of orbiting electrons determing the nature of chemical reactions. (See Huxley, 1940 for a more complete discussion of the history of classification systems).

The history of classification repeats a common theme in many different disciplines. First an investigators finds some aspect of the phenomenon under study that appears interesting and that manifests a certain degree of regularity across all the phenomena under investigation. He then attempts to organize all the known items or materials in an ordered fashion along the dimension he has selected. If a classification scheme is successful, it will both make intuitive sense and generate hypotheses about the nature of the items being classified.

Unfortunately, the various attempts to classify visual illusions have not proved to be particularly fruitful. These classifications can be divided into two groups. The first group is based on the nature of the illusory distortions. Boring (1942) reviewed most of the early attempts to classify illusions according to the kind of distortion involved. He concluded that most of these early efforts reduce to two classes of distortion: illusions of extent and illusions of direction, with some aberrant or complicated cases that do not fit either category. This general separation into two classes is the procedure that we have used in Chapters 2 and 3 of this volume.

There are a number of more recent attempts to establish a typology of visual illusions according to type of distortion. For instance, Oyama (1960) utilized three major classifications. The first included illusions of angle, direction, straightness, and curvature—the equivalent of Boring's illusions of direction. The remaining two classes were produced by subdividing illusion of extent into illusions of length and distance and illusions of size and area. Oyama then divided each general heading into subclasses in which virtually every major illusion pattern falls into a separate subgrouping.

Robinson's (1972) first general grouping included illusions of extent and area, with separate subheadings under which most of the major illusion figures, including the Mueller-Lyer, the Ponzo, the Delboeuf, the Oppel-Kundt, illusions of area, and the moon illusion, are used as prototypes for a subgrouping. His second major grouping predominantly involved illusions of angle and direction, under which are the Zoellner, the Orbison figures, and the Poggendorff illusion. Robinson's third section, "Other Illusions," contained illusions such as the horizontal-vertical illusion and the flattening of arcs of a circle.

Luckiesh (1922/1965) used a mixed classification scheme in which he proposed three categories that referred to characteristics of the stimulus configuration itself (illusions of interrupted extent, such as the Oppel-Kundt illusion; illusions of location in the visual field, such as the horizontal-vertical illusion; and illusions of contour, such as the Mueller-Lyer illusion) and two categories that refer to particular mechanisms of illusion formation (illusions of contrast, such as the Ebbinghaus and Delboeuf illusions; and illusions of perspective, such as the Sander parallelogram and the Orbison configurations).

The second type of classification scheme involves a mechanism rather than an end product. A number of authors have tried to classify illusions solely in terms of hypothesized underlying mechanisms. The first attempt of this kind seems to have been made by Wundt (1898), who divided illusions into two classes: constant illusions arising from the structure of the ocular muscles and normally adaptive for extracting information from the environment, and variable illusions that are due to patterns of eye movements over the configuration. Since there were no objective eye movement data available when this classification system was proposed, the assignment of any given illusion to one of the two classes had to be done largely on speculative grounds. Later research has not confirmed the usefulness of this typology.

Tausch (1954) attempted to define all illusions in terms of a single underlying mechanism, suggesting that all visual illusions can be classified in terms of a depth-processing mechanism such as those we described in Chapter 7. Since Tausch reduced all illusory distortions to a single mechanism, the problem of classification solved itself in his scheme: All illusions must lie along the single contiuum, hence no typology that divides distortions into separate classes is necessary.

Piaget (1969) used his theory of centrations (described in Chapter 11) to classify illusions into two groups: primary illusions, which consist of all illusions that diminish in magnitude with increasing age, and secondary illusions, which increase in magnitude with increasing age. As we saw in Table 5.1, however, there is a decrease in illusion magnitude as an individual grows older for most of the illusions for which developmental data exist. Only the Ponzo illusion consistently shows an increase in magnitude with age, whereas a number of illusions show both an increase and a decrease as a function of age. Thus, if one were to use Piaget's classification scheme, almost all the classical configurations would be classified as primary illusions, which seems to be a rather unlikely organization.

The proposals that attempted to classify illusions in terms of underlying mechanisms have, unfortunately, not been very successful. However, the purely descriptive classification schemes have been equally unsuccessful, perhaps owing to the fact that all the descriptive typologies that have been proposed have been based on the type of perceived distortion, with some attempt to form subgroupings based on apparent commonalities of pattern. This latter approach can lead to difficulties. As we saw in Chapters 2 and 3, it is frequently the case that similar patterns of relationships lead to different types of distortion. For example, the Delboeuf illusion, which is an illusion of area, can easily be seen as a variant of the Baldwin illusion (or vice versa), which is an illusion of linear extent. Similarly, the Zoellner illusion can be seen as an illusion of directional contrast in much the same way as the Ebbinghaus illusion can be seen as an illusion of size contrast. Furthermore, as described in the beginning of Chapter 3, almost any illusion of extent can easily be transformed into an illusion of direction. It seems likely that classification of illusions on the basis of the type of distortion will not in the long run prove to be a very fruitful approach.

Because no fruitful approach to a generally agreed-on taxonomy for visual illusions has emerged so far, it may be possible to use the idea that illusions are multiply caused and that any distortion may involve several mechanisms and levels of processing to establish a classification of illusory distortions that is behaviorally meaningful. Consider the following hypothetical state of events. Suppose there are two underlying illusion formation mechanisms. For convenience, we will simply call them A and B. It seems reasonable to classify illusions caused predominantly by mechanism A into one group and to classify illusions caused predominantly by mechanism B into another. Of course, because both mechanisms may be operating in any one configuration, there will be some cross talk between the classes. Nevertheless, if we could obtain two groupings each based on the predominant mechanism, we could have both a meaningful division and perhaps some insight into the nature of illusion formation.

As we have seen with previous attempts to develop this type of classification, there is a problem in that we must first be able to define the underlying mechanisms. If the specific mechanisms are not correctly identified, the classification scheme is doomed to failure. However, even this difficulty is not insurmountable. To continue with our hypothetical example, suppose that an individual is highly responsive to mechanism A and only weakly responsive to mechanism B. He would show a large illusion magnitude for illusions predominantly based on A but little distortion on illusions incorporating B. Another individual not as responsive to mechanism A but very responsive to mechanism B should produce the opposite results. Notice that by using individual differences in responsiveness in this way we could provide illusion magnitudes that covary as a function of the underlying mechanism. We could use this covariation as a means of segregating illusions into A and B groups. This mode of analysis, based on a preliminary acceptance of the multiplicity of mechanisms operating in visual illusions, suggests a means of producing a classification system. If there are large individual differences in visual illusion magnitude, and if these differences may be presumed to depend on variations in an observer's sensitivity to a given mechanism or his propensity toward the use of a given strategy, then we need not know the underlying mechanism in advance. We can simply group illusions together on the basis of those distortions that tend to vary together in magnitude with individuals.

Any illusion researcher can easily verify that there are large individual differences in the responsiveness of observers to various illusions. Variability is, in fact, the bane of every experimenter working in this area. Coren, Girgus, Ehrlichman, and Hakstian (1976) decided to try to use these individual differences in illusion response among subjects to produce a taxonomy of illusions based on the rationale described above.

Coren et al. (1976) selected twelve of the most common illusion forms: the Poggendorff, the Wundt, the Zoellner, the Ebbinghaus, the Delboeuf, the Ponzo, the Jastrow, the Baldwin, the horizontal-vertical, the Oppel-Kundt, the divided line, and the Sander parallelogram, as shown in Figure 13.1. They also decided to use 11 variants of the Mueller-Lyer illusion, as shown in Figure 13.2. A reasonably large set of classical illusion figures was used to permit meaningful groupings to emerge, and a large number of variants of a single illusion was used to ascertain whether altered forms of a given illusion actually comprise variations of the same underlying illusion mechanism. Because all these illusion patterns, except for the Poggendorff illusion, contain both a segment that is usually overestimated and a segment that is usually underestimated, separate measurements were taken of the two illusion components. All illusion judgments were designed so that they required estimations of linear extent for the data to be comparable for purposes of analysis. Two judgments on each of the 45 different illusion configurations were made by 221 observers.

A factor analytic technique was then used to generate the classification scheme. The initial correlation matrix of 990 unique correlations produced 951 positive correlations and no significant negative correlations. Such a correlation matrix seems to imply that there is a large degree of similarity and covariation among most illusion distortions and that, for this set of configurations, illusion judgments are highly interrelated. Since the same mechanism may be involved to a greater or lesser extent in many illusions, such a positive manifold of correlations is perhaps not very surprising. This high degree of correlation further suggests that any classification scheme derived from this matrix would not contain exclusive groupings but rather classes that show some interrelations. With this in mind, Coren et al. (1976) decided to analyze the data using an oblique factor analysis procedure, hoping that this procedure would permit the separation of illusions into meaningful groups, even though some of the groups might not be completely independent of one another.

The analysis revealed that there were five factors present, as shown in Table 13.1, in which the factor coefficients above 0.40 are starred. Because most of the illusions used have a segment that is usually overestimated and a segment

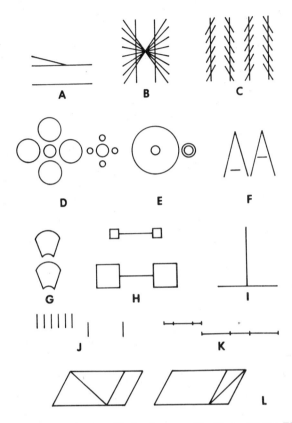

FIG. 13.1.   Twelve common illusion forms used by Coren, Girgus, Ehrlichman, and Hakstian (1976). (A) The Poggendorff illusion; (B) the Wundt
illusion; (C) the Zoellner illusion; (D) the Ebbinghaus illusion; (E) the Delboeuf illusion; (F) the Ponzo illusion; (G) the Jastrow illusion; (H) the
Baldwin illusion; (I) the horizontal-vertical illusion; (J) the Oppel–Kundt
illusion; (K) the divided-line illusion; (L) the Sander parallelogram.

that is usually underestimated, we have indicated which segment is involved by
a plus sign for the normally overestimated segment and a minus sign for the
normally underestimated segment. Notice in Table 13.1 that virtually all the
illusion patterns tested load highly on one, and only one, factor, which is en-
couraging if one hopes to offer a classification scheme based on these results.

If the multicausal approach is valid, the extracted factors will, it is hoped,
make sense in light of the various structural and strategic mechanisms we have
discussed in the preceding chapters. Let us begin by considering the first factor,
where we find high coefficients for the Poggendorff illusion and for both measurements on the Wundt and Zoellner illusions. In addition, the apparently
longer segment of the Sander parallelogram loads here, as does the apparently

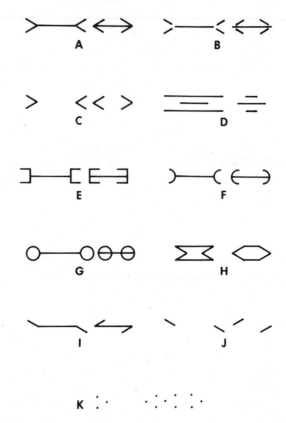

FIG. 13.2.   Eleven variants of the Mueller–Lyer illusion used by Coren, Girgus, Ehrlichman, and Hakstian (1976).

longer segment of the divided line illusion. If we ignore the latter two for the moment, it is interesting to see that the Poggendorff, Wundt, and Zoellner illusions are all illusions involving intersecting line elements. In addition, these distortions involve the apparent direction of a line, thus producing the deviation in the Poggendorff transversal, the apparent nonparallelism in the Zoellner illusion, and the apparent bowing of the lines in the Wundt illusion. All these distortions in apparent direction seem to be most easily explained by the structural mechanisms discussed in Chapters 4, 5, and 6—blur due to optical aberrations, lateral inhibitory interactions on the retina, and perhaps interactions among orientation-specific cortical feature detectors. In effect, one can derive each of these illusions by simply postulating the type of contour displacements and opening up of acute angles that these mechanisms predict. Why one segment of the Sander parallelogram and one segment of the divided line illusion also load on this factor is not immediately clear. However, the other five high factor pattern coefficients do suggest that Factor I involves structural, contour interactive mechanisms. Coren et al. (1976) designate this first grouping as *shape and direction illusions*, although they might be more descriptively called *angular expansion illusions* since they may all be predicted by the expansion of angles in intersecting line configurations. It seems likely that other shape and directional distortions found in intersecting line figures such as the Orbison or Jastrow-Lipps illusions would also load on this factor.

The second factor looks quite different. In this factor, we find high coefficients for both the over- and underestimated segments of the Delboeuf and the Ebbinghaus illusions and for the apparently longer segments of the Ponzo and Jastrow illusions. The apparently smaller section of the Jastrow illusion just misses the criterion cut-off with a factor coefficient of 0.38. This factor appears to be quite homogeneous and readily suggests a theoretical interpretation because all the illusion forms loading on this factor seem to involve judgments of relative size. We have frequently seen that the Ebbinghaus and the Delboeuf illusions are the configurations most frequently interpreted in terms of cognitive assimilation and contrast mechanisms, such as those discussed in Chapters 8, 9, and 10. In addition, the size differences in the Jastrow illusion may well be due to the contrast between the longer segment of the lower figure and the shorter segment of the upper figure. We have already suggested a possible contrast-assimilation explanation for the Ponzo configuration when we introduced the *pool and store* model in Chapter 10. Because this factor seems to involve cognitive contrast mechanisms, in which a target appears to be larger when surrounded by small elements and smaller when surrounded by large elements, Coren et al. (1976) designated this class as containing *size contrast illusions*, although they actually contain both the contrast and assimilation components of these configurations. Illusions involving contrast between the sizes of angles would also presumably fall into this category.

Factors III and IV present a slightly more complex situation. To begin with, they are highly related, with a correlation of 0.73. This is perhaps not surprising when one considers the fact that most of the high pattern coefficients on these factors represent variants of the Mueller-Lyer illusion.

Factor III shows high pattern coefficients for all 11 variants of the apparently longer segment of the Mueller-Lyer illusion. The only apparently shorter segment that intrudes on this factor is the circle version. In addition, both segments of the Baldwin illusion, which may easily be interpreted as variants of the apparently longer segment of the Mueller-Lyer illusion with boxed ends, appear on this factor. Yet this factor is not purely a Mueller-Lyer classification. The apparently longer segment of the horizontal-vertical illusion and the apparently longer segment of the Oppel-Kundt illusion also appear on this factor. Thus this factor seems to represent a tendency toward overestimation of linear extents. The specific mechanism underlying this grouping is not immediately clear because quite different mechanisms usually have been proposed to explain the Mueller-Lyer, horizontal-vertical, and Oppel-Kundt illusions. Coren et al. (1976) have called this factor *overestimation illusions*.

TABLE 13.1
Factor Pattern for 45 Illusion Measures

	I	II	III	IV	V
Poggendorff	.42*	.07	.01	.03	.05
Wundt	.76*	.13	−.05	.03	.09
Wundt−	.51*	.39	.05	−.20	−.05
Zoellner+	.84*	.02	−.28	.16	−.04
Zoellner−	.74*	.11	.01	−.04	.00
Delboeuf−	−.08	.81*	.16	−.18	.13
Delboeuf+	−.10	.62*	−.04	.29	−.10
Ebbinghaus−	.23	.57*	.01	.01	.07
Ebbinghaus+	.15	.69*	−.25	.07	.04
Ponzo+	.07	.62*	.09	.08	.04
Ponzo−	.05	.20	.13	−.03	.66*
Jastrow+	.08	.49*	.15	.27	.08
Jastrow−	.01	.38	.07	.29	.15
Baldwin+	.02	−.22	.58*	.30	.13
Baldwin−	.02	.21	.64*	.04	−.02
Horiz-Vert+	.24	−.06	.67*	.00	−.10
Horiz-Vert−	.05	.12	.36	.38	−.08
Oppel-Kundt+	.07	.07	.46*	.15	.12
Oppel-Kundt−	.04	−.05	.21	.68*	−.05
Standard ML+	.04	−.03	.69*	.18	−.16
Standard ML−	−.12	.16	.23	.49*	.00
Exploded ML+	−.05	−.12	.51*	.36	.15
Exploded ML−	.12	.13	.15	.62*	.07
No Shaft ML+	−.07	−.07	.74*	.14	.00
No Shaft ML−	.02	.17	.14	.50*	.06
Piaget ML+	.24	−.03	.70*	.06	.05
Paget ML−	.85	−.10	.11	.68*	.20
Curved ML+	−.11	.04	.62*	.24	.19
Curved ML−	−.12	.03	.11	.59*	.30
Box ML+	−.10	.11	.59*	.17	−.02
Box ML−	−.19	.19	.34	.39	−.04
Circle ML+	−.08	−.07	.64*	.16	.19
Circle ML−	−.33	.06	.49*	.31	−.01
Lozenge ML+	−.15	−.07	.70*	−.04	.12
Lozenge ML−	.02	.00	−.23	.96*	.01
Sanford ML+	.07	.13	.81*	−.03	−.02
Sanford ML−	.05	.02	.05	.62*	.27
Minimal ML+	.03	.12	.49*	.28	.25
Minimal ML−	−.07	.22	.01	.63*	.21
Coren ML+	−.03	.02	.85*	.20	.04
Coren ML−	.22	.00	.19	.56*	−.03
Divided Line+	.45*	.09	.13	.05	.03
Divided Line−	.02	.16	−.16	.15	.69*
Sander Parallelogram+	.56*	−.09	.28	.27	−.10
Sander Parallelogram−	.18	−.06	.00	−.08	.16
Factor Variance	3.57	3.99	9.04	7.34	1.84

It is interesting to contrast Factor III with Factor IV. On Factor IV we find nine of the 11 apparently shorter variants of the Mueller-Lyer illusion, with the remaining two apparently shorter segments just missing the criterion with factor coefficients above 0.30. In addition, the apparently shorter segment of the Oppel-Kundt illusion appears on this factor, whereas the apparently shorter segment of the horizontal-vertical illusion just misses the criterion with a factor pattern coefficient of 0.32. Since this factor seems to represent a set of distortions associated with the underestimation of linear extents, Coren et al. (1976) have called it *underestimation illusions.*

It is not clear why Factors III and IV segregate themselves in this fashion. To be sure, the high correlation between them indicates that the underlying mechanisms for these two illusory classes may be related. Since the two factors contain separate halves of the same distortion, they would be expected to manifest some relationship on purely logical grounds. This, however, makes it particulatory interesting that the apparently longer and apparently shorter halves of these configurations load on separate factors at all. It has been suggested previously, based on the fact that the two halves of the Mueller-Lyer do not covary in the same fashion in response to certain parametric manipulations, that they may in fact be separate distortions (Sekuler & Erlebacher, 1971). However, no similar suggestion has been made about the horizontal-vertical or the Oppel-Kundt illusions.

Since Factor V shows only two significant coefficients, it provides the most tentative classification. Only the apparently shorter segment of the Ponzo illusion and the apparently shorter segment of the divided line illusion load on this factor. It is possible to view both of these figures as enclosed segments that occupy only a small portion of the total enclosed space. We may be dealing with the comparison of an element with a global frame of reference. Since Coren et al. (1976) did not include many frame of reference illusions in their stimulus set, they may not have provided the conditions for an adequate assessment of this factor, which they have tentatively labeled *frame of reference illusions.* If this is correct, illusions such as the rod and frame should also fall into this classification.

It seems that Coren et al. (1976) have provided a classification scheme with five bins into which illusory distortions may be sorted. Two of these bins—the one labeled *shape and direction illusions* and the one labeled *size contrast illusions*—seem to suggest underlying mechanisms. When we consider the remaining three, two are highly related—*overestimation* and *underestimation illusions*—and seem logical, although these labels are merely descriptive of the distortions that manifest themselves, and no underlying mechanism immediately suggests itself. The fifth and final bin—*frame of reference illusions*—must be seen as being merely suggestive at this point.

It is possible to do a further analysis of these data. Table 13.2 shows the intercorrelations among the five factors shown in Table 13.1. A second-order factor analysis performed on these data revealed that two factors were adequate to explain the higher level covariation shown in Table 13.2. If one now projects the primary pattern coefficients shown in Table 13.1 onto these two second-order factors, two meta factors or global groupings emerge, as shown in Table 13.3. These two second-order factors are not totally independent because they are correlated with $r = 0.49$.

The first global factor, which we have labeled Factor A, includes both the over- and underestimated segments of almost all the variants of the Mueller-Lyer illusion, both segments of the horizontal-vertical illusion, both segments of the Oppel-Kundt illusion, and one segment of the Baldwin and Sander illusions. Thus this factor seems to involve nearly all the illusions of linear extent tested. On the other hand, Factor B contains the Delboeuf, the Ebbinghaus, the Ponzo, the divided line, the Wundt, and the Zoellner illusions, with the Jastrow illusion just missing the criterion value. It is clear that this factor predominantly involves illusions of area, shape, and direction. Earlier investigators who grouped illusions into two categories, one involving illusions of extent and the other involving illusions of shape, may have been on the right track, at least in terms of global classifications.

Thus we may globally group illusions into two classes: illusions of linear extent and illusions of shape and direction. It is only with the finer groupings that emerge from the primary factor analysis that hypotheses about underlying mechanisms seem possible.

The reader may wonder why we have devoted an entire chapter to a single set of experimental findings. In part it is because the problem of the classification of visual illusions is such an important one. The primary reason, however, stems from the underlying rationale for this study rather than from the particular findings. To develop this classification scheme, Coren et al. (1976) first had to accept the fact that illusions are multiply caused and thus result from the contribution of many diverse factors that interact to produce the final percept. Given many sources of distortion, it seemed likely that different individuals might show different levels of structural involvement or different dispositions toward the use of particular strategies. Hence the very individual differences

TABLE 13.2
Correlations between Factors Extracted
for Illusion Classification

	I	II	III	IV	V
I	–	.45	.12	.24	.26
II	.45	–	.32	.48	.38
III	.12	.32	–	.73	.18
IV	.24	.48	.73	–	.31
V	.26	.38	.18	.31	–

TABLE 13.3
High Order Factor Pattern Loadings
for 45 Illusion Measures

	A	B
Poggendorff	.00	.34
Wundt+	.07	.46*
Wundt−	.20	.61*
Zoellner+	.00	.51*
Zoellner−	.10	.54*
Delboeuf−	−.11	−.74*
Delboeuf+	.26	.51*
Ebbinghaus−	.04	.60*
Ebbinghaus+	.18	−.60*
Ponzo+	.05	.50*
Ponzo−	−.19	−.46*
Jastrow+	.09	.34
Jastrow−	.36	.37
Baldwin+	.18	−.28
Baldwin−	−.50*	−.11
Horiz-Vert+	.52*	.10
Horiz-Vert−	.62*	.10
Oppel-Kundt+	.52*	.13
Oppel-Kundt−	.78*	.09
Standard ML+	.72*	.04
Standard ML−	.62*	−.16
Exploded ML+	.08	−.25
Exploded ML−	.44*	−.06
No Shaft ML+	.48*	−.16
No Shaft ML−	.31	−.06
Piaget ML+	.61*	.15
Piaget ML−	.71*	.26
Curved ML+	.74*	−.04
Curved ML−	.65*	.14
Box ML+	.65*	−.01
Box ML−	.65*	.02
Circle ML+	.68*	−.04
Circle ML−	.68*	.01
Lozenge ML+	.57*	−.04
Lozenge ML−	.67*	.11
Sanford ML+	.61*	−.11
Sanford ML−	−.50*	.09
Minimal ML+	.64*	−.01
Minimal ML−	.58*	.09
Coren ML+	.52*	−.03
Coren ML−	.63*	.17
Divided Line+	−.13	−.48*
Divided Line−	.24	.45*
Sander Parallelogram+	−.41*	−.34
Sander Parallelogram−	−.10	−.01

that ordinarily add to the variability of the data in illusion studies could be used to establish a taxonomy by ascertaining which illusions covary systematically. Unlike previous classifications, which relied on either direction of perceived distortion or theoretical predispositions, this classification scheme uses behavioral data to develop a coherent taxonomy.

Such a classification scheme may have taken so long to appear because of the tendency among investigators to try to explain all illusions with a single mechanism. However, if there is one thing we have learned during the course of our review of the data to this point, it is that there is no *one* mechanism responsible for all illusory distortions.

14 Illusions: Implications and Extrapolations

It may seem somewhat paradoxical that the phenomena we have been discussing in the preceding chapters are called *illusions*. One might ask how we can call something that is a universal and predictable experience of all human beings an illusion. Why should it be the case that if I judge a line with outward-turned wings as being longer than another line with no wings, despite the fact that the former casts a longer retinal image, I am said to be manifesting an illusion, whereas if I judge a six-foot-tall man a few feet away from me to be the same size as another six-foot-tall man across the room, despite the fact the latter casts a smaller retinal image, my percept is not said to be illusory at all? Why is it the case that I am said to be experiencing an illusion of shape when a target, drawn to be physically square on a piece of paper yet intersected by some slanting lines, is encoded as if it were trapezoidal, yet I am said to be perceiving "normally" when I perceive the top of my desk as being rectangular when in fact it casts a trapezoidal image on my retina? In each of these cases, one is forced to ask "Which is the illusion?" and "Which percept is normal?" Since both classes of percept are manifested by all normal perceivers, it seems reasonable to classify both instances as examples of "normal" perception. In this light, it is interesting to recall Gregory and Wallace's (1963) investigation of the visual capacity of an individual whose sight had been restored by an operation after he had been blind since birth. When Gregory and Wallace found that this individual did not manifest the usual distortion in the Mueller-Lyer, the Zoellner, or the Poggendorff configurations, they concluded that his vision was abnormal. In other words, "normals' see these arrays as distorted and the absence of illusion is abnormal.

To the extent that the perception of illusory distortions, such as those we have presented in earlier chapters, constitutes a clearly definable aspect of normal perception, it would seem reasonable to expect that any theory of perception that claims that it can explain how form and extent are perceived should also be able to explain the perception of illusions. Let us pick up where Chapter 1 left off and see how several contemporary approaches to perception handle the problem of visual illusions.

PERCEPTUAL THEORIES AND ILLUSIONS

In this section we consider a number of contemporary theories of visual perception that claim to have some generality, in order to see how they treat the problem of visual illusions. Total coverage of all perceptual theories extant in contemporary psychology would clearly be impossible in a single chapter. However, we will briefly describe several of the dominant theorietical viewpoints.

Information Pick-Up Theories

The information pick-up approach actually stems rather directly from a much older theory of perception known as naïve realism, which was based on the assumption that the conscious percept is simply a copy of the external reality. This position, of course, is quickly refuted by the very existence of visual illusions. In both naïve realism and the more contemporary theories that have evolved from it, the observer is a relatively passive receiver of information. The function of the perceptual system is merely to select the portions of the external ambient array that are to be processed, in much the same way that a photographer can point his camera at the sections of the external environment that he wants to record. Neither the photographer nor the perceiver can alter the nature of the inputs; they may only selectively attend. In such a theoretical framework, it is clear that the selection procedure can omit certain features of the stimulus from processing but cannot add any features not present in some form in the physical stimulus.

Perhaps the most ardent supporters of the information pick-up viewpoint are the Gibsons (E.J. Gibson, 1969; J.J. Gibson, 1950, 1959, 1966). For these theorists, perceptual learning and change occur simply because the observer learns new patterns of information selection. It should be clear that this position is no better able to handle the existence of illusions than is the naïve realistic viewpoint from which it springs. In fact, Gibson (1950) explicitly states that his theory is concerned with veridical perception rather than illusions.

Feature Analyzers and Fourier Analysis

There are a number of contemporary theories that seem to adopt the general tenets of naïve realism, utilizing a framework consistent with contemporary knowledge of visual physiology. The primary stimulation for such theories probably stems from the pioneer work of Hubel and Wiesel (1962), who discovered that specific cells in the striate cortex are maximally stimulated by lines of a given orientation. Further experimental work revealed that some cortical cells were selectively responsive to aspects of the stimulus that were even more complex, such as contour length, direction of movement, or even radius or curvature. It appeared that the brain contained specific templates against which features of the stimulus could be matched. Theorists who attempt to analyze the perception of form based on such feature analyzers tend to adopt the viewpoint that features in the stimulus are first directly analyzed by specifically tuned cortical cells and then synthesized into the final percept.

The feature analysis viewpoint is capable of explaining some illusions of direction if it can be assumed that there are lateral neural interactions among cortical cells, such as those we dealt with at length in Chapter 6. It may also be possible for such theories to deal with the existence of subjective contours, if one can find features in this type of stimulus array that activate cells normally representing complete lines, although there are some subjective configurations that this viewpoint clearly cannot handle (Gregory, 1972).

It is quite difficult, within the framework of feature analysis theories, to deal with size illusions such as the Ebbinghaus or Jastrow. One is at a loss to isolate the appropriate feature or to specify the nature of the interaction that results in the distortion. In addition, these theories must presume that very degraded stimuli, such as subjective contours or dot configurations, can provide enough stimulus information to activate the orientation-specific units, despite the fact that the neurophysiological data do not support such a presumption. Thus, at best, feature analysis theories can handle only some subsets of illusory distortions.

There is another form of analysis also seemingly based on the naïve realism assumption that the percept is determined by stimulus characteristics. This may be viewed as an alternate form of feature analysis. Since the time of Helmholtz, it has been known that the ear analyzes compound sounds into their sine wave components. Mathematically, this process is called *Fourier analysis*. It is possible to decompose visual patterns mathematically into spatial sine wave frequencies in a similar manner, using Fourier analysis. For this reason, it has been suggested that the visual system analyzes visual patterns into their sine wave components in much the same way as the auditory system analyzes compound sounds (Cornsweet, 1970).

However, the visual system presumably does not analyze the pattern perfectly because it is well known that the visual system fails to transmit high frequency components to the cortex because of the optical limitations of the eye and may fail to transmit some very low frequency components to the cortex because of neural interactions on the retina. The mathematical function that describes how these frequencies are altered as they pass through the visual system is called the modulation transfer function (Cornsweet, 1970).

Ginsburg (1971) hypothesized that the visual system's attenuation of the high frequency components of visual patterns is responsible for some visual illusions. He reasoned that, if this were the case, illusion stimuli presented on an oscilloscope screen, with the high frequency components filtered out, would show actual contour shifts of the kind usually reported perceptually. He was able to show that such shifts did, in fact, occur for the Mueller-Lyer and Hering illusions.

However, removing the high frequency components of a visual stimulus is analogous to blurring the contours of that stimulus. As we discussed in Chapter 4, such blurring causes shifts in the maxima of stimulation at corners and vertices and thus would lead to the kinds of shifts reported by Ginsburg (1971) for any intersecting line illusion.

However, neither optical aberrations nor Fourier analysis can predict illusory distortions in any configurations that are not composed of converging line segments, including such figures as Coren's dot form or Piaget's horizontal line form of the Mueller-Lyer illusion. Similarly, size illusions, such as the Ebbinghaus, the Jastrow, or the divided line illusion, cannot be predicted by such analyses. In addition, when Ginsburg (1975) attempted to use a Fourier analysis procedure on a subjective contour-inducing configuration, the predictive ability of this technique clearly broke down. The analysis led to a complex lattice or net-like grid of line over the array. However, in such patterns one perceives only apparent contours, not a complicated interwoven pattern of lines. Thus it seems clear that any theory based on spatial frequency analysis is somewhat limited in its applicability to illusions.

Perception as Hypothesis and Ecological Cue Validity

Perception as hypothesis is a global description that encompasses the large class of perceptual theories that argue that associations between patterns of stimulation and object characteristics are built up as the result of an individual's experience with the physical world. On the basis of the available input, the observer makes a guess or forms a hypothesis about the nature of the target. This hypothesis is then represented in consciousness as a percept. It is quite clear that this set of theories is similar to that originally offered by Helmhotz (1856, 1860, 1866/1962) and revived by the transactional theorists (Ames, 1946, 1951) as we discussed in Chapters 1 and 7.

According to this set of theories, the perception that occurs is the result of a process whereby observers extract the appropriate information from the current input and formulate a hypothesis about it, which is then attributed to the object in consciousness. To the extent that the information extraction process is subject to distortion, illusions are likely to arise. For example, in such theories, size constancy arises because observers extract relative size and distance information from the current input and formulate a hypothesis about the object's actual size. An inappropriate hypothesis about the object's distance or size will result in a distortion of the represented extent in consciousness. In a similar fashion, subjective contours may arise from the hypothesis that the gaps in the inducing stimulus are due to an object in front of the figural components hiding parts of it. Illusions of direction may arise from misapplied hypotheses about the distance or orientation of contours relative to the observer.

Unfortunately, the suggestion that transactions or interactions with the environment form the basis of hypothesis formation strategies is too general to permit precise predictions. It has proved difficult to specify in advance which characteristics of the environment are relevant and thus which type of hypothesis will result. Most explanations of illusory distortions based on this type of theory have, therefore, been formulated on a *post hoc* basis. Some attempts at more precise specification have been offered by researchers using a picture perception approach to illusions, as we discussed in Chapter 7.

An interesting variant on the perception as hypothesis theme was provided by Brunswik (1956). He noted that certain cues in the input array tend to correlate with certain physical properties of the environment. Thus converging lines in the array (perspective) usually indicate recession in distance. According to this theory, we learn about the validity of such cues as a function of our experience. For this theory, distortions arise when a cue normally correlated with some aspect of environmental change is inappropriate for the present stimulus pattern. Thus, according to this theory, targets superimposed upon an array of converging lines on a flat piece of paper are processed as if they were at different distances, resulting in a size distortion.

Like perception as hypothesis, perception based on the validity of ecological cues can explain illusions of direction, extent, and subjective contours. This theory has the added advantage that it provides a specific predictive mechanism, assuming that it is possible to determine which cues in the environment are based on our experience with them, normally utilized for perception.

Perception as a Constructive Process, Phase Sequences, and Schematic Maps

A number of theorists have proposed that, through interaction with the environment, the observer builds up memory traces for previously processed visual stimuli and that these stored representations are then utilized to process subsequent visual inputs. Hebb (1949) was one of the first theorists to propose such a system. He suggested that neural networks, known as cell assemblies, which correspond to specific stimulus features, are gradually built up. These cell assemblies are then combined into phase sequences that represent more complex parts of objects or even entire objects. In some respects, a cell assembly is an empirically formed feature analyzer. However, this theory differs from feature analysis theory in that both cell assemblies and phase sequences are probably capable of handling the existence of subjective contours. The nature of the interactions among these hypothetical stored representations has not been sufficiently specified to permit the prediction of most illusory phenomena of extent or direction.

Similar problems arise with more recent proposals that perception is a constructive process based on interactions with the environment (Hochberg, 1968; Neisser, 1967). Unlike Hebb, these theorists did not try to specify an underlying physiological component for the perceptual process. However, they talked about perception in terms of matches between the incoming perceptual stimulation and stored representations of previous perceptual processing. These stored representations, which Hochberg (1968) called schematic maps, specify both the features of the objects and the relationships between the features. Hochberg proposed that the observer hypothesizes which schematic map will provide the best fit to the incoming stimulus information. The incoming information is then matched to the information in the map and, if the fit is a reasonable one, the perception itself is based on the complete map. Like Hebb's theory, however, these theories of constructive perception have been primarily concerned with veridical perception and the problem of illusions has, for the most part, been ignored.

Information Processing

There is one contemporary approach to perception that probably does not warrant designation as a theory but rather should be called an approach or a methodology. This viewpoint was originally designed by Shannon (1948) and Wiener (1949) to describe the operation of radio and telephone systems. Its application has been attempted with many kinds of information-processing systems, including perceptual ones. In this approach, a communications system is divided into levels or stages of processing. One first begins with a stimulus (for instance, a voice spoken into a microphone) which is then transmitted in some physical form (the radio waves) to a decoding mechanism (the radio receiver) and then translated into the final indentification response (in the nervous system of the listener). It is but a small step to identify such stages as analogous to a perceptual system such as vision, where the stimulus object is transmitted as light rays to the eye and then processed by the visual system of the observer. The fidelity of the final phenomenological response is measured by its correlation with the original stimulus. Systematic distortions would indicate the presence of illusions. Thus an information processing approach assumes that, if the appropriate techniques could be devised, it should be possible to sample and examine the contents of stimulation at every stage, at every point in time, and at every level in the nervous system. By systematically comparing these samples at different times and locations with the original stimulus and with the perceiver's phenomenological report, it should be possible to indicate the nature of the processing that the stimulus undergoes.

Such an approach suggests that we may be forced to deal with many sources of distortion, at many points in the visual processing system, each leading to a systematic form of nonveridicality in consciousness. It should be clear to the reader that, in many respects, this entire volume has followed an information-processing approach as it attempted to synthesize illusions from a variety of structural and strategy mechanisms.

Overview

We should now glance back across the five contemporary theoretical approaches we have briefly outlined above to see how well they deal with the problem of visual illusions. At least one approach, information pick-up, explicitly denies any interest in illusions. Phase sequences and schematic maps may be able to handle subjective contours (by treating them as real contours) but have not been formulated in a way designed to deal with most other illusions. Perception as a hypothesis-testing procedure can explain the presence of illusions but lacks predictive specificity. Feature analysis and Fourier analysis can explain some intersecting line illusions but do not seem to be able to handle other kinds of configurations. The information-processing approach, although it cannot properly be called a theory, seems to provide the most fruitful avenue for the study of illusory phenomena.

Thus, despite the prevalence of visual illusions in normal perception, most contemporary theories have treated them as if they were special cases, not to be dealt with directly or utilized to form the core of perceptual theory. Yet it is interesting that virtually every contemporary perceptual theory finds it necessary to explain size and shape constancy, which, as we have noted, may merely be another form of illusion.

ILLUSIONS AS EXPERIMENTAL TOOLS

Most of this treatise attempts to analyze illusions as a part of the normal perceptual process. It is reasonable, therefore, to expect that they can serve as important tools in the study of visual perception. At the very least they serve as test cases for the more general theories of perception, since any theory must be able to explain visual illusions in order to be complete.

The methodological importance of illusions lies in their ability to provide a way of separating the subjective experience of a visual input from the emitted response. An example of how this may be done involves the question of whether information that is not available in consciousness may be encoded at some level in the visual system. This is often referred to as subliminal perception. Illusions are useful in this context since the magnitude of the distortion varies continuously and the illusion strength can thus provide a measure of the effectiveness of the "unseen" stimulus. With this in mind, a number of experimenters have employed the Mueller-Lyer illusion, exposing it in such a manner that the test shafts were clearly visible but the illusion-inducing wings were at subthreshold levels. Under these conditions, even though observers do not report seeing the wings, they manifest a measurable illusory distortion in the length of the test shaft. Bressler (1931) was even able to demonstrate that the magnitude of the illusion decreased as the wings, already below the threshold of consciousness, were made still fainter and hence presumably became less effective stimuli for the visual system. Smith and Henriksson (1955) conducted a similar experiment using a variant of the Ehrenfel's illusion in which a square is superimposed upon a series of converging lines (Figure 3.1D). In this experiment, the lines were presented briefly, followed by the square. When data from the observers who never reported seeing the lines were analyzed, the usual distortion of the square into an apparent trapezoid was found. Taken together, these experiments indicate that stimuli too degraded to elicit any report of conscious perception still have the ability to enter into the visual processing sequence at some level of effectiveness. Since the directions of the distortion of test items are not usually known to naïve subjects, it is unlikely that the observer can affect the result by consciously manipulating his response in order to "please" the experimenter, a problem that arises frequently when recognition stimuli are used in subliminal perception experiments.

An interesting modification on this basic paradigm extends the usefulness of this approach beyond the investigation of subliminal stimuli. Trimble and Eriksen (1966) utilized an illusion configuration in a signal detection paradigm in order to address the difficult problem of what is meant by a perceptual threshold. Generally speaking, accepted psychological practice is to use a statistical criterion for the determination of the threshold point, rather than requiring the complete conscious awareness of the stimulus. A stimulus that is detected 50% of the time is usually said to be "at threshold." Between the point at which the observer reports the stimulus 0% of the time and the point at which he reports it 50% of the time, it is clear that some stimulus information, of which the subject is occasionally aware, is being processed. Let us now ask the threshold question in a different manner. Suppose that a stimulus is no longer effective in altering any aspect of the visual response. Under these circumstances, it seems reasonable to conclude that the stimulus is *functionally* subthreshold. Using the Mueller-Lyer figure, Trimble and Eriksen (1966) varied the luminosity of the fins and found that, when the stimulus levels were low enough to give a d' of less than 1 the usual illusory distortion was no longer reported. Above these levels, the illusion manifests itself to a measurable degree. This suggests that, below this signal detection cut-off, the usual visual processes are not sufficiently aroused to produce the "normal" distortion. Thus a d' of less than 1 may serve as an index of the point at which stimuli lose their effectiveness in the visual channels. Hence this point may represent the "functional threshold."

Miller, Hennessey, and Leibowitz (1973) utilized a different paradigm to study the limits of conscious experience. They used a group of subjects who were highly hypnotizable and reportedly capable of negative hallucinations. A negative hypnotic hallucination essentially involves a procedure by which parts of the figure are hypnotically ablated so that the observer reports that he is no longer consciously aware of the stimulus. Critics of this procedure have asked whether the lack of response represents merely a change in verbal report or an actual change in the percept. It is clear that this question has important implications for the understanding of the nature of hypnosis. In this particular experiment, observers were hypnotized and asked to suppress the inducing lines in the Ponzo illusion. Despite the fact that the inducing lines were no longer reported in consciousness, the usual distortion was obtained, implying that the hypnotically erased information was still being processed within the visual system in the usual manner.

The three preceding problems—subliminal perception, functional threshold, and hypnotic hallucinations—provide interesting examples of the usefulness of illusions as experimental tools.

There are other ways in which illusion paradigms might be used as secondary indicators of the nature of the percept under circumstances where the direct response measures produce ambiguous results. For example, children develop the concepts of "bigger" and "smaller" quite early and readily express them linguistically. There are a variety of more complex concepts that children seem to have difficulty expressing until they are older, including the notions of similarity or complexity. Illusion manipulations could be used to circumvent the difficulty of explaining the meaning of "similarity" to a young child. For instance, Coren and Miller (1974) noted that the magnitude of the Ebbinghaus illusion diminished as the similarity between the test and inducing forms diminished. It thus seems likely that one could invert the process and use the magnitude of the illusion as a dependent variable in order to obtain estimates of the similarity between test and inducing stimuli in children too young to make similarity ratings. They need only be old enough to make comparative size ratings.

Another instance of the use of illusions for "nonillusory" research comes from Coren and Girgus (1977), who reviewed the systematic variations in illusion magnitude obtained as one altered some of the stimulus parameters within the configurations. They then correlated these changes with stimulus properties within pictures, which allowed them to draw a number of conclusions about the nature of size constancy scaling in picture perception. These results were then checked against actual data from picture perception, revealing several places where size constancy in pictures differs from size constancy in natural settings.

These are but a few examples of how illusions may be used as an index to monitor other psychological factors. Theoretically, by using illusion magnitude as a dependent variable, one ought to be able to assess changes in the amplitude of the response of any of the mechanisms initially responsible for the formation of the distortion. In a sense, it should be possible to develop techniques that use the magnitude of converging line illusions to investigate the amount of blur in the retinal image, the gain of lateral inhibition, or the interaction, fatigue, and satiation of cortical units responsive to specific stimulus features. In terms of the investigation of perceptual strategies, it ought to be possible to use illusions as an estimate of the efficiency of comparative judgmental processes or pictorial depth perception. Illusion decrement might be useful as an index of the efficiency of a sensory motor learning. Unfortunately, too few studies have made use of these resources.

Of more than a thousand papers published on the topic of illusions since the middle of the nineteenth century, most have been attempts to present new illusory distortions or to explain illusory distortions already known, while only a few investigators have attempted to use illusions as tools for investigating other psychological processes. Perhaps this displays a reluctance stemming from the fact that many psychologists feel that we know too little about the mechanisms involved in illusion formation to use them as a tool to investigate other perceptual phenomena. Still these same investigators often use variations of size constancy as an index of higher level processing, despite the fact that our knowledge in this area is no more certain. We unhesitatingly use variations in reaction time as a dependent measure, despite the fact that the basic mechanisms underlying the transition from stimulus to final response still remain a mystery. These latter techniques are useful nonetheless, because they manifest systematic changes in speed, strength, or accuracy as a function of secondary manipulations, thus serving as indices of changes in the mechanisms under consideration. It is, thus, the pattern of change in constancy scaling, reaction time, or even illusion magnitude that may serve as an index of changes in the process under study and thus provide us with new tools for the exploration of the perceptual process.

A BACKWARD GLANCE FORWARD

The illusion configurations that we have dealt with in this book are, in actuality, merely lines scattered across paper surfaces. The reason that they have provoked so much attention, speculation, theorizing, and experimentation is because the phenomenology they elicit is not at all simple but involves many levels of information processing and analysis within the visual system. The interactions between the physical relationships displayed on the surface of the paper and our phenomenological representation of the lines still remain to be fully explained.

Nonetheless, some psychologists seem to consider these phenomena as being too "lightweight" or "unimportant" to warrant serious study when there are more "practical" problems that need to be dealt with. The theoretical importance of the phenomena should be clear to the reader by now, and one need not go far to show how real-world problems arise from the faulty phenomenology that is characteristic of illusions.

On December 4, 1965, a TWA Boeing 707 and an Eastern Airlines Lockheed 1049C were enroute to John F. Kennedy International Airport and to Newark

Airport, respectively. Both were converging on the New York area, the Boeing 707 at its assigned altitude of 11,000 feet and the Lockheed at its assigned altitude of 10,000 feet. At that time, the area was overcast and the cloud tops protruded above a height of 10,000 feet. The clouds were generally higher in the north than in the south and seemed to form an upward-sloping bar of white against the blue background of the sky. Within a few moments of each other, the crews of both aircraft perceived what appeared to be an imminent collision between the two planes. They rapidly began evasive maneuvers. The Lockheed aircraft pulled up, and the Boeing rolled first to the right and then to the left. The two aircraft collided at approximately 11,000 feet. The structural damage to the Lockheed was sufficient to force it to land in an open field, where it was destroyed by impact and fire. There were four fatalities and forty-nine nonfatal injuries. The U.S. Civil Aeronautics Board attributed the collision to a misjudgment of altitude separation by the crew of the Lockheed aircraft because of an "optical illusion" created by the upward-sloping contours of the cloup tops. Four persons died and 49 were injured through the operation of a simple effect that we mimic on paper with simple lines and call the Poggendorff illusion. Perhaps the idea that visual illusions are interesting but relatively unimportant oddities of perception is itself merely another illusion.

References

Adam, J. A note on the visual illusions of direction. *Australian Journal of Psychology,* 1964, *16,* 53–56.

Adrian, E. D., & Matthews, R. The action of light on the eye: III. The interaction of retinal neurones. *Journal of Physiology,* 1928, *65,* 273–298.

Ames, A. Some demonstrations concerned with the origin and nature of our sensations (what we experience). Hanover, New Hampshire, 1946 (mimeographed).

Ames, A. Visual perception and rotating trapezoidal window. *Psychological Monographs,* 1951, #324.

Ames, A., & Proctor, C. A. Dioptrics of the eye. *Journal of the Optical Society of America,* 1921, *5,* 22–35.

Ames, L. B., Learned, J., Metraux, R., & Walker, R. Development of perception in the young child as observed in responses to the Rorschach test blots. *Journal of Genetic Psychology,* 1953, *82,* 183–204.

Anderson, N. H. A simple model for information integration. In R. P. Abelson et al. (Eds.), *Theories of cognitive consistency: A sourcebook.* Chicago: Rand McNally, 1968.

Anderson, N. H. Averaging model applied to the size–weight illusion. *Perception and Psychophysics,* 1970, *77,* 153–170.

Aristotle. De memoria et reminiscenta. In J. I. Beare (Trans.), W. D. Ross (Ed.), *The works of Aristotle III.* Oxford: Clarendon Press, 1931.

Aubert, H. *Grundzuege der physiologischen Optik.* Leipzig: Engelmann, 1876.

Auerbach, F. Erklaerung der Brentano'schen optischen Tauschung. *Zeitschrift fur Psychologie,* 1894, *7,* 152–160.

Avery, G. C., & Day, R. H. Basis of the horizontal-vertical illusion. *Journal of Experimental Psychology,* 1969, *81,* 376–280.

Baldwin, J. M. The effect of size contrast upon judgements of positions in the retinal field. *Psychological Review,* 1895, *2,* 224–259.

Barclay, R., & Comalli, P. Age differences in perceptual learning on the Mueller–Lyer illusion. *Psychonomic Science,* 1970, *19,* 323–325.

Barlow, H. B., Fitzhugh, R., & Kuffler, S. W. Change of organization in the receptive fields of the cats retina during dark adaptation. *Journal of Physiology,* 1957, *137,* 327–337.

Bates, M. A study of Mueller–Lyer illusion, with special reference to paradoxical movement and the effect of attitude. *American Journal of Psychology*, 1923, *34*, 46–72.

Bayer, C. A., & Pressey, A. W. Geometric illusions as a function of pigmentation of the fundus oculi and target size. *Psychonomic Science*, 1972, *26*, 77–79.

Beh, H. C., & Wendroth, P. M. The effect of variation of frame shape on the angular function of the rod-and-frame illusion. *Perception & Psychophysics*, 1972, *11*, 35–37.

Beh, H. C., Wendroth, P. M., & Purcell, A. T. The angular function of a rod-and-frame illusion. *Perception and Psychophysics*, 1971, *9*, 353–355.

Bekesy, G. von. The ear. *Scientific American*, August, 1957.

Bekesy, G. von. Neural inhibitory units of the eye and skin. Quantitative description of contrast phenomena. *Journal of the Optical Society of America*, 1960, *50*, 1060–1070.

Bekesy, G. von. *Sensory inhibition.* Princeton, N.J.: Princeton University Press, 1967.

Benussi, V. Zur Psychologie des Gestalterfassens (die Müller–Lyersche Figur). In A. Meinong (Ed.), *Untersuchurgen zur Gegenstands Theorie und Psychologie.* Leipzig: Johann Ambrosius Burth, 1904.

Berliner, A., & Berliner, S. The distortion of straight and curved lines in geometric fields. *American Journal of Psychology*, 1948, *61*, 153–166.

Berry, J. W. Temme and Eskimo perceptual skills. *International Journal of Psychology*, 1966, *1*, 119–128.

Berry, J. W. Ecology, perceptual development and the Mueller–Lyer illusion. *British Journal of Psychology*, 1968, *59*, 205–210.

Berry, J. W. Mueller–Lyer susceptibility: Culture, ecology, race? *International Journal of Psychology*, 1971, *6*, 193–197.

Biervliet, J. J. van. Nouvelles measures des illusions visuelles chez les adultes et chez les enfants. *Revue Philosophique.* 1896, *41*, 169–181.

Binet, A. La mesure des illusions visuelles chez les enfants. *Revue Philosophique*, 1895, *40*, 11–25.

Bishop, P. O., Burke, W., & Davis, R. Activation of single lateral geniculate cells by stimulation of either optic nerve. *Science*, 1959, *130*, 506–507.

Blakemore, C., Carpenter, R. H. S., & Georgeson, M. A. Lateral inhibition between orientation detectors in the human visual system. *Nature* (London), 1970, *228*, 37–39.

Blix, M. Die sog. Poggendorff's optische Fauschungen. *Skandinauisches Archiv fur Physiologie*, 1902, *13*, 193–228.

Bock, R. D., & Kolakowski, D. A. Further evidence of sex-linked major-gene influence on human spatial visualizing ability. *American Journal of Human Genetics*, 1973, *25*, 1–14.

Bogen, J. E. The other side of the brain, II: An oppositional model. *Bulletin of the Los Angeles Neurological Societies*, 1969, *34*, 135–162.

Boring, E. G. *Sensation and perception in the history of experimental psychology.* New York: Appleton-Century-Crofts, 1942.

Bornstein, M. Color vision and color naming: A psychophysical hypothesis of cultural difference. *Psychological Bulletin*, 1973, *80*, 257–285.

Brentano, F. Ueber ein optisches Paradoxen. *Journal of Psychology*, 1892, *3*, 349–258.

Bressler, J. Illusion in the case of subliminal visual stimulation. *Journal of General Psychology*, 1931, *5*, 244–251.

Brindley, G. S., & Merton, P. A. The absence of position sense in the human eye. *Journal of Physiology*, 1960, *153*, 127–130.

Brown, J. F., & Voth, A. C. The path of scan movement as a function of the vector field. *American Journal of Psychology*, 1937, *49*, 543–563.

Brunot, C. Les illusions optiques. *Revue Scientifique Paris*, 1893, 3 Ser., *52*, 210–212.

Brunswik, E. *Wahrnehmung und Gegenstandswelt: Grundlegung einer Psychologie von Gegenstand her.* Leipzig: Deuticke, 1934.

Brunswik, E. *Perception and the representative design of psychological experiments* (2nd ed.). Berkeley: University of California Press, 1956.

Burnham, C. A. Decrement of the Mueller–Lyer illusion with saccadic and tracking eye movements. *Perception and Psychophysics,* 1968, *3,* 424–426.

Burns, B. D., & Pritchard, R. Geometrical illusions and the response of neurones in the cat's visual cortex to angle patterns. *Journal of Physiology,* 1971, *213,* 599–616.

Byram, G. M. The physical and photochemical basis of visual resolving power. I. The distribution of illumination in retinal images. *Journal of the Optical Society of America,* 1944, *34,* 571–591. (a)

Byram, G.M. The physical and photochemical basis of visual resolving power. II. Visual acuity and the photochemistry of the retina. *Journal of the Optical Society of America,* 1944, *34,* 718–738. (b)

Cameron, E. H., & Steele, W. M. The Poggendorff illusion. *Psychological Review,* 1905, 83–111.

Campbell, F. W., & Gubisch, R. W. Optical quality of the human eye. *Journal of Physiology* (London), 1966, *186,* 558–578.

Carlson, J. A. Effect of instructions and perspective-drawing ability on perceptual constancies and geometrical illusion. *Journal of Experimental Psychology,* 1966, *72,* 874–879.

Carter, D. J., & Pollack, R. H. The great illusion controversy: A glimpse. *Perceptual and Motor Skills,* 1968, *27,* 705–706.

Chapanis, A., & Manken, D. A. The vertical-horizontal illusion in a visually rich environment. *Perception and Psychophysics,* 1967, *2,* 249–255.

Chiang, C. A new theory to explain geometrical illusions produced by crossing lines. *Perception and Psychophysics,* 1968, *3,* 174–176.

Clem, R. K., & Pollack, R. H. Illusion magnitude as a function of visual field expsoure. *Perception and Psychophysics,* 1975, *17,* 450–454.

Coltheart, M. Visual feature-analyzers and aftereffects of tilt and curvature. *Psychological Review,* 1971, *78,* 114–121.

Cooper, L. A., & Weintraub, D. J. Delboeuf-type circle illusions: Interactions among luminance, temporal characteristics and inducing-figure variations. *Journal of Experimental Psychology,* 1970, *85,* 15–82.

Coren, S. The influence of optical aberrations on the magnitude of the Poggendorff illusion. *Perception and Psychophysics,* 1969, *6,* 185–186.

Coren, S. Lateral inhibition and the Wundt–Hering illusion. *Psychonomic Science,* 1970, *18,* 341. (a)

Coren, S. Lateral inhibition and geometric illusions. *Quarterly Journal of Experimental Psychology,* 1970, *22,* 274–278. (b)

Coren, S. A size contrast illusion without physical size difference. *American Journal of Psychology,* 1971, *84,* 565–566.

Coren, S. Subjective contour and apparent depth. *Psychological Review,* 1972, *79,* 359–367.

Coren, S., & Festinger, L. An alternative view of the "Gibson normalization effect." *Perception and Psychophysics,* 1967, *2,* 621–626.

Coren, S., & Girgus, J. S. Density of human lens pigmentation: In vivo measures over an extended age range. *Vision Research,* 1972, *12,* 343–346. (a)

Coren, S., & Girgus, J. S. Differentiation and decrement in the Mueller–Lyer illusion. *Perception and Psychophysics,* 1972, *12,* 466–470. (b)

Coren, S., & Girgus, J. S. Illusion decrement in intersecting line fugures. *Psychonomic Science,* 1972, *26,* 108–110. (c)

Coren, S., & Girgus, J. S. Visual spatial illusions: Many explanations. *Science,* 1973, *179,* 5034.

Coren, S., & Girgus, J. S. Transfer of illusion decrement as a function of perceived similarity. *Journal of Experimental Psychology*, 1974, *102*, 881–887.

Coren, S., & Girgus, J. S. A size illusion based upon a minimal interposition cue. *Perception*, 1975, *4*, 251–254.

Coren, S., & Girgus, J. S. Perceptual development: A distorted view. In K. F. Riegel & J. A. Meacham (Eds.), *The developing individual in a changing wolrd. Vol. 1. Historical and cultural issues.* The Hague: Mouton, 1976.

Coren, S., & Girgus, J. S. Illusions and constancies. In W. Epstein (Ed.), *Stability and constancy in visual perception: Mechanisms and processes.* New York: Wiley, 1978.

Coren, S., Girgus, J. S., Ehrlichman, H., & Hakstian, A. R. An empirical taxonomy of visual illusions. *Perception and Psychophysics*, 1976, *20*, 129–137.

Coren, S., & Hoenig, P. Eye movements and decrement in the Oppel–Kundt illusion. *Perception and Psychophysics*, 1972, *12*, 224–225.

Coren, S., & Miller, J. Size contrast as a function of figural similarity. *Perception and Psychophysics*, 1974.

Coren, S., & Porac, C. Family correlations in visual-geometric illusions. *Behavior Genetics*, 1977, *7*, 50.

Coren, S., & Theodor, L. H. Subjective contour: The inadequacy of brightness contrast as an explanation. *Bulletin of the Psychonomic Society*, 1975, *6*, 87–89.

Cornsweet, T. N. *Visual perception.* New York: Academic Press, 1970.

Craig, F. E. Variations in the illusion of filled and unfilled tactual space. *American Journal of Psychology*, 1931, *43*, 112–114.

Crosland, H. R., Taylor, H. R., & Newsom, J. Practice and improvability in the Mueller–Lyer illusion in relation to intelligence. *Journal of Genetic Psychology*, 1929, *2*, 290–306.

Dawson, J. L. M. *Psychological effects of social change in a West African community.* Unpublished doctoral thesis, Oxford University, 1963.

Dawson, J. L. Cultural and physiological influences upon spatial-perceptual processes in West Africa: I. *International Journal of Psychology*, 1967, *2*, 115–128.

Dawson, J. L. Effects of sex hormones on cognitive style in rats and men. *Behavior Genetics*, 1972, *2*, 21–42.

Day, R. H. On the stereoscropic observation of geometric illusion. *Perceptual and Motor skills*, 1961, *13*, 247–258.

Day, R. H. The effects of repeated trials and prolonged fixation on error in the Mueller–Lyer figure. *Psychological Monographs*, 1962, *76* No. 14 (Whole No. 533). (a)

Day, R. H. Excitatory and inhibitory processes as the basis of contour shift and negative after-effect. *Psychologia*, 1962, *5*, 185–193. (b)

Day, R. H. Inappropriate constancy explanation of spatial distortions. *Nature*, 1965, *207*, 891–893.

Day, R. H. Visual spatial illusion: A general explanation. *Science*, 1972, *175*, 1335–1340.

Day, R. H., & Dickinson, R. G. The Poggendorff illusion: Apparent misalignment which is not attributable to apparent orientation of the transversals. *Quarterly Journal of Experimental Psychology*, 1975, *27*, 551–557.

Delabarre, E. B. A method of recording eye movements. *American Journal of Psychology*, 1897, *9*, 572–574.

Delboeuf, J. L. R. Sur une nouvelle illusion d'optique. *Academie Royale des Sciences, de Lettres et des Beaux Arts de Belgique. Bulletins*, 1892, *24*, 545–558.

Dengler, M. A test of constancy scaling theory in a modified Mueller–Lyer illusion. *Perception and Psychophysics*, 1972, *12*, 339–341.

Denton, J. J. The influence of visual pattern on perceived speed. *Road Research Laboratory Report*, LR409, 1971.

Deregowski, J. B. Difficulties in pictorial depth perception in Africa. *British Journal of Psychology*, 1968, *57*, 195–204.

Deregowski, J. B. Perception of the two-pronged trident by two- and three-dimensional perceivers. *Journal of Experimental Psychology*, 1969, *82*, 9–13.

Deregowski, J. B. Illusion and Culture. In R. L. Gregory & G. H. Gombrich (Eds.), *Illusion in nature and art*. New York: Charles Scribner Sons, 1973.

Deregowski, J. B., Muldrow, E. S., & Muldrow, W. F. Pictorial recognition in a remote Ethiopian population. *Perception*, 1973, *1*, 417–425.

DeSisto, M. J., & Moses, F. L. Saccadic eye movement response to Mueller–Lyer stimuli. Paper presented at the meeting of the Eastern Psychological Association, Washington, D.C., 1968.

DeValois, R. Color vision mechanisms in the monkey. *Journal of General Physiology*, 1960, *43* (supplement part 2), 115–128.

Dewar, R. E. The effect of angle between the oblique lines on the decrement of the Mueller–Lyer illusion with extended practice. *Perception and Psychophysics*, 1967, *2*, 426–428. (a)

Dewar, R. E. Stimulus determinants of the magnitude of the Mueller–Lyer illusion. *Perceptual and Motor Skills*, 1967, *24*, 708–710. (b)

Dewer, R. E. Distribution of practice and the Mueller–Lyer illusion. *Perception and Psychophysics*, 1968, *3*, 246–248.

Diogenes Laertius. *Lives and opinions of eminent philosophers*. (R. D. Hicks, trans.). Cambridge, Mass.: Harvard University Press, 1925.

Ditchburn, R. W., & Ginsborg, B. L. Vision with a stabilized retinal image. *Nature*, 1952, *170*, 36–37.

Dominguez, K. A. A study of visual illusions in the monkey. *Journal of Genetic Psychology*, 1954, *85*, 105–127.

Doyle, M. Perceptual skill development: A possible resource for the intellectually handicapped. *American Journal of Mental Deficiency*, 1967, *71*, 776–782.

Ducharme, R., Delorme, A., & Boulard, M. The Oppel–Kundt illusion in the white rat. *Perceptual and Motor Skills*, 1967, *24*, 1271–1276.

Duecker, G. Untersuchugen uber geometrisch-optische Tauschugen bei Wirbeltieren. *Tierpsychologie*, 1966, *23*, 452–496.

Ebbinghaus, H. *Grundzuege der Psychologie*, Vols. I & II. Leipzig: Viet, 1902.

Ebert, P. C., & Pollack, R. H. Magnitude of the Mueller–Lyer illusion as a function of lightness contrast, viewing time, and fundus pigmentation. *Psychonomic Science*, 1972, *26*, 347–348.

Ebert, P. C., & Pollack, R. H. The effect of lightness contrast, tachistoscopic duration and fundus pigmentation on the magnitude of the Mueller–Lyer illusion. *American Journal of Optometry and Archives of American Academy of Optometry*, 1973, *50*, 872–878. (a)

Ebert, P. C., & Pollack, R. H. Some factors affecting magnitude of the Mueller–Lyer illusion. *Perceptual and Motor Skills*, 1973, *37*, 433–434. (b)

Ehrenfels, C. V. Ueber Gestaltqualitaten. *Vierteljahrsschrift fur Wissenchaftliche Philosophe*, 1890, *14*, 249.

Ehrenstein, W. *Probleme der ganzheit psychologischen Wahrenhumungslehre*. Leipzig: Barth, 1954.

Einthoven, W. Eine einfache physiologische Erklarung fur verschiedene geometrisch-optische Tauschungen. *Pfluger's Archiv fur Physiologie*, 1898, *71*, 1–43.

Ellis, H. D. Illusions, aftereffects, and iconic memory. *Psychonomic Science*, 1969, *17*, 328–245.

Ercoles–Guzzoni, A. M., & Fiorentini, A. Stimultaneous contrast effect produced by nonuniform coloured fields. *Fondazioni Giorgio Ronchi, Florence. Atti*, 1958, *13*, 135–144.

Eriksson, E. S. A field theory of visual illusions. *British Journal of Psychology*, 1970, *61*, 451–466.

Erlebacher, A., & Sekuler, R. Explanation of the Mueller–Lyer illusion: Confusion theory examined. *Journal of Experimental Psychology*, 1969, *80*, 462–467.

Evans, C. R., & Marsden, R. P. A study of the effect of perfect retinal stabilization on some well-known visual illusions, using the after-image as a method of compensating for eye movements. *British Journal of Physiological Optics*, 1966, *23*, 242–248.

Farquar, M., & Leibowitz, H. W. The magnitude of the Ponzo illusion as a function of age for large and for small stimulus configurations. *Psychonomic Science*, 1971, *25*, 97–99.

Fechner, G. *Elements of Psychophysics*. (H. Adler, trans.). New York: Holt, 1966. (Originally published, 1860.) New York: Holt, 1966.

Fellows, B. J. Reversal of the Mueller–Lyer illusion with changes in length of the interfins line. *Quarterly Journal of Psychology*, 1967, *19*, 208–214.

Fellows, B. J. The reverse Mueller–Lyer illusion and "enclosure." *British Journal of Psychology*, 1968, *59*, 369–372.

Festinger, L., Burnham, C. A., Ono, H., & Bamer, D. Efference and the conscious experience of perception. *Journal of Experimental Psychology Monograph*, 1967, (Whole No. 637).

Festinger, L., White, C. W., & Allyn, M. R. Eye movements and decrement in the Mueller–Lyer illusion. *Perception and Psychophysics*, 1968, *3*, 376–382.

Fick, A. *De errone quodam optic asymmetria bulbi effecto* Marburg: Koch, 1851.

Filehne, W. Die geometrische-optischen Tauschungen als Nachwirkungen der im koperlichen sehen erworbenen Erfahrung. *Zeitschrift fur Psychologie und Physiologie der Sinnesorgane*, 1898, *17*, 15–61.

Fisher, G. H. Gradients of distortion seen in the context of the Ponzo illusion and other contours. *Quarterly Journal of Experimental Psychology*, 1968, *20*, 212–217.

Fisher, G. H. Towards a new explanation for the geometrical illusions. I. The properties of contours which induce illusory distortion. *British Journal of Psychology*, 1969, *60*, 170–187. (a)

Fisher, G. H. An experimental study of angular subtension. *Quarterly Journal of Experimental Psychology*, 1969, *21*, 356–366. (b)

Fisher, G. H. An experimental and theoretical appraisal of the perspective and size-constancy theories of illusions. *Quarterly Journal of Experimental Psychology*, 1970, *22*, 631–652.

Fisher, G. H. Geometrical illusions and figural after-effects: II. The mechanism and its location. *Vision Research*, 1971, *11*, 289–309.

Fisher, G. H. Towards a new explanation for the geometrical illusions: II Apparent depth or contour proximity? *British Journal of Psychology*, 1973, *64*, 607–621.

Fisher, G. H., & Lucas, A. Illusions in concrete situations: I. Introduction and demonstrations. *Ergonomics*, 1969, *12*, 11–24.

Fisher, G. H., & Lucas, A. Geometrical illusions and figural after-effects. The distorting and distorted components of illusions. *Vision Research*, 1970, *10*, 393–404.

Fraisse, P., Ehrlich, S., & Vurpillot, E. Etudes de la centration perceptive par la method tachistoscopique. *Archives de Psychologie*, 1956, *35*, 193–214.

Fraisse, P., & Vautrey, P. The influence of ages, sex, and specialized training on the vertical-horizontal illusion. *Quarterly Journal of Experimental Psychology*. 1956, *8*, 114–120.

Francois, J. *Heredity in ophthalmology*. St. Louis: C.V. Mosby Co., 1961.

Fraser, J. A new illusion of direction. *British Journal of Psychology*, 1908, *8*, 49–54.

Freeman, K. *The pre-Socratic philosophers: A companion to Diels Fragment der Vorsokratiker*, 3rd edition. Oxford: Basil, Blackwell, 1953.

Fry, G. A. Mechanisms subserving simultaneous brightness contrast. *American Journal of Optometry*, 1948, *25*, 162–178.

Fry, G. A. *Blur of the retinal image.* Columbus, Ohio: Ohio State University Press, 1953.

Ganz, L. Lateral inhibition and the location of visual contours: An analysis of figural after-effects. *Vision Research,* 1964, *4,* 465–481.

Ganz, L. Is the figural after-effect? *Psychological Bulletin,* 1966, *66,* 151–165. (a)

Ganz, L. Mechanism of the figural after-effects. *Psychological Review,* 1966, *73,* 128–150. (b)

Gaudreau, J., Lavoie, G., & Delorme, A. La perception des illusions de Mueller–Lyer et d'Oppel–Kundt chez les deficients mentaux. *Canadian Journal of Psychology,* 1963, *14,* 249–256.

Gazzaniga, M. S., Bogan, J. E., & Sperry, R. W. Dyspraxia following division of the cerebral commissures. *Archives of Neurology,* 1967, *16,* 606–612.

Georgeson, M. A., & Blakemore, C. Apparent depth and the Mueller–Lyer illusion. *Perception,* 1973, *2,* 225–234.

Gibson, E. J. *Principles of perceptual learning and development.* New York: Appleton-Century-Crofts, 1969.

Gibson, J. J. Adaptation, after-effect and contrast in the perception of tilted lines: II. Simultaneous contrast and the areal restriction of the after-effect. *Journal of Experimental Psychology,* 1937, *20,* 553–569.

Gibson, J. J. *Perception of the visual world.* Boston: Houghton Mifflin, 1950.

Gibson, J. J. What is form? *Psychological Review,* 1951, *58,* 403–412.

Gibson, J. J. Perception as a function as a function of stimulation. In S. Koch (Ed.), *Psychology a study of a science I.* New York: McGraw-Hill, 1959.

Gibson, J. J. *The senses considered as perceptual systems.* Boston: Houghton Mifflin, 1966.

Giering, H. Das Augenmass bei Schalkindern. *Zeitschrift fur Psychologie,* 1905, *39,* 42–87.

Gillam, B. A depth processing theory of the Poggendorff illusion. *Perception and Psychophysics,* 1971, *10,* 211–216.

Gillam, B. The nature of size scaling in the Ponzo and related illusions. *Perception and Psychophysics,* 1973, *14,* 353–357.

Ginsburg, A. P. Psychological correlates of a model of the human visual system. *Proceedings 1971 Naecon,* 1971, 283–290.

Ginsburg, A. P. Is the illusory triangel physical or imaginary? *Nature,* 1975, *257,* 219–220.

Girgus, J. S., & Coren, S. Peripheral and central components in the formation of visual illusions. *American Journal of Optometry and Archives of the American Optometric Society,* 1973, *50,* 533–580. (a)

Girgus, J. S., & Coren, S. The stability of forms under conditions of illusory distortion. *Perceptual and Motor Skills,* 1973, *37,* 715–719. (b)

Girgus, J. S., & Coren, S. Depth cues and constancy scaling in the horizontal-vertical illusion: The bisection error. *Canadian Journal of Psychology,* 1975, *29,* 59–65.

Girgus, J. S., & Coren, S. Age differences and the Poggendorff illusion: The effect of angle size and distance between the parallels. Paper delivered at the meeting of the Canadian Psychological Association, Toronto, June, 1976.

Girgus, J. S., Coren, S., & Agdern, M. The interrelationship between the Ebbinghaus and Delboeuf illusions. *Journal of Experimental Psychology,* 1972, *95,* 453–455.

Girgus, J. S., Coren, S., Durant, M., & Porac, C. The assessment of components involved in illusion formation using a long term decrement procedure. *Perception and Psychophysics,* 1975, *18,* 144–148.

Girgus, J. S., Coren, S., & Fraenkel, R. Levels of perceptual processing in the development of visual illusions. *Developmental Psychology,* 1975, *11,* 268–273.

Girgus, J. S., Coren, S., & Horowitz, L. Peripheral and central components in variants of the Mueller–Lyer illusion. *Perception and Psychophysics,* 1973, *13,* 157–160.

Gogel, W. C. Depth adjacency and the Ponzo illusion. *Perception and Psychophysics,* 1975, *17,* 125–132.

Goldstein, M. B., & Weintraub, D. J. The parallel-less Poggendorff: Virtual contours put the illusion down but not out. *Perception and Psychophysics,* 1973, *11,* 353–354.

Gollin, E. S. Some research problems for developmental psychology. *Child Development,* 1956, *27,* 223–235.

Graham, C. H. Vision III: Some neural correlations. In C. Murchison (Ed.), *Handbook of General Experimental Psychology.* Worcester, Mass.: Clark University Press, 1934.

Granit, R. *Sensory mechanisms of he retina.* New York: Oxford University Press, 1947.

Green, R. T., & Hoyle, E. M. The Poggendorff illusion as a constancy phenomenon. *Nature,* 1963, *200,* 611–612.

Green, R. T., & Hoyle, E. M. Adaptation level and the optico-geometric illusions. *Nature,* 1964, *201,* 1200–1201.

Green, R. T., & Hoyle, E. M. The influence of spatial orientation on the Poggendorff illusion. *Acta Psychologica* (Amsterdam), 1965, *22,* 348–366.

Gregor, A. J., & McPherson, D. A. A study of susceptibility to geometric illusion among cultural subgroups of Australian aborigines. *Psychologia Africana,* 1965, *11,* 1–13.

Gregory, R. L. Distortion of visual space as inappropriate constancy scaling. *Nature,* 1963, *199,* 678–680.

Gregory, R. L. Visual illusions. In B. Foss (Ed.), *New horizons in psychology.* Baltimore: Penguin Books, 1966.

Gregory, R. L. Perceptual illusions and brain models. *Proceedings of the Royal Society,* 1968, Section B, *171,* 279–296. (a)

Gregory, R. L. Visual illusions. *Scientific American,* 1968, *219,* 66–76. (b)

Gregory, R. L. *The intelligent eye.* London: Weidenfeld & Nicolson, 1970.

Gregory, R. L. Cognitive contours. *Nature,* 1972, *238,* 51.

Gregory, R. L., & Harris, J. B. Illusory contours and stereo depth. *Perception and Psychophysics,* 1974, *15,* 411–416.

Gregory, R. L., & Wallace, J. G. Recovery from early blindness: A case study. *Experimental psychology Society Monographs* (Cambridge), 1963, No. 2.

Griggs, R. Constancy scaling theory and the Mueller–Lyer illusion: More disconfirming evidence. *Bulletin of the Psychonomic Society,* 1974, *4,* 168–170.

Gruber, H. E. The relation of perceived size to perceived distance. *American Journal of Psychology,* 1954, *67,* 411–426.

Gubisch, R. W. Optical performance of the human eye. *Journal of the Optical Society of America,* 1967, *57,* 407–415.

Hake, A. W., Faust, G. W., McIntyre, J. S., & Murray, H. G. Relational perception and modes of perceiver operation. *Perception and Psychophysics,* 1967, *2,* 469–478.

Hamilton, V. Susceptibility to the Mueller–Lyer illusion and its relationship to differences in size constancy. *Quarterly Journal of Experimental Psychology,* 1966, *18,* 63–72.

Hanley, C., & Zerbolio, D. J. Developmental changes in five illusions measured by the up-and-down method. *Child Development,* 1965, *36,* 437–452.

Harris, C. S., & Gibson, A. R. Is orientation-specific color adaptation in human vision due to edge detector, after-images or "dipoles"? *Science,* 1968, *162,* 1506–1507.

Hartline, H. K. The receptive fields of optic nerve fibers. *American Journal of Physiology,* 1940, *130,* 690–699.

Hartline, H. K., Wagner, H. G., & Ratliff, F. Inhibition in the eye of Limulus. *Journal of General Physiology,* 1956, *39,* 651–673.

Hatwell, Y. Etude de quelques illusions geometriques tactiles chez les aveugles. *L'Anee Psychologique,* 1960, *60,* 1–27.

Hayami, H., & Miya, K. On the Gestalt apprehension of the Mueller–Lyer figure. *Japanese Journal of Psychology,* 1937, *12,* 525–552.

Hebb. D. O. *The organization of behavior.* New York: Wiley, 1949.

Heinemann, E. G., Tulving, E., & Nachmias, J. The effect of oculomotor adjustments on apparent size. *American Journal of Psychology*, 1959, *72*, 32–45.

Heiss, A. Zum Problem der isolierenden abstraktion. *Neue Psychologie Studien*, 1930, *4*, 285–318.

Helmholtz, H. von. *Populare wissenschraft Vortage*. 1881 (E. Atkinson, trans.). *Popular lectures on scientific subjects*. Longmans, Green: New York, 1903.)

Helmholtz, H. von. *Handbuch der Physiologischen Optik*. Leipzig: Voss, Part I (1856), Part II (1860), Part III (1866). (Translated and republished, New York: Dover, 1962.)

Helson, H. *Adaptation–level theory: An experimental and systematic approach to behavior*. New York: Harper, 1964. (a)

Helson, H. Current trends and issues in adaptation-level theory. *American Psychologist*, 1964, *19*, 26–38. (b)

Hemmendinger, L. Perceptual organization and development as reflected in the structure of Rorschach test responses. *Journal of Projective Techniques*, 1953, *17*, 162–170.

Hering, E. *Beitrage zur Psychologie, Vol. I*. Leipzig: Engleman, 1861.

Herter, K. Weitere Dressurversuche an Fischen. *Zeitschrift fur Verleichende Physiologie*, 1930, *11*, 730–748.

Heuse, G. A. Etudes Psychologiques sur les noirs soudanais et guineens. *Revue de Psychologie des Peuples*, 1957, *12*, 35–68.

Heymans, G. Quantitative Untersuchungen ueber das optische Paradoxen. *Zeitschrift fur Psychologie*, 1896, *9*, 221–255.

Hicks, G. D., & Rivers, W. H. R. The illusion of compared horizontal and vertical lines. *British Journal of Psychology*, 1908, *2*, 243–260.

Hochberg, J. In the minds eye. In R. N. Haber (Ed.), *Contemporary theory and research in visual perception*. New York: Holt, Rinehart & Winston, 1968.

Hochberg, J., & Brooks, V. Pictorial recognition as an unlearned ability: A study of one child's performance. *American Journal of Psychology*, 1962, *75*, 624–628.

Hoenig, P. The effects of eye movements, fixation and figure size on decrement in the Mueller–Lyer illusion. Unpublished doctoral thesis, The New School for Social Research, 1972.

Hofmann, F. F., & Bielchowsky, A. Ueber die Einstellung der scheinbaren Horizontalen und Vertikalen bei Betrachtung eines von schraegen Konturen erfuellten Gesichtsfeldes. *Pflueger's Archiv fur die gesamte Physiologie des Menschen und der Tiere*, 1909, *126*, 453–475.

Holt-Hansen, K. Hering's illusion. *British Journal of Psychology*, 1961, *52*, 317–321.

Hotopf, W. H. The size-constancy theory of visual illusions. *British Journal of Psychology*, 1966, *57*, 307–318.

Hotopf, W. H. N., & Ollereanshaw, C. The regression to right angles tendency and the Poggendorff illusion, I. *British Journal of Psychology*, 1972, *63*, 359–365. (a)

Hotopf, W. H. N., & Ollereanshaw, C. The regression to right angles tendency and the Poggendorff illusion, II. *British Journal of Psychology*, 1972, *63*, 367–379. (b)

Hubel, D. H., & Wiesel, T. N. Receptive fields of single neurones in the cat's striate cortex. *Journal of Physiology*, 1959, *148*, 574–591.

Hubel, D. H., & Wiesel, T. N. Integrative action in the cat's lateral geniculate body. *Journal of Physiology*, 1961, *155*, 385–398.

Hubel, D. H., & Wiesel, T. N. Receptive fields, binocular interaction and functional architecture in the cat's visual cortex. *Journal of Physiology*, 1962, *160*, 106–154.

Hubel, D. H., & Wiesel, T. N. Receptive fields and functional archtecture of monkey striate cortex. *Journal of Physiology*, 1968, *195*, 215–243.

Hubel, D. H., & Wiesel, T. N. Stereoscopic vision in macaque monkey. *Nature*, 1970, *225*, 41–42.

Hudson, W. Pictorial depth perception in subcultural groups in Africa. *Journal of Social Psychology*, 1960, *52*, 183–208.

Hudson, W. Pictorial perception and educational adaptation in Africa. *Psychologia Africana*, 1962, *9*, 226–239.

Hudson, W. The study of the problem of pictorial perception among unacculturated groups. *International Journal of Psychology*, 1967, *2*, 89–107.

Huggins, W. H., & Licklidor, J. G. R. Place mechanisms in auditory frequency analysis. *Journal of the Acoustical Society of America*, 1951, *23*, 290–299.

Humphrey, N. K., & Morgan, M. J. Constancy and the geometric illusions. *Nature*, 1965, *206*, 744–746.

Huxley, J. S. *The new systematics.* Oxford: Clarendon Press, 1940.

Ikeda, H., & Obanai, T. Figural after-effect, retroactive effect and simultaneous illusion. *Japanese Journal of Psychology*, 1955, *26*, 235–246.

Imai, S. Illusions in the figure consisting of straight and curved lines, I. *Japanese Journal of Psychology*, 1956, *27*, 147–149. (a)

Imai, S. Illusions in the figure consisting of straight and curved lines, II. *Japanese Journal of Psychology*, 1956, *27*, 235–237. (b)

Imai, S. Experiments on negative optical illusions in the Zoellner figure. *Tokyo Metropolitan University*, 1962, No. 30, 31–44.

Ivanoff, A. Les aberrations de chromatisme et de sphericite de l'oeil. *Revue d'optique théoretique et instrumentale*, 1947, *26*, 145–171.

Jahoda, G. Geometric illusions and environment: A study in Ghana. *British Journal of Psychology*, 1966, *57*, 193–199. (a)

Jahoda, G. Retinal pigmentation, illusion susceptibility and space perception. *International Journal of Psychology*, 1971, *6*, 199–208.

Jastrow, J. A study of Zoellner's figures and other related illusions. *American Journal of Psychology*, 1891, *4*, 381–398.

Jastrow, J. On the judgment of angles and positions of lines. *American Journal of Psychology*, 1892, *5*, 214–221.

Jenkin, N., & Hyman, R. Attitude and distance-estimation as variables in size matching. *American Journal of Psychology*, 1959, *72*, 68–76.

Judd, C. H. An optical illusion. *Psychological Review*, 1898, *5*, 286–294.

Judd, C. H. Practice and its effects on the perception of illusions. *Psychological Review*, 1902, *8*, 27–39.

Judd, C. H. The Mueller–Lyer illusion. *Psychological Review Monograph Supplement*, 1905, No. 29, 55–82.

Julesz, B. *Foundations of cyclopean perception.* Chicago: University of Chicago Press, 1971.

Kanizsa, G. Marzini quasi-percettivi in campi con stimolazione omegenea. *Revista di Psicologia*, 1955, *49*, 7–30.

Kanizsa, G. Contours with gradients or cognitive contours? *Italian Journal of Psychology*, 1974, *1*, 93–112.

Kilbride, P. L., & Leibowitz, H. W. Factors affecting the magnitude of the Ponzo illusion among the Baganda. *Perception and Psychophysics*, 1975, *17*, 543–548.

Kilbride, P. L., & Robbins, M. C. Linear perspective, pictorial depth perception and education among the Baganda. *Perceptual and Motor Skills*, 1968, *27*, 601–602.

Kilbride, P. L., Robbins, M. C., & Freeman, R. B. Pictorial depth perception and education among Baganda schoolchildren. *Perceptual and Motor Skills*, 1968, *26*, 1116–1118.

Kimura, D. Dual function asymmetry of the brain in visual perception. *Neuropsychologia*, 1966, *4*, 275–285.

Kimura, D. Manual activity during speaking: I. Right-handers. II. Left-handers. *Neuropsychologia*, 1973, *11*, 45–55.

Kobayashi, T. Analytical study of displacement in visual perception: I. *Japanese Psychological Research*, 1956, No. 3, 37—47.

Koehler, W. *The task of Gestalt psychology*. Princeton, N.J.: Princeton University Press, 1967.

Koehler, W., & Fishback, J. The destruction of the Mueller—Lyer illusion in repeated trials: I. An examination of two theories. *Journal of Experimental Psychology*, 1950, *40*, 267—281. (a)

Koehler, W., & Fishback, J. The destruction of the Mueller—Lyer illusion in repeated trials: II Satiation patterns and memory trace. *Journal of Experimental Psychology*, 1950, *40*, 938—410. (b)

Koehler, W., & Wallach, H. Figural after-effects: An investigation of visual processes. *Proceedings of the American Philosophical Society*, 1944, *88*, 269—357.

Koffka, K. *Principles of Gestalt Psychology*. New York: Harcourt, 1935.

Krantz, D. H., & Weintraub, D. J. Factors affecting perceived orientation of the Poggendorff transversal. *Perception and Psychophysics*, 1973, *14*, 511—517.

Krauskopf, J. Light distribution in human retinal images. *Journal of the Optical Society of America*, 1962, *52*, 1046—1050.

Kristof, W. Ein Umschlag der Heringschen Tauschung bei Abwandlung der Vorlage. *Zeitschrift fur experimentalle und angewandter Psychogie*, 1960, *7*, 68—75.

Kristof, W. Ueber die Einordnung geometrisch-optischer Taeuschungen in die Gestzmaessigkeit der visuellen Wahrnehmung. *Part I. Archiv fur die gesante Psychologie*, 1961, *113*, 1—48.

Kuennapas, T. M. An analysis of the "horizontal-vertical illusion." *Journal of Experimental Psychology*, 1955, *49*, 134—140. (a)

Kuennapas, T. M. Influence of frame size on apparent length of a line. *Journal of Experimental Psychology*, 1955, *50*, 168—170. (b)

Kuennapas, T. M. Vertical-horizontal illusion and surrounding field. *Acto Psychologica*, 1957, *13*, 35—41.

Kuennapas, T. M. Influence of head inclination on the vertical-horizontal illusion. *Journal of Psychology*, 1958, *46*, 179—185.

Kuennapas, T. M. The vertical-horizontal illusion in artificial visual fields. *Journal of Psychology*, 1959, *47*, 41—48.

Kuffler, S. W. Neurons in the retina: Organization, inhibition and excitation problems. *Cold Spring Harbor Symposia on Quantitative Biology*, 1952, *17*, 281—292.

Kundt, A. Unterschungen ueber Auginmass und optische Tauschungen. *Poggendorff Analle*, 1863, *120*, 118—158.

Lakowski, R. Is the deterioration of colour discrimination with age due to lens or retinal changes? *Die Farbe*, 1962, *11*, 69—86.

Lashley, K. S., Chow, K., & Semmes, J. An examination of the electrical field theory of cerebral integration. *Psychological Review*, 1951, *58*, 123—136.

Laska, W. Uebereinige optische Urtheilstaeuschungen. *Archiv fuer Anatomie und Physiologie*, 1890, *14*, 326—328.

Lawson, R. B., Cowan, E., Gibbs, T. D., & Whitmore, C. G. Stereoscopic enhancement and erasure of subjective contours. *Journal of Experimental Psychology*, 1974, *103*, 1142—1146.

Leibowitz, H. W. Sensory, learned, and cognitive mechanisms of size perception. *Annals of the New York Academy of Science*, 1971, *188*, 47—62.

Leibowitz, H., Brislin, R., Perlmutter, L., & Hennessy, R. Ponzo perspective illusion as a manifestation of space perception. *Science*, 1969, *166*, 1174—1176.

Leibowitz, H. W., & Gwozdecki, J. The magnitude of the Poggendorff illusion as a function of age. *Child Development*, 1967, *38*, 573—580.

Leibowitz, H. W., & Heisel, M. A. L'evolution de l'illusion de Ponzo en fonction de l'age. *Archives de Psychologie, Geneve,* 1958, *36,* 328–331.

Leibowitz, H. W., & Judisch, J. M. The relationship between age and the magnitude of the Ponzo illusion. *American Journal of Psychology,* 1967, *80,* 105–109.

Leibowitz, H. W., & Pick, H. A. Cross-cultural and educational aspects of the Ponzo illusion. *Perception and Psychophysics,* 1972, *12,* 430–432.

Leibowitz, H., & Toffey, S. The effect of rotation and tilt on the magnitude of the Poggendorff illusion. *Vision Research,* 1966, *6,* 101.

Levy–Agresti, G., & Sperry, R. W. Differential perceptual capacities in major and minor hemispheres. *Proceedings of the National Academy of Sciences,* 1968, *61,* 1151.

Lewis, E. O. The effect of practice on the perception of the Mueller–Lyer illusion. *British Journal of Psychology,* 1908, *2,* 294–306.

Lewis, E. O. Confluxion and contrast effects in the Mueller–Lyer illusion. *British Journal of Psychology,* 1909, *3,* 21–41.

Lipps, T. *Raumausthetik und geometrisch-optische Taeuschungen.* Leipzig: Barth, 1897.

Lotze, R. *Medicinische psychologie.* Leipzig: Weidmann, 1852.

Luckiesh, M. *Visual illusions.* Princeton, New Jersey: Van Nostrand, 1922. (Republished, New York: Dover, 1965.)

Ludvigh, E. Perception and contour. U.S. Naval School of Medicine, 1953, Project No. NM 011 075.01.04, Report No. 4.

Maheux, M., Townsend, J. C., & Gresock, C. J. Geometric factors in illusions of direction. *American Journal of Psychology,* 1960, *73,* 535–543.

Massaro, D. W. Constancy scaling revisited. *Psychological Review,* 1973, *80,* 303.

Massaro, D. W., & Anderson, N. H. A test of a perspective theory of geometrical illusions. *American Journal of Psychology,* 1970, *83,* 567–575.

Massaro, D. W., & Anderson, N. H. Judgmental model of the Ebbinghaus illusion. *Journal of Experimental Psychology,* 1971, *81,* 147–151.

McKeever, W. F., & Huling, M. D. Right hemisphere superiority in graphic reproduction of briefly viewed dot figures. *Perceptual and Motor Skills,* 1971, *31,* 201–202. (a)

McKeever, W. F., & Huling, M. D. Lateral dominance in tachistoscopic word performances obtained with simultaneous bilateral input. *Neuropsychologia,* 1971, *9,* 15–20. (b)

Merryman, C. T., & Restle, F. Perceptual displacement of a test mark toward the larger of two visual objects. *Journal of Experimental Psychology,* 1970, *84,* 311–318.

Miller, R. J., Hennessey, R. T., & Leibowitz, H. W. The effect of hypnotic ablation of the background on the magnitude of the Ponzo perspective illusion. *International Journal of Clinical and Experimental Hypnosis,* 1973, *21,* 180–191.

Milner, B. Interhemispheric differences in the localization of psychological processes in man. *British Medical Bulletin,* 1971, *27,* 272–277.

Moed, G. Satiation theory and the Mueller–Lyer illusion. *American Journal of Psychology,* 1959, *72,* 609–611.

Morant, R. B., & Aronoff, J. Starting position, adaptation and visual framework as influencing the perception of verticality. *Journal of Experimental Psychology,* 1966, *71,* 684–686.

Morgan, P. A study in perceptual differences among cultural groups in Southern Africa using tests of geometric illusions. *Journal of the National Institute of Personnel, Johannesburg,* 1959, *8,* 39–43.

Morinaga, S. Untersuchungen ueber die Zoellnersche Tauschung. *Japanese Journal of Psychology,* 1933, *8,* 195–243.

Morinaga, S. 'Paradox of displacement' in optical illusion. Paper presented at the meeting of the Japanese Psychological Association, 1954.

Morinaga, S. Optical illusions and figural after-effects. Paper presented at the meeting of the Japanese Psychological Association, 1955.

Morinaga, S. An examination of the conditions determining size-contrast. Paper presented at the meeting of the Japanese Psychological Association, 1956.

Morinaga, S., Noguchi, K. & Ohishi, A. The horizontal-vertical illusion and the relation of spatial and retinal orientations. *Japanese Psychological Research*, 1962, *4*, 25–29.

Motokawa, K. *Physiology of color and pattern vision.* Springer-Verlag: New York, 1970.

Motokawa, K., & Ogawa, T. The electrical field in the retina and pattern vision. *Tohoku Journal of Experimental Medicine*, 1962, *78*, 209–221.

Mountcastle, V. B. Modality and topographic properties of single neurons of cat's somatic sensory cortex. *Journal of Neurophysiology*, 1957, *20*, 408–434.

Mountjoy, P. T. Effects of exposure time and intertrial interval upon decrement to the Mueller–Lyer illusion. *Journal of Experimental Psychology*, 1958, *56*, 97–102.

Mueller–Lyer, F. C. Optische Urteilstauschungen. *Dubois-Reymonds Archive fuer Anatomie und Physiologie*, 1889, Supplement Volume, 263–270.

Mueller, J. H. *Beitrage zur vergleichenden Physiologie des Gesichtsinnes.* Leipzig: Knobloch, 1826. (a)

Mueller, J. H. *Ueber die phantastichen Gesichtserscheinungen.* Coblenz: Holscher, 1826. (b)

Mueller, J. H. *Handbuch der physiologie des menschen.* Coblenz: Holscher, 1834–1840.

Muensterberg, H. Die verscholene sehaehbrettfigur. *Zeitscrift fur Psychologie*, 1897, *15*, 184–188.

Mundy–Castle, A. C., & Nelson, G. K. A neuropsychological study of the Knyssa forest workers. *Psychologia Africana*, 1962, *9*, 240–272.

Murray, F. B. Conservation of illusion-distance length and illusion strength. *Psychonomic Science*, 1967, *7*, 65–66.

Nakagawa, D. Mueller–Lyer illusion and retinal induction. *Psychologia*, 1958, *1*, 167–174.

Neisser, U. *Cognitive psychology.* New York: Appleton-Century-Crofts, 1967.

Newman, C. V., & Newman, B. M. The Ponzo illusions in pictures with and without suggested depth. *American Journal of Psychology*, 1974, *87*, 511–516.

Ni, C. F. The effect of combining some geometrical optical illusions. *Journal of Genetic Psychology*, 1934, *10*, 472–476.

Noelting, G. Rechersches sur le developpement des perceptions: XL. La structuration progressive de la figure Meuller–Lyer en fonction de la repetition chez l'enfant et l'adulte. *Archives de Psychologie*, Geneve, 1960, *37*, 313–413.

Obonai, T. Contributions to the study of psychophysical induction. III. Experiments on the illusion of filled space. *Japanese Journal of Psychology*, 1933, *8*, 699–721.

Obonai, T. Induction effects in estimates of extent. *Journal of Experimental Psychology*, 1954, *47*, 57–60.

Ohwaki, S. On the destruction of geometrical illusions in stereoscopic observation. *Tohuku Psychologica folia*, 1960, *29*, 24–36.

Oppel, J. J. Ueber geometrisch-optische Tauschungen. *Jahresbericht des Frankfurter Vereins*, 1854–1855, 37–47.

Orbison, W. D. Shape as a function of the vector field. *American Journal of Psychology*, 1939, *52*, 31–45. (a)

Orbison, W. D. The correction of an omission in "Shape as a Function of the Vector Field." *American Journal of Psychology*, 1939, *52*, 309. (b)

Ornstein, R. *The psychology of consciousness.* San Francisco: Freeman, 1972.

Over, R. A comparison of haptic and visual judgements of some illusions. *American Journal of Psychology*, 1966, *79*, 590–595.

Oyama, T. Japanese studies on the so-called gemetrical-optical illusions. *Psychologia*, 1960, *3*, 7–20.

Oyama, T. The effect of hue and brightness on the size-illusion of concentric circles. *American Journal of Psychology*, 1962, *75*, 45–55.

Papert, S. Centrally produced geometrical illusions. *Nature* (London), 1961, *191*, 733.

Parker, N. I., & Newbigging, P. L. Magnitude and decrement of the Mueller–Lyer illusion as a function of pre-training. *Canadian Journal of Psychology*, 1963, *17*, 134–140.

Parrish, C. S. The cutaneous estimation of open and filled space. *American Journal of Psychology*, 1895, *6*, 514–520.

Parrish, M., Lundy, R. M., & Leibowitz, H. W. Hypnotic age-regression and magnitudes of the Ponzo and Poggendorff illusions. *Science*, 1968, *159*, 1375–1376.

Pastore, N. *Selective history of theories of visual perception, 1650–1950.* New York: Oxford University Press, 1971.

Piaget, J. *The mechanisms of perception.* (G. N. Seagrine, trans.). New York: Basic Books, 1969.

Piaget, J., & von Albertini, B. Recherches sur le developpement des perceptions: XI. L'illusion de Mueller–Lyer. *Archives de Psychologie, Geneve*, 1950, *33*, 1–48.

Piaget, J., & Bang, V. Research on the development of perceptions: XLI. The evolution of the illusion of divided spaces with tachistoscopic presentation. *Archives de Psychologie, Geneve*, 1961, *38*, 1–21. (a)

Piaget, J., & Bang, V. Comparaison des mouvements oculaires et des centrations du regard chez l'enfan et chez l'adulte. *Archives de Psychologie, Geneve*, 1961, *38* (Whole no. 150), 167–200. (b)

Piaget, J., Bang, V., & Matalon, B. Note on the law of the temporal maximum of some optico-geometric illusions. *American Journal of Psychology*, 1958, *71*, 277–282.

Piaget, J., Lambercier, M., Boesch, E., & von Albertini, B. Recherches sur le developpement des perceptions: I. Introduction a l'etude des perceptions chez l'enfant et analyse d'une illusion relative a la perception visuelle de cercles concentriques (Delboeuf). *Archives de Psychologie, Geneve*, 1942, *29*, 1–107.

Piaget, J., Maire, F., & Privat, F. Recherches sur le developpement des perceptions: XVIII. La resistance des bonnes formes a l'illusion de Mueller–Lyer. *Archives de Psychologie, Geneve*, 1954, *34*, 155–202.

Piaget, J., Matalon, B., & Bang, V. Research on the development of perceptions: VLII. The evolution of the horizontal-vertical illusion from its constituent elements and the Delboeuf illusion in tachistoscopic presentation. *Archives de Psychologie, Geneve*, 1961, *38*, 23–68.

Piaget, J., & Osterrieth, P. A. Recherches sur le developpement des perceptions: XVII. L'evolution de l'illusion d'Oppel–Kundt en fonction de l'age. *Archives de Psychologie, Geneve*, 1953, *34*, 1–38.

Piaget, J., & Pene, F. Essai sur l'illusion de la mediane des angles en tant que mesure de l'illusion des angles. *Archives de Psychologie*, 1955, *35*, 77–92.

Pierce, H. The illusion of the kindergarten patterns, *Psychological Review*, 1898, *5*, 233–253.

Pike, A. R., & Stacey, B. G. The perception of luminous Mueller–Lyer figures and its implications for the misapplied constancy theory. *Life Sciences*, 1968, *7*, 355–362.

Pintner, R., & Anderson, M. M. The Mueller–Lyer illusion with children and adults. *Journal of Experimental Psychology*, 1916, *1*, 200–210.

Pitblado, C. B., & Kaufman, L. On classifying the visual illusions. In L. Kaufman (Ed.), *Contour descriptor properties of visual shape.* Sperry Rand Research Center Report SRRC-CR 67-43, prepared for Air Force Cambridge Research Laboratories, Project, No. 4645, 1967, 32–53.

Pollack, R. H. Figural after-effects: Quantitative studies of displacement. *Australian Journal of Psychology*, 1958, *10*, 269–277.

Pollack, R. H. Contour detectability thresholds as a function of chronological age. *Perceptual and Motor Skills*, 1963, *17*, 411–417.

Pollack, R. H. Simultaneous and successive presentation of elements of the Mueller–Lyer figure and chronological age. *Perceptual and Motor Skills*, 1964, *19*, 303–310.

Pollack, R. H. Effects of figure-ground contrast and contour orientation on figural marking. *Psychonomic Science*, 1965, *2*, 369–370.

Pollack, R. H. Some implications of ontogenetic changes in perception. In J. Flavell & D. Elkind (Eds.), *Studies in cognitive development, Essays in honor of Jean Piaget*. New York: Oxford University Press, 1969.

Pollack, R. H. Mueller–Lyer illusion: Effect of age, lightness contrast and hue. *Science*, 1970, *170*, 93–95.

Pollack, R. H., & Chaplin, M. R. Effects of prolonged stimulation by components of the Mueller–Lyer figure upon the magnitude of the illusion. *Perceptual and Motor Skills*, 1964, *18*, 377–382.

Pollack, R. H., & Magerl, G. E. A binocular viewing apparatus for sensory threshold studies in children. *Perceptual and Motor Skills*, 1965, *20*, 127–130.

Pollack, R. H., & Silvar, S. D. Magnitude of the Mueller–Lyer illusion in children as a function of pigmentation of the fundus oculi. *Psychonomic Science*, 1967, *8*, 83–84. (a)

Pollack, R. H., & Silvar, S. D. Racial differences in the pigmentation of the fundus oculi. *Psychonomic Science*, 1967, *7*, 159–160. (b)

Ponzo, M. Urteilstausehungen ueler Mengen. *Archiv Gestalt Psychologie*, 1928, *65*, 129–162.

Porac, C., & Coren, S. The assessment of motor control in sighting dominance using an illusion decrement procedure. *Perception and Psychophysics*, 1977, *21*, 341–346.

Porac, C., & Robertson-Mann, B. An inquiry into the role of depth processing in the formation of subjective contours. Paper delivered at the meetings of the Western Psychological Association, Los Angeles, April, 1976.

Pressey, A. W. A theory of the Mueller–Lyer Illusion. *Perceptual and Motor Skills*, 1967, *25*, 569–572. (a)

Pressey, A. W. A theory of the Mueller–Lyer illusion. *Perceptual and Motor Skills*, 1967, *25*, 641–644. (b)

Pressey, A. W. The assimilation theory applied to a modification of the Mueller–Lyer illusion. *Perception and Psychophysics*, 1970, *8*, 411–412.

Pressey, A. W. An extension of assimilation theory to illusions of size, area and direction. *Perception and Psychophysics*, 1971, *9*, 172–176.

Pressey, A. W. Evidence for the role of attentive fields in the perception of illusions. *Quarterly Journal of Experimental Psychology*, 1974, *26*, 464–471.

Pressey, A. W., & den Heyer, K. Observations on Chaing's "new" theory of geometrical illusions. *Perception and Psychophysics*, 1968, *4*, 313–314.

Pressey, A. W., & Sweeney, O. Age changes in the Poggendorff illusion as measured by a method of reproduction. *Psychonomic Science*, 1970, *19*, 99–100.

Pritchard, R. M. Visual illusions viewed as stabilized retinal images. *Quarterly Journal of Experimental Psychology*, 1958, *10*, 77–81.

Quina, K., & Pollack, R. H. Effects of test line position and age on the magnitude of the Ponzo illusion. *Perception and Psychophysics*, 1972, *12*, 253–256.

Quina, K., & Pollack, R. H. Attraction of parallels as a function of intercontour distance. *Perceptual and Motor Skills*, 1973, *36*, 934.

Ratliff, F. *Mach bands: Quantitative studies on neural networks in the retina*. New York: Holden-Day, 1965.

Reid, T. *Essays on the intellectual powers of man*. Edinburgh, 1785.

Restle, F. Instructions and the magnitude of an illusion: Cognitive factors in the frame of reference. *Perception and Psychophysics*, 1971, *9*, 31–32. (a)

Restle, F. Visual illusions. In M. H. Appley (Ed.), *Adaptation-level theory*. New York: Academic Press, 1971. (b)

Restle, F., & Merryman, C. T. An adaptation-level theory account of a relative-size illusion. *Psychonomic Science,* 1968, *12,* 229–230. (a)

Restle, F., & Merryman, C. T. Distance and an illusion of length of line. *Journal of Experimental Psychology,* 1968, *81,* 297–303. (b)

Revesz, G. System der optischen und hoptischen Raumtauschungen. *Zeitschrift fur Psychologie,* 1934, *131,* 296–375.

Rivers, W. H. R. Vision. In A. C. Haddon (Ed.), *Reports of the Cambridge Anthropological Expedition to the Torres Straits, Vol. II, Part I.* Cambridge: Cambridge University Press, 1901.

Rivers, W. H. R. Observations on the senses of the Todas. *British Journal of Psychology,* 1905, *1,* 321–396.

Robinson, J. O. Retinal inhibition in visual distortion. *British Journal of Psychology,* 1968, *59,* 29–36.

Robinson, J. O. *The psychology of visual illusion.* London: Hutchinson and Co., 1972.

Rock, I. *Orientation and form.* New York: Academic Press, 1973.

Rock, I., & McDermott, W. The perception of visual angle. *Acta Psychologica,* 1962, *22,* 119–134.

Rodwan, A. S. Accuracy in size judgments as a function of location in the visual field and the duration of viewing. *Psychonomic Science,* 1968, *10,* 277–278.

Ruddock, K. H. The effect of age upon colour vision. II. Changes with age in light transmission of the ocular media. *Vision Research,* 1965, *5,* 47–58.

Rudel, R. G., & Teuber, H. L. Decrement of visual and haptic Mueller–Lyer illusion on repeated trials: A study of cross-modal transfer. *Quarterly Journal of Experimental Psychology,* 1963, *15,* 125–131.

Ruessel, A. Geometric-optical illusions in children. *Deutsche, Gesellschaft fur Psychologie. Bericht Veberden Kongress, Leipzig,* 1934, *13,* 169–170.

Said, F. S., & Weale, R. A. The variation with age of the spectral transmissivity of the living human crystalline lens. *Gerontologia,* 1959, *3,* 213–231.

Sander, F. Optische Taeuschungen und Psychologie. *Neue Psycholische Studien,* 1926, *1,* 159–167.

Sanford, E. C. *A course in experimental psychology. Part I: Sensation and perception.* Boston: Heath, 1901.

Santastefano, S. A developmental study of the Delboeuf illusion. *Perceptual and Motor Skills,* 1963, *17,* 23–44.

Schiller, P., & Weiner, M. Binocular and stereoscopic viewing of geometric illusions. *Perceptual and Motor Skills,* 1962, *13,* 739–747.

Schumann, F. Beitrage zur Analyse der Gesichtswahrnehmungen. *Zeitschrift fur Psychologie,* 1900, *23,* 1–32; *24,* 1–33.

Schumann, F. Beitrage zur Analyse der Gesichtswahrnehmungen. *Zeitschrift fur Psychologie,* 1904, *36,* 161–185.

Seashore, C. E. Carl Emil Seashore. In C. Murchison (Ed.), *A history of psychology in autobiography.* New York: Russell and Russell, 1961.

Segall, M. H., Campbell, D. T., & Herskovits, M. J. Cultural differences in the perception of geometric illusions. *Science,* 1963, *139,* 769–771.

Segall, M. H., Campbell, D. T., & Herskovits, M. J. *The influence of culture on visual perception.* Indianapolis, Indiana: Bobbs-Merrill, 1966.

Sekuler, R., & Erlebacher, A. The two illusions of Mueller–Lyer: Confusion theory reexamined. *American Journal of Psychology,* 1971, *84,* 477–481.

Selinka, R. Der Ubergang von der ganz heitlichen zur analytischen Auffassung im kindesalter. *Zeitschrift fur Pedagogische Psychologie und Vugendkunde,* 1939, *40,* 256–278.

Seltzer, W. J., & Sheridan, C. L. Effects of inspection figure persistence of a figural aftereffect. *Psychonomic Science,* 1965, *2,* 279–280.

Shannon, C. E. A mathematical theory of communication. *Bell System Technical Journal*, 1848, *27*, 379–423.

Sheard, C. S. The chromatic aberration of the eye: The chromatic variations in the interval of the sturm and applied phenomena as determined by the subjective method of skras-copy. *Journal of the Optical Society of America.* 1926, *12*, 79–82.

Sickles, W. R. Experimental evidence for the electrical character of visual fields derived from a quantitative analysis of the Ponzo illusion. *Journal of Experimental Psychology*, 1942, *30*, 84–91.

Sjostrom, K. P., & Pollack, R. H. The effect of simulated receptor aging on two visual illusions. *Psychonomic Science*, 1971, *23*, 147–148.

Skinner, B. F. *About behaviorism.* New York: Knopf, 1974.

Smith, G. J. W., & Henriksson, M. The effect on an established percept of a perceptual process beyond awareness. *Acta Psychologica*, 1955, *11*, 346–355.

Smith, O. W., Smith, P. C., & Hubbard, D. Perceived distance as a function of the method of representing perspective. *American Journal of Psychology*, 1958, *71*, 662–674.

Smith, R. *A compleat system of opticks.* (2 vols.) Cambridge: C. Crownfield, 1738.

Smith, S. M., Brown, H. D., Toman, J. E. P., & Goodman, L. S. The lack of cerebral effects of d-tubocurarine. *Anesthesiology*, 1947, *8*, 1–14.

Spearman, C. *Psychology down the ages.* London: MacMillan, 1937.

Sperry, R. W., & Milner, N. Pattern perception following insertion of mica plates into visual cortex. *Journal of Comparative and Physiological Psychology*, 1955, *48*, 463–469.

Spitz, H. H. Ganz's hypothesis on figural aftereffects. *American Journal of Psychology*, 1967, *80*, 462–464.

Springbett, B. M. Some stereoscopic phenomena and their implications. *British Journal of Psychology*, 1961, *52*, 105–109.

Stiles, W. S., & Burch, N. P. L. Colour-matching investigation: Final report (1958). *Optica Acta*, 1959, *6*, 1–26.

Stratton, G. M. Symmetry, linear illusions, and the movements of the eye. *Psychological Review*, 1906, *13*, 81–96.

Sun, S. Age differences in the Mueller–Lyer illusion. *Acta Psychologica Sinica*, 1964, *3*, 223–228.

Tajfel, H. Social and cultural factors in perception. In G. Lindzey & E. Aronson (Eds.), *The handbook of social psychology.* Reading, Mass.: Addison-Wesley, 1969.

Tausch, R. Optische Taeuschungen als artifizielle Effekte der Gestaltungsprozesse von Groessen-und Formenkonstanz in der natuerlichen Raumwahrnehmung. *Psychologica Forschung*, 1954, *24*, 299–348.

Taylor, J. A. Drive theory and manifest anxiety. *Psychological Bulletin*, 1956, *53*, 303–320.

Thiery, A. Uber geometrisch-optische Tauschungen. *Philosophische Studien*, 1896, *12*, 67–126.

Titchener, E. B. *Experimental psychology: A manual of laboratory practice.* New York: Macmillan, 1901–1905.

Tolansky, S. *Optical illusions.* New York: Pergamon Press, 1964.

Trimble, R., & Eriksen, C. W. "Subliminal cues" and the Mueller–type illusion. *Perception and Psychophysics*, 1966, *1*, 401–404.

Verriest, G. Further studies on acquired deficiency of colour discrimination. *Journal of the Optical Society of America*, 1963, *53*, 185–195.

Virsu, V. Tendencies to eye movement and misperception of curvature, direction and length. *Perception and Psychophysics*, 1971, *9*, 65–72.

Vitruvius, P. *De archetectura* (F. Granger, trans.). New York: Putnam, 1931.

Vurpillot, E. L'influence de la signification du materiel sur l'illusion de Poggendorff. *Annee Psychologie*, 1957, *57*, 339–357.

Vurpillot, E. Piaget's law of relative centrations. *Acta Psychologica.* 1959, *16*, 403–430.

Vurpillot, E. L'organization perceptive: son role dans l'evolution des illusions optico-geometriques. *Etudes de psychologie et de philoslphie, XVI,* Paris: Librarie Philosophique J. Vrin, 1963.

Waardenburg, P. J., Franceschetti, A., & Klein, D. *Genetics and Ophthalmology.* Oxford: Blackwell Scientific Publications, 1961.

Wagner, H. L. Simultaneous and successive contour displacements. Doctoral thesis, University of Wales, 1969.

Waite, H., & Massaro, D. W. Test of Gregory's constancy scaling explanation of the Mueller–Lyer illusion. *Nature,* 1970, *227,* 733–734.

Wallace, G. K., & Crampin, P. J. The effect of background density of the Zoellner illusion. *Vision Research,* 1969, *9,* 167–179.

Walters, A. A gentic study of geometrical optical illusions. *Genetic Psychology Monographs,* 1942, *25,* 101–155.

Wapner, S., & Werner, H. *Perceptual development: An investigation within the framework of sensory-tonic field theory.* Worcester: Clark University Press, 1957.

Wapner, S., Werner, H., & Comalli, P. W. Perception of part–whole relationships in middle and old age. *Journal of Gerontology,* 1960, *15,* 412–416.

Ward, L. M., & Coren, S. The effect of optically induced blur on the magnitude of the Mueller–Lyer illusion. *Bulletin of the Psychonomic Society,* 1976, *7,* 483–484.

Ward, L. M., & Lockhead, G. R. Sequential effects and memory in category judgments. *Journal of Experimental Psychology,* 1970, *84,* 27–34.

Ward, L. M., & Lockhead, G. R. Response system processes in absolute judgment. *Perception and Psychophysics,* 1971, *9,* 73–78.

Ward, L. M., Porac, C., Coren, S., & Girgus, J. S. The case for misapplied constancy scaling: Depth associations elicited by illusion configurations. *American Journal of Psychology,* 1977, *90,* 609–620.

Watson, J. B. Psychology as a behaviorist views it. *Psychological Review,* 1913, *20,* 158–177.

Watson, J. B. *Psychology from the standpoint of a behaviorist.* Philadelphia: Lippincott, 1919.

Watson, J. B. *Behaviorsim.* Chicago: University of Chicago Press, 1930.

Weber, E. H. *De pulsu, resorptione, auditu et tactu: annotationes anatomicae et physiologicae.* Leipzig, 1834.

Weintraub, D. J. Rectangle discriminability: Perceptual relativity and the law of Pragnanz. *Journal of Experimental Psychology,* 1971, *88,* 1–11.

Weintraub, D. J., & Cooper, L. A. Coming of age with the Delboeuf illusion: Brightness contrast, cognition and perceptual development. *Developmental Psychology,* 1972, *6,* 187–197.

Weintraub, D. J., & Krantz, D. H. The Poggendorff illusion: Amputations, rotations, and other perturbations. *Perception and Psychophysics,* 1971, *10,* 257–264.

Weintraub, D. J., Tong, L., & Smith, A. J. Mueller–Lyer size versus size reflectance contrast illusion: Is the age-related decrement caused by a declining sensitivity to brightness contours? *Developmental Psychology,* 1973, *8,* 6–15.

Weintraub, D. J., Wilson, B. A., Greene, R. D., & Palmquist, M. J. Delboeuf illusion: Displacement versus diameter, arc deletions and brightness contrast. *Journal of Experimental Psychology,* 1969, *80,* 505–511.

Wendroth, P. M. The effects of tilted outline frames and intersecting line patterns on judgments of vertical. *Perception and Psychophysics,* 1973, *14,* 242–248.

Werner, H., & Wapner, S. Toward a general theory of perception. *Psychological Review,* 1952, *59,* 324–338.

Werner, H., & Wapner, S. Studies in physiognomic perception: I. Effect of configurational dymanics and meaning-induced sets on the position of the apparent median plane. *Journal of Psychology,* 1954, *38,* 51–65.

Werner, H., Wapner, S., & Chandler, K. A. Experiments on sensory-tonic field theory of perception: II. Effect of supported and unsupported tilt of the body on the visual perception of verticality. *Journal of Experimental Psychology*, 1951, *42*, 346–350.

Wertheimer, M. Experimentelle Studien uber das Schen von Bewegung. *Zeitschrift fur psychologie*, 1912, *61*, 161–265.

Westheimer, G. Optical and motor factors in the formation of the retinal image. *Journal of the Optical Society of America*, 1963, *62*, 86–93.

Westheimer, G., & Campbell, F. W. Light distribution in the image formed by the living human eye. *Journal of the Optical Society of America*, 1962, *52*, 1040–1045.

White, K. G. Implicit contours in the Zoellner illusion. *American Journal of Psychology*, 1972, *85*, 421–424.

Whitmore, C. L. G., Lawson, R. B., & Kozora, C. E. Subjective contours in stereoscopic space. *Perception and Psychophysics*, 1976, *19*, 211–213.

Wiener, N. *Cybernetics.* New York: Wiley, 1949.

Wickelgren, B. G. Brightness contrast and length perception in the Mueller–Lyer illusion. *Vision Research*, 1965, *5*, 141–150.

Winch, W. H. The vertical-horizontal illusion in school children. *British Journal of Psychology*, 1907, *2*, 220–225.

Winslow, C. N. Visual illusions in the chick. *Archives of Psychology*, 1933, *153*, 80.

Witasek, S. Ueber die Natur der geometrisch-optischen Taeuschungen. *Zeitschift fur Psychologie*, 1898, *19*, 81–174.

Witkin, H. A. Perception of body position and of the position of the visual field. *Psychological Monographs*, 1949, *63*, 1–46.

Witkin, H. A. A cognitive-style approach to cross-cultural research. *International Journal of Psychology*, 1967, *2*, 233–250.

Witkin, H. A., & Asch, S. E. Studies in space orientation. III. Perception of the upright in the absence of a visual field. *Journal of Experimental Psychology*, 1948, *38*, 603–614. (a)

Witkin, H. A., & Asch, S. E. Studies in space perception. IV. Further experiments on perception of the upright with displaced visual fields. *Journal of Experimental Psychology*, 1948, *38*, 762–782. (b)

Witkin, H. A., Dyk, R. B., Faterson, H. F., Goodenough, D. R., & Karp, S. A. *Psychological differentiation.* New York: Wiley, 1962.

Witkin, H. A., Goodenough, D. R., & Karp, S. A. *Developmental changes in perception.* Unpublished study described in Witkin, Dyk, Faterson, Goodenough & Karp, 1962.

Witkin, H. A., Lewis, H. B., Hertzman, M., Machover, K., Meissner, P. B., & Wapner, S. *Personality through perception.* New York: Harper, 1954.

Wober, M. Confrontation of the H-V illusion and a test of 3-dimensional pictorial perception in Nigeria. *Perceptual and Motor Skills*, 1970, *31*, 105–106.

Worrall, N. A test of Gregory's theory of primary constancy scaling. *American Journal of Psychology*, 1974, *87*, 505–510.

Worrall, N., & Firth, D. Extension cues in open and closed figures. *Quarterly Journal of Experimental Psychology*, 1971, *23*, 311–315.

Wuersten, H. Recherches sur le developpement des perceptions: IX. L'evolution des comparaisons de longueurs de l'enfant a l'adulte avec variation d'angle entre la vertcale et l'horizontale. *Archives de Psychologie, Geneve*, 1947, *32*, 1–444.

Wundt, W. *Lectures on human and animal psychology.* (J. E. Greighton & E. B. Titchener, trans.). London: Swan Sonnenschein, 1894.

Wundt, W. Die geometrisch-optischen Taeuschungen. *Akademie der Saechs, Wissenschaften, Leipzig. Abnandlungem*, 1898, *24*, 53–178.

Yarbus, A. L. *Eye movements and vision.* New York: Plenum Press, 1967.

Yokose, Z. The law of the "field" in visual form perception (I) A theoretical formula to seek the field strength of the form and its experimental proof. *Japanese Psychological Research*, 1954, *1*, 55–64.

Yokose, Z. Theoretical formula of vector-field and its experimental proof. *Psycholgia*, 1957, *1*, 17–21.

Yokose, Z., & Kawamura, H. A study of the direction of the field force in shape perception. Report No. 1, *Japanese Journal of Psychology*, 1952, *23*, 133–142.

Zanforlin, M. Some observations on Gregory's theory of perceptual illusions. *Quarterly Journal of Experimental Psychology*, 1967, *19*, 193–197.

Zigler, E. Size estimates of circles as a function of size of adjacent circles. *Perceptual and Motor Skills*, 1960, *11*, 47–53.

Zoellner, F. Ueber eine neue Art von Pseudoskopie und ihre Beziehung zu den von Plateau and Oppel beschriebenen Bewegungsphaenomenon. *Annalen der Physik,* 1860, 500–525.

Author Index

Subject Index